Praise for *Divider-in-Chief*

"Kate Obenshain's new book *Divider-in-Chief* is an outstanding exposé of the hypocrisy, cynicism, and extremism of the Obama administration. He claimed to be a uniter, but Kate's book identifies where and how he has been the ultimate divider of Americans. If Obama is shown the door after the 2012 election, Kate's book will be one of the reasons why—everyone needs to read this before November!"

—**Sean Hannity**

"Kate Obenshain has written one of the best takedowns of Obama I've read. If you have friends still bedazzled by the fraudulent rhetoric of hope and change, give them this book, and wipe that smile right off their face. *Divider-in-Chief* reveals the radical presidency of Barack Obama for exactly what it is—the most divisive, polarizing, and balkanizing in American history."

—**David Limbaugh**, nationally syndicated columnist and *New York Times* bestselling author, most recently of *The Great Destroyer: Barack Obama's War on the Republic*

"Kate Obenshain has written a penetrating and astute book about the Obama political method. Highly recommended."

—**Peter Schweizer**, *New York Times* bestselling author of *Throw Them All Out*

"Here is the book to have handy as Obama pursues his re-election strategy of dividing Americans along lines of race, religion, sex, and economic class. As Obenshain notes, 'Whether Obama wins or loses, the country he promised to unite, the nation he pledged to heal, will be far more deeply divided than on the day he took office in 2009.'"

—**David Freddoso**, editorial page editor of the *Washington Examiner* and *New York Times* bestselling author of *The Case against Barack Obama*

"Kate Obenshain's new book, *Divider-in-Chief*, is more than a must-read. It's *required* reading! Kate proves what many Americans have now learned the hard way. So-called 'hope and change' was a smokescreen for Barack Obama's premeditated attack on the very foundations of our Republic. Instead of bringing the nation together, as he promised, we now see President Obama is truly the Divider-in-Chief. If you care about our nation, its future, and what will be left for our children and grandchildren, you need to read this book."

—**Allen West**, Florida Congressman

"Kate Obenshain's *Divider-in-Chief* is a devastating portrait of America's most polarizing president. She exposes his advertised politics of civility and unity as an utter sham—a demagogic plot that not only divides Americans from each other but also divides them from the founding principles of the country."

—**George Neumayr**, contributing editor, the *American Spectator* and co-author with Phyllis Schlafly of *No Higher Power: Obama's War on Religious Freedom*

DIVIDER
-IN-
CHIEF

DIVIDER
-IN-
CHIEF

THE FRAUD OF HOPE AND CHANGE

KATE OBENSHAIN

Since 1947
REGNERY
PUBLISHING, INC.
An Eagle Publishing Company • Washington, DC

Library of Congress Cataloging-in-Publication Data
Obenshain, Kate.
  Divider-in-chief : the fraud of hope and change / by Kate Obenshain.
    p. cm.
  Includes bibliographical references and index.
  ISBN 978-1-62157-011-0 (alk. paper)
  1. United States--Politics and government--2009- 2. Obama, Barack. 3. Presidents--United States. I. Title.
  JK275.O34 2012
  973.932092--dc23
  [B]
                                        2012028237

Published in the United States by
Regnery Publishing, Inc.
One Massachusetts Avenue NW
Washington, DC 20001
www.Regnery.com

Manufactured in the United States of America

10 9 8 7 6 5 4 3 2 1

Books are available in quantity for promotional or premium use. Write to Director of Special Sales, Regnery Publishing, Inc., One Massachusetts Avenue NW, Washington, DC 20001, for information on discounts and terms, or call (202) 216-0600.

Distributed to the trade by
Perseus Distribution
387 Park Avenue South
New York, NY 10016

For Henry, Paul, Stone, and Lucy

Contents

The Divisive President

The idea of Barack Obama the uniter is a lie; the notion of Obama the post-partisan president is a farce.

Obama was supposed to be a new kind of politician—America's first post-partisan president. But instead he's been a president who's astonishingly willing to jump into the trenches—to sling mud at his political enemies, launch attacks on other branches of government, and blacklist news organizations that criticize him.

Obama has sown division within and between religious groups; pitted women against one another; ignored laws he dislikes; cynically exploited class, race, faith, and even his own family for transparently political purposes; and shut down debate over important and controversial issues, in particular the government takeover of one-sixth of the economy through Obamacare.

This book is about broken promises and shattered hopes. And I decided to write it because, though Obama has abandoned unity and post-partisanship, millions of Americans remain unaware of his betrayals. In fact, many Americans take at face value the liberal talking point that claims conservatives and Republicans are chiefly to blame for the divisiveness in politics. This book is not an indictment of division in political discourse. Our country was founded on differences of opinion—starkly contrasting ideas that were articulated passionately, openly, and with integrity. It was through the free and open exchange of ideas that our founders determined the best course.

But Obama's call for post-partisanship has as its goal the subjugation of differing points of view to the ideology of radical leftism. In ObamaWorld, partisanship can be transcended only when everyone agrees with Barack Obama.

With his attempt to force religious institutions to violate their core beliefs by covering their employees' birth control, sterilizations, and abortion-inducing drugs, Obama has made a political calculation that appealing to secular and liberal female voters is more important than the constitutional rights of believers.

The day he publicly endorsed same-sex marriage—a decision he claimed was rooted in his faith and inspired by "Christ sacrificing himself on our behalf"[1]—Obama immediately jumped on a plane to attend a Hollywood fundraiser, where he raised nearly $15 million off the announcement.[2]

He's taken credit for the successes and heroism of others, and blamed others, including his predecessor and even the public, when his own initiatives have failed. When congressional Republicans wouldn't compromise on tax cuts, he began referring to them as "hostage-takers."[3]

Democrats tried to rally liberal voters to the polls ahead of the 2010 mid-term elections by releasing a video of Obama imploring "young people, African-Americans, Latinos, and women" to unite and go to the polls for Democrats just like they did back in 2008.[4]

The video was a desperate and cynical attempt to energize voters with an "us versus them" appeal. Obama ran for president as a post-partisan, post-racial uniter. But his instinct was to respond to the coming disaster by dividing on the grounds of age, race, ethnicity, and sex.

Obama's re-election campaign is also based on pandering to key constituencies—young people, ethnic and racial minorities, radical feminists, gays, environmentalists, public employee unions—while demonizing Republicans, conservative women, business owners, portions of the media, religious organizations, and any other group or institution that challenges his agenda or threatens his power.

Because Obama spends so much of his time catering to special interests, he has very little time to focus on the national interest, in particular reviving the economy and creating jobs.

Obama has embraced a slash and burn approach to his 2012 re-election bid. As early as August 2011, the Obama campaign signaled it would focus on, according to *Politico*, "a ferocious personal assault on Mitt Romney's character and business background."[5]

> The dramatic and unabashedly negative turn is the product of political reality. Obama remains personally popular, but pluralities in recent polling disapprove of his handling of his job, and Americans fear the country is on the wrong track. His aides are increasingly resigned to running for reelection in a glum nation. And so the candidate who ran on "hope" in 2008 has little choice four years later but to run a slashing, personal campaign aimed at disqualifying his likeliest opponent.[6]

"Unless things change and Obama can run on accomplishments," a prominent Democratic strategist aligned with the White House told *Politico*, "[Obama] will have to kill Romney."[7]

To that end, the Obama campaign hired Stephanie Cutter as deputy campaign manager to oversee the campaign's daily combat operation. Cutter is famous among Democrats for her "Dresden-esque" campaign tactics, referring to the Allies' overwhelming and indiscriminate bombing of Dresden, Germany, at the end of World War II.

"What Obama and his team have accepted is that, while there's a lot to be said for changing politics and elevating the discourse, your most important job as president is to defend your priorities," the *New Republic*'s Noam Scheiber wrote.[8] "And the way you do that is to win."

The Obama way—sowing division to get his way—is essentially un-democratic. Obama seeks to avoid any honest back-and-forth, the messiness of Congress and democracy. He does this by encouraging divisiveness. So, for instance, if he can convince the American people that Republicans are anti-woman, then he can shut down debate on any issues involving women. He won't need to argue the merits of an idea; he wins without uttering a single cogent thought merely by impugning the motives of the other side.

But that's not the way our system works. Our two-party system, our republican form of government, is successful because it is premised on contrasting ideas that offer the American people clear choices. The idea that wins a majority of the people (or their elected representatives) to its side, wins. The system falls apart *not* when differing ideas exist and are debated vigorously, but rather when the debate is shut down.

When the debate is either carried out in an undemocratic way—behind closed doors where special interests and money rather than ideas or the people's interests prevail—or is shut down through scare tactics and division, democracy is diminished. What Obama has done by trying to stifle debate and hide his true intentions is not only divisive, it is also completely contradictory to the essence of America and what makes her great.

This book is meant to be a thoughtful, clear-eyed examination of Obama's first term. My hope is that it shines light on the ways Obama has betrayed his promises of unity and post-partisanship and instead embraced division and polarization as a method of governing and campaigning.

Obama is not the first president to practice the politics of division. But he is the first to do so with so much tenacity and skill, and such complete disregard for our democracy. Obama is indeed a new kind of politician: he is the most divisive president in modern history—one whose divisiveness promises to cut even deeper as the 2012 campaign reaches its climax.

CHAPTER ONE

The Community Organizer President

*There were those who argued that because I had spoken
of a need for unity in this country that our nation
was somehow entering into a period of post-partisanship.
That didn't work out so well.*

—President Barack Obama, remarks at Vermont Avenue Baptist
Church, Washington, D.C., January 17, 2010

On January 20, 2009, nearly two million people huddled on the National Mall in frigid Washington, D.C., to witness Barack Obama's swearing in as the forty-fourth president of the United States.

For many Americans, Obama had come to personify the hopes of a battered and weary nation. Inexperienced and un-vetted, Obama won not because he possessed executive experience or foreign policy expertise, but rather because he promised a unique capacity to transcend politics, unite divided factions, and heal the nation.

Rising to the podium after his swearing-in, the new president declared:

On this day, we gather because we have chosen hope over fear, unity of purpose over conflict and discord. On this day, we come to proclaim an end to the petty grievances and false promises, the recriminations and worn-out dogmas that for far too long have strangled our politics.[1]

Obama's call to unity of purpose had by then become familiar—it was a variation on a theme he had visited again and again at key moments during his political rise.

"Now even as we speak, there are those who are preparing to divide us, the spin masters and negative ad peddlers who embrace the politics of anything goes," he told the audience in his show-stealing speech at the 2004 Democratic National Convention.

> Well, I say to them tonight, there is not a liberal America and a conservative America; there is the United States of America. There is not a black America and white America and Latino America and Asian America; there is the United States of America.
>
> The pundits, the pundits like to slice and dice our country into red states and blue states: red states for Republicans, blue states for Democrats. But I've got news for them, too. We worship an awesome God in the blue states, and we don't like federal agents poking around our libraries in the red states.
>
> We coach little league in the blue states and, yes, we've got some gay friends in the red states. There are patriots who opposed the war in Iraq, and there are patriots who supported the war in Iraq.
>
> We are one people, all of us pledging allegiance to the stars and stripes, all of us defending the United States of America. In the end, that's what this election is about. Do we participate in a politics of cynicism, or do we participate in a politics of hope?[2]

Hope, unity, and post-partisanship weren't merely key parts of Obama's message. They were his entire message. Obama's 2006 autobiography, *The Audacity of Hope*, is a 350-page lament for the highly polarized politics Obama encountered when he reached the U.S. Senate in 2004. The book, which became Obama's presidential campaign manifesto, is also an indictment of the grievance politics that dominates the political left. "I reject a politics that is based solely on racial identity, gender identity, sexual orientation or victimhood generally," Obama wrote in the prologue.[3]

The unity theme pervaded Obama's 2008 presidential run. Early in the campaign, he told Iowans, "I don't want to pit red America against blue America—I want to be the president of the United States of America."[4]

On Super Tuesday, he claimed that his candidacy prompted many Americans to realize that "maybe we don't have to be divided by race and region and gender … that we can come together and build an America that gives every child everywhere the opportunity to live out their dreams."[5]

And at Grant Park in Chicago on the night of his election, Obama pledged to Republicans, "I will listen to you, especially when we disagree. Let us resist the temptation to fall back on the same partisanship and pettiness and immaturity that has poisoned our politics for too long."[6] In part due to such lofty rhetoric, Obama began his presidency with a 68 percent job approval rating—"one of the better initial ratings of post-World War II presidents," according to the Gallup polling firm.[7]

Of course, by the most objective measure, Obama had not united the country. The nearly 70 million votes he had received were more than any presidential candidate in U.S. history.[8] But more than two-thirds of eligible voters did not cast a ballot for Barack Obama. That included more than 61 million Americans who voted for somebody other than Obama,[9] and another 90 million eligible voters who found the idea of Obama as president so rousing that they couldn't even drag themselves to the voting booth on Election Day.[10]

Obama was, as many conservatives pointed out, an unlikely uniter. Rhetoric aside, his record was that of a rigid, doctrinaire liberal with almost no history of bucking his party. According to National Journal, Obama had the Senate's most liberal voting record in 2007, the year he started running for president.[11]

What's more, Obama had cut his political teeth in the corrupt machine politics of Chicago and had already shown hints of a nastier, more divisive side. "If they bring a knife to the fight, we bring a gun," he told a crowd of supporters in Philadelphia about how to counter Republican attacks, "because from what I understand, folks in Philly like a good brawl."[12]

During the transition period after the election, before he was sworn in as president, Obama selected Chicago scrapper Rahm Emanuel—a.k.a. "Rahmbo"—as his chief of staff. The profanity-spewing Emanuel was known for employing ruthless, brass-knuckle tactics. Obama had chosen a political enforcer as his chief "uniter."

Still Organizing after All These Years

During the 2008 campaign, it was evident to clear-eyed observers that Obama was applying to politics the lessons he had learned as a community organizer in Chicago. Obama was a disciple of Saul Alinsky, the Chicago-based radical community organizer who from the 1930s to his death in 1972 helped shape the activist left. As a community organizer himself, Obama helped train hundreds of other young activists in Alinsky's methods in the 1980s.

In *Rules for Radicals*, a primer for young leftwing activists, Alinsky explained that a community organizer's task is to take "apathetic workers" and stir discontent with the status quo, fanning "resentments and hostilities by a number of means."[13] But he must do so carefully. As Stanley Kurtz writes in *Radical-in-Chief*, "Community organizers in the tradition of Saul Alinsky keep their political beliefs to themselves. They make a point of presenting themselves as pragmatists in search of 'commonsense solutions for working families.'"[14]

But, Kurtz continues, "though commonsense pragmatism unfettered by ideology is their public theme, Alinskyites use polarization as a tactic. Organizers search for 'enemies'—businessmen and political leaders who can either offer the group something valuable or serve as 'targets' for anger. Targets are sometimes baited to strike back, thus further enraging the group."[15]

During his years as a community organizer, Obama became an expert in Alinksy's tactics of division. Mike Kruglik, a community organizer who worked with Obama in the 1980s, told the *New Republic* that Obama was "the undisputed master of agitation … with probing, sometimes personal questions, he would pinpoint the source of pain in their lives, tearing down their egos just enough before dangling a carrot of hope that they could make things better."[16]

Obama didn't leave the world of community organizing behind when he entered politics. He has called his years as a community organizer the best education of his life. Politics was the natural next step to organizing an ever larger community. Or, in Obama's own words, "What if a politician were to see his job as that of an organizer, as part teacher and part advocate, one who does not sell voters short but who educates them about the real choices before them?"[17]

In her book *The Obamas*, Jodi Kantor reports that when the president saw his old community organizing boss Jerry Kellman at a White House party, he happily pulled him aside and said, "I'm still organizing." Kantor adds, "It had echoes of what Valerie Jarrett had told me once—'The senator still thinks of himself as a community organizer.'"[18]

From Unity to Division

Once ensconced in the Oval Office, President Obama quickly abandoned all pretense of post-partisanship.

Just three days into his administration, Obama met with Republican congressional leaders and told them to quit listening to radio talk show host Rush Limbaugh. Then, when Minority Whip Eric Cantor laid out familiar conservative arguments about taxes, Obama shot back, "I won. I will trump you on that."[19]

During his first few days in office, Obama ignored Republican objections and made enormously contentious decisions. He issued an executive order to close Guantanamo Bay prison in Cuba and another to restore taxpayer funding of overseas abortion groups. He supported a controversial United Nations declaration on sexual orientation and gender identity and lifted a ban on taxpayer funding of research using stem cells from human embryos. Hardly the stuff of compromise.

After just two months in office, Pew Research Center found that, "for all his hopes about bipartisanship, Barack Obama has the most polarized early job approval of any president in the past four decades."[20]

A year later, Gallup found that Obama had had the most polarizing first year of any president in the pollster's history. "The 65 percentage point gap between Democrats' (88 percent) and Republicans' (23 percent) average job approval ratings for Barack Obama is easily the largest for any president in his first year in office, greatly exceeding the prior high of 52 points for Bill Clinton," Gallup reported.[21]

Obama's remarkable transformation from uniter to divider has not gone unnoticed. As Florida Senator Marco Rubio told a group of South Carolina Republicans about Obama in May 2012:

> For all the policy disagreements that we may have with the president, it is hard to understate how much he inspired people across this country four years ago, with his promises to unite America and lift it up. The man who today occupies the White House and is running for president is a very different person. We have not seen such a divisive figure in modern American history as we have over the last three and a half years.[22]

In May 2012, former Democratic representative Artur Davis, a former Obama ally and early endorser of his presidential run, switched political parties. "If I were to run again, it would be as a Republican," he wrote in an online post. Echoing Rubio, he said, "Frankly, the symbolism of Barack Obama winning has not given us the substance of a united country.... I have taken issue with an administration that has lapsed into a bloc by bloc appeal to group grievances when the country is already too fractured."[23]

A flashpoint for Obama's divisiveness was the Affordable Care Act, a.k.a. Obamacare, Obama's signature legislative initiative. As Kantor reveals in *The Obamas*, the president didn't care that his proposal was unpopular. "Rahm Emanuel saw a disaster in the making. He spent the final week of July mounting what another aide called a 'nonstop campaign' to convince the president to scale back his efforts on health care," she writes.[24] But to no avail. "The president plunged ahead anyway."

> Around that time, Obama gathered with a group of aides around a table in the office of Phil Schiliro, the legislative affairs director, to discuss the bill's chances.... The advisers in the room had dozens of years of legislative experience among them, and they could not quite see a route to successful passage. A feeling of discouragement settled in around the table.
>
> "You know what, I feel lucky," said the president, sitting at one end of the table. "This is going to pass." I feel lucky? Barack Obama was highly rational and deliberative, and yet he was ending the meeting with a profession of blind faith. For five years, things had broken his way again and again; was he still able to imagine that things would turn out otherwise?
>
> "...I don't care if I'm a one-term president," Obama told his senior staff. Forget the polls, he told political advisors.[25]

In other words, forget the American people. Let's do whatever is necessary to fundamentally transform America's economy in a statist direction. Obama's ideology trumped the rhetoric of unity.

CHAPTER TWO

The Blame-Shifter-in-Chief

Besides the 2008 presidential election, Barack Obama's most conse-quential election occurred not in 2004 (when he won his U.S. Senate seat) or in 1996 (when he won his Illinois State Senate seat), but in 1989, when he was elected president of the *Harvard Law Review.* That election gave Obama his first taste of national prominence and helped him secure a contract to write his first autobiography, *Dreams from My Father.*

What's most interesting about Obama's *Harvard Law Review* election is that Obama was seen as the compromise candidate. The *Law Review* staff was split between conservatives and liberals, and Obama won because, as one former staff member put it to David Remnick in *The Bridge*, "There was a general sense that he didn't think [conservatives] were evil people, only misguided people, and he would credit us for good faith and intelligence."[1]

Christine Spurell, an outspoken liberal Harvard Law student, com-plained to Obama about not getting the position she wanted on his staff. She told Remnick that Obama explained to her it was because she was "'too confrontational, too abrasive—qualities that he could not bear,' she said."[2] Spurell continued: "I had no patience for the idiots on the other side and Barack did, which annoyed me, even angered me sometimes, but it made him the better person, certainly a better one to be president of the *Law Review*."[3]

Running for president, Obama sounded much like the compromise candidate of two decades earlier. He promised he would put an end to the type of politics that "breeds division and conflict and cynicism" and would help us "rediscover our bonds to each other and get out of this constant, petty bickering that's come to characterize our politics."[4]

He pledged to work with the other side. In March 2008, he said, "I'm a big believer in working with the other side of the aisle. Even if we've got a majority of Democrats, I think it's very important to listen to Republicans, to respect them.... I want to have a weekly meeting with Republican and Democratic leaders to talk about the economy, to talk about foreign policy, so that we're actually trying to solve problems away from the TV cameras, not trying to score political points."[5]

On election night, he told Republicans, "I will listen to you, especially when we disagree. Let us resist the temptation to fall back on the same partisanship and pettiness and immaturity that has poisoned our politics for too long."[5]

In the initial days of his presidency, Obama took the unusual step of traveling to Capitol Hill to meet with the Republican House caucus to hear their ideas and concerns for the economy. Vice President Joe Biden was deployed to do the same in the Senate.

But when that little bit of outreach didn't yield immediate results, Obama gave up. As Jonathan Alter relates in *The Promise*: "For Obama this was the greatest surprise of 2009. '[It wasn't that] I thought that my political outreach and charm would immediately end partisan politics,' the president said. 'I just thought that there would be enough of a sense of urgency that at least for the first year there would be an interest in governing. And you just didn't see that.'"[6]

Since then, Obama has done very little aisle-crossing, and has been remarkably willing to blame others for his failures and to threaten those who don't agree with him or do his will.

In February 2009, Obama warned the country's mayors that he would "call them out" and use the "full power" of the presidency to expose and crack down on them if they misused the economic stimulus dollars.[7]

Later that year, he began telling congressional Republicans to get out of his way as he tried to fix the economy. "I don't want the folks who created the mess to do a lot of talking," he told a crowd at a campaign event for Virginia gubernatorial candidate Creigh Deeds.[8] "I want them to get out of the way so we can clean up the mess. I don't mind cleaning up after them, but don't do a lot of talking."[9] So much for "listening to you especially when we disagree."

He called Republicans "hostage-takers" for demanding certain tax cuts in a tax cut compromise in 2010. "It's tempting not to negotiate with hostage takers unless the hostage gets harmed," Obama said at a press conference. "In this case, the hostage was the American people."[10]

During the debt ceiling crisis in the summer of 2011, as Democrats and Republicans debated whether and how much to raise the limit on the amount of debt the federal government could take on, Obama condescended to Republicans. He told them it was time to "pull off the band aid. Eat our peas."[11]

Then he took them to task for taking a recess with the debt ceiling deadline looming, comparing them to children. "Malia and Sasha generally finish their homework a day ahead of time," he said. "Malia is 13, Sasha is 10.... They don't wait until the night before.... Congress can do the same thing."[12]

When Republican Representative Paul Ryan of Wisconsin unveiled his budget in 2011, Obama criticized it and demonized those who supported it. "Their vision is less about reducing the deficit than it is about changing the basic social compact in America," he said.[13] He alleged that the budget pits "children with autism or Down syndrome" against "every millionaire and billionaire in our society."[14]

In 2012 Obama compared Republican presidential candidates who pushed for the production of more domestic oil to "founding members of the Flat Earth Society."[15]

He has characterized the Republican philosophy as "We are better off when everybody is left to fend for themselves and play by their own rules."[16] The Republican vision, according to Obama, is to leave elderly Americans unable to afford nursing home care, and to leave poor children and children with disabilities to "fend for themselves." The GOP favors "dirtier" air and water. And Republicans in Congress consistently "put party before country."[17]

Obama and his Democratic allies suffered two major electoral defeats during Obama's first term. And after each, instead of taking a new path toward the promised conciliation and compromise, Obama doubled down on his divisive agenda and was impervious to advice or criticism.

In January 2010, Republican State Senator Scott Brown defeated Democratic state Attorney General Martha Coakley to win the Massachusetts Senate seat long held by Ted Kennedy. Obama dismissed what was indisputably a historic defeat, blaming it on his predecessor, George W. Bush. "The same thing that swept Scott Brown into office swept me into office," he explained. "People are angry, and they're frustrated. Not just because of what's happened in the last year or two years, but what's happened over the last eight years."[18]

After describing the Democrats' historic losses in the 2010 mid-term elections as a "shellacking," Obama said, "I am very eager to sit down with members of both parties.... No party has a monopoly on wisdom."[19] But, once again, the conciliation didn't last long.

Obama met with various Washington, D.C., veterans and insiders, according to David Corn, author of *Showdown: The Inside Story of How Obama Fought Back Against Boehner, Cantor, and the Tea Party*. Vernon Jordan, the preeminent Washington fixer, told Obama he had been overly partisan. And, as Corn wrote:

Some of these interlocutors reiterated the widespread gripe that the Obama White House was too insular. Obama was told he should get out more, strengthen his relationships with other Washington power players, be less aloof from the capital's permanent establishment.

"Obama didn't care about the criticism that he was too insular," a White House aide said. "He didn't give a shit."

"There's no question he believes he's doing exactly the right thing," said Tom Daschle. "He looks back with great satisfaction over the first two years." Obama's lack of regret infuriated some members of his own White House. "It has the feel of a husband struggling as he apologizes to his wife because he knows he is supposed to apologize," one top aide said. "In his heart, he thinks it is his wife's fault."[20]

Obama hosted a lunch with congressional Democrats who had lost their seats in 2010. This group, too, was struck by Obama's lack of regret. "In retrospect we can look back and say we could have done things differently, but I had a very ambitious agenda," Representative Jim Oberstar recalled Obama saying.[21] "'In the end this is for the greater good of the country.' He seemed entirely sure he knew what was best for the country; he seemed to think that he was a better judge than the public."[22]

The feeling among some in Congress was that Obama regarded them with contempt, because Obama views himself as being superior to other politicians, and he feels they should bend to his will. Obama found solidarity with his wife in his low regard for Congress. As Jodi Kantor explains in *The Obamas*, "It was one of the areas where the Obamas seemed to reinforce and stoke each other: the president's opinion of Capitol Hill legislators was low, and his wife's was lower."[23]

In his bestselling book *The Amateur*, Ed Klein was told by a former State Department official, "I've been in a lot of meetings with [Obama] on foreign policy. While I was in the room, he'd get phone calls from heads of state, and more than once I heard him say, 'I can't believe I've got to meet with all these congressmen from Podunk city to get my bills passed.'"[24]

Blaming Bush

Obama has blamed George W. Bush for seemingly every setback of his administration—so much so that it's become a sort of national joke. In fact, even three and a half years into his administration, and into his run for re-election, Obama continues to make "It's Bush's fault" his go-to explanation not only for the financial crisis and the 2007–2009 recession, but also for the subsequent years of stagnation.

Anytime he talks about the economy, Obama is either "cleaning up the mess" left by Bush or rescuing America from a "financial disaster" that he "inherited" from Bush. Even after taking ownership of the unemployment crisis by ramming the stimulus through, promising that unemployment would not rise above 8 percent, he continued to blame Bush as unemployment rose beyond his self-imposed marker.

While it was reasonable for Obama to tie financial conditions to Bush in the initial stages of his presidency, at some point, say after two years, much of the Bush blaming became implausible, then downright laughable.

The only concession Obama has made to growing doubts that Bush can be blamed for everything is to blame him more obliquely. An example was in one of his weekly radio addresses in June 2011. "I wish I could tell you there was a quick fix to our economic problems," he said. "But the truth is, we didn't get into this mess overnight, and we won't get out of it over-night. It's going to take time."[25]

Having embraced the campaign motto "Forward," you'd assume the Obama campaign would stop looking backward to blame Bush. But you'd be wrong. Obama was still indirectly blaming Bush in June 2012. At a campaign stop in Golden Valley, Minnesota, Obama said, "We're still fighting our way back. Our economy is still facing serious head winds."[26]

Blaming the Public

Obama and his allies have a tendency to blame the public for the administration's failures. Liberal comedian and million-dollar Obama contributor Bill Maher has complained that Americans "are not bright enough to really understand the issues."[27]

In early 2010, when Obama was having a hard time advancing his agenda, *Slate*'s Jacob Weisberg wrote a piece called "Down with the People: Blame the childish, ignorant American public—not politicians—for our political and economic crisis."[28] He wrote, "The biggest culprit in our current predicament" is "the childishness, ignorance and growing incoherence of the public at large."[29]

Joe Klein of *Time* magazine couldn't believe the American public could oppose Obama's stimulus package. He said the opposition was "yet further evidence that Americans are flagrantly ill-informed... and, for those watching FOX News, misinformed. It is very difficult to have a democracy without citizens. It is impossible to be a citizen if you don't make an effort to understand the most basic activities of your government. It is very difficult to thrive in an increasingly competitive world if you're a nation of dodos."[30]

Obama has also gotten into the act. He told Massachusetts donors that Democrats' problems can be chalked up to the fact that people are "hardwired not to always think clearly when we're scared. And the country is scared."[31]

Obama has a habit of blaming his political troubles on voters' ignorance and impulsiveness. When he started losing primaries to Hillary Clinton in 2008, he told a group of San Francisco donors—in comments that are now notorious but remain revealing about Obama's base assumptions—that Midwesterners cling to guns, religion, and xenophobia as a way to explain their frustrations.

More recently, the president explained his poor fundraising performance in May 2012 to donors on an Air Force One conference call, implying the people's ignorance is to blame: "In 2008 everything was new and exciting about our campaign.... And now I'm the incumbent president. I've got gray hair." Rather than accepting responsibility for people's angst over the economy and their inclination to hold him at least partially responsible, Obama patronizes and shifts more blame: "It turns out change is hard, especially when you've got an obstructionist Republican Congress."[32]

Obama holds a remarkable distinction as a president who appears less presidential with every passing year. As professor James W. Ceaser has noted, "Obama has reversed the usual process of growth and maturation, appearing today far more like a candidate for the presidency... than he did during the latter stages of his campaign."[33]

The president's ego and blame-shifting are among his most obvious characteristics: he will readily claim credit for success, no matter how implausible; but when things go wrong, he'll shift the blame, point his finger, and, above all, attack his opponents. Many Americans did not see Obama for what he was in 2008, listening only to his siren song of hope, change, and reconciliation. It will be harder to fool them in 2012.

CHAPTER THREE

Spiking
the Football

E go is Barack Obama's defining characteristic. It is also his greatest liability.

At the Catholic Charities Al Smith dinner in New York in October 2008, Obama joked, "If I had to name my greatest strength, I guess it would be my humility. Greatest weakness, it's possible that I'm a little too awesome."[1] The joke elicited raucous laughter from the assembled guests. It was funny because it contained an admission from Obama that he is often a little too full of himself.

In his book *From Promise to Power*, David Mendell linked Obama's robust ego to his mother. She worried that her biracial son would lack self-esteem without his father present. So she went to great lengths to shore up Obama's confidence. "As a consequence, there was no shortage of self-esteem," Obama once told Mendell with a wry smile.[2]

As a candidate in October 2008, Obama said, "Like any politician at this level, I've got a healthy ego."[3] Obama's staff members have remarked on his high estimation of himself and his abilities. When David Plouffe, who would become Obama's campaign manager, first interviewed for a job with him in 2006, then-Senator Obama told him straightforwardly: "I think I could probably do every job on the campaign better than the people I'll hire to do it."[4]

Obama said something similar to Patrick Gaspard, whom he hired to be the campaign's political director. "I think that I'm a better speechwriter than my speechwriters. I know more about policies on any particular issue than my policy directors. And I'll tell you right now that I'm gonna think I'm a better political director than my political director."[5]

To be fair, given the way Obama was treated during his political rise by liberals and the media, it's easy to see why he'd be so self-assured. Take just one example from the 2008 election: *Newsweek* editor Evan Thomas called Obama a "brave" and "great teacher" who "stands above everybody." Thomas later elaborated, saying, "I mean in a way Obama's standing above the country, above—above the world, he's sort of God."[6]

According to the book *Game Change*, by John Heilemann and Mark Halperin, Obama surrounded himself with aides who treated him like a deity: "After his election as Senator a lot of requests came in for him to speak, many of them fundraisers for other candidates.... His aides were 'praying it wouldn't go to Obama's head; his ego was robust enough already. They even conferred on the senator a new nickname: Black Jesus.'"[7]

Obama was held in even higher esteem abroad. After having held office just two weeks, Obama was nominated for the Nobel Peace Prize. When the committee awarded him the prize in October 2009, it highlighted Obama's "extraordinary efforts to strengthen international diplomacy and cooperation between peoples."[8]

Obama's ego prompted him to make many audacious promises, such as his claim upon receiving the Democratic nomination:

> I am absolutely certain that generations from now we will be able to look back and tell our children that this was the moment when we began to provide care for the sick and good jobs to the jobless; this was the moment when the rise of the oceans began

to slow and our planet began to heal; this was the moment when we ended a war and secured our nation and restored our image as the last, best hope on earth.[9]

Obama's towering ego and unflinching self-confidence were no doubt helpful in getting him to the White House. But those characteristics often and easily tip into arrogance and overconfidence. It's clear he no longer feels the need to win people to his side; rather, he tries by sheer force of his personality to compel others to follow him.

Taking Credit

In July 2009, the Chicago White Sox's Mark Buehrle pitched a perfect game—only the twenty-first Major League baseball pitcher ever to achieve that feat. Barack Obama is a White Sox fan, and he took the opportunity to call Buehrle to congratulate him. Obama, according to administration press secretary Robert Gibbs, told Buehrle, "Maybe [the perfect game] was because I wore the White Sox jacket at the All-Star Game."[10]

It was a joke, of course, but, like the joke he made at the Al Smith dinner, it revealed an uncomfortable truth: that Obama is so self-centered, he takes credit for successes that have little or nothing to do with him.

Obama always puts himself center stage. Dinesh D'Souza, in his book *Obama's America,* offered a prime example of Obama's ego, of how everything is always about him, writing:

My own favorite incident revealing Obama's high opinion of himself occurred in India, when the president spoke at a business roundtable in Mumbai. Indian entrepreneur Bhupendra Kansagra was speaking, and Obama was trying to guess where his remarks were headed.

Kansagra: Welcome, Mr. President, to India. As a fellow Kenyan, I'm very proud to see that you have made...

Obama: [laughing] Made something of myself?

>**Kansagra:** … India the focus of your drive for exports out of the U.S.[11]

On a more serious note, Obama was scandalously silent when Iranian citizens risked, and some lost, their lives to protest Iran's sham elections in 2009—yet he still took credit for the protests. Senior Obama advisers let it be known that Obama's Cairo speech a few months earlier had, according to them, inspired the protesters.

"There clearly is in the region a sense of new possibilities. I was struck in the aftermath of the president's speech that there was a connection. It was very sweeping in terms of its reach," one senior administration official told the *Washington Post*. Obama said that "obviously after the speech that I made in Cairo we tried to send a clear message that we think there is the possibility of change" in Iran.[12]

Another example: even after he blocked the Keystone oil project, Obama took credit for expediting construction of a portion of the Keystone XL oil pipeline. "President Obama claiming credit for speeding up the Keystone pipeline is like Al Gore saying he invented the Internet," said Oklahoma Republican congressman John Sullivan.[13]

Team Obama has even gone so far as to take credit for *Republican* victories. Republicans won governor races in New Jersey and Virginia in 2009 that were commonly viewed as repudiations of Obama. But Obama senior adviser David Axelrod argued that the Republican in the Virginia race, Bob McDonnell, won because he ran "not as a Sarah Palin Republican, but more as a Barack Obama centrist."[14] This after Obama and the left tried to defeat McDonnell by playing up the Republican's unmistakably Christian, conservative values.

Obama Spikes the Football

Almost everyone acknowledges that Obama made the right decision in pulling the metaphorical trigger to kill Osama bin Laden. But Obama and his allies seem to believe Obama should also get credit for pulling the actual trigger in the assassination.

Immediately after the raid, in May 2011, Obama repeatedly said that he wouldn't release photos of Osama bin Laden's dead body. "It is important to make sure that very graphic photos of somebody who was shot in the head are not floating around as an incitement to additional violence or as a propaganda tool," Obama told Steve Kroft of *60 Minutes*.[15] "We don't trot out this stuff as trophies… we don't need to spike the football. Given the graphic nature of these photos it would create a national security risk."

But though he never released the photos, Obama constantly reminds voters about his decision, often politicizing it. In an ad called "One Chance," Bill Clinton says Obama took "the harder and the more honorable path" in ordering the bin Laden assassination. Then subtitles appear that ask, "Which path would Mitt Romney have taken?" Obama himself has even implied Romney would not have given the go-ahead.[16]

"It's now sad to see the Obama campaign seek to use an event that unified our country to once again divide us in order to try and distract voters' attention from the failures of his administration," said Romney spokeswoman Andrea Saul.[17]

Serving and former U.S. Navy SEALs criticized Obama for taking credit for the killing and then exploiting it for his re-election campaign. Ryan Zinke, a former commander in the U.S. Navy who spent twenty-three years as a SEAL and led a SEAL Team 6 assault unit, told *Daily Mail* reporter Toby Harnden, himself a veteran of the Royal Navy: "The decision was a no brainer. I applaud him for making it but I would not overly pat myself on the back for making the right call. I think every president would have done the same. He is justified in saying it was his decision but the preparation, the sacrifice—it was a broader team effort."[18]

Zinke suggested that Obama was exploiting bin Laden's death for his re-election bid. "The President and his administration are positioning him as a war president using the SEALs as ammunition," he said. "It was predictable."[19]

Even some liberals condemned Obama's politicization of the bin Laden killing. Arianna Huffington, who runs the left's premiere news website, the *Huffington Post*, told CBS: "We should celebrate the fact that they did such a great job. It's one thing to have an NBC special from the Situation Room... all that to me is perfectly legitimate, but to turn it into a campaign ad is one of the most despicable things you can do."[20]

Campaigning in Portsmouth, New Hampshire, Romney responded to a shouted question about the bin Laden raid by saying, "Even Jimmy Carter would have given that order."[21] (I'm not so sure.)

A serving SEAL Team member said: "Obama wasn't in the field, at risk, carrying a gun. As president, at every turn he should be thanking the guys who put their lives on the line to do this. He does so in his official speeches because his speechwriters are smart. But the more he tries to take the credit for it, the more the ground operators are saying, 'Come on, man!' It really didn't matter who was president. At the end of the day, they were going to go."[22]

Chris Kyle, a former SEAL sniper with 160 confirmed and another 95 unconfirmed kills to his credit, told the *Daily Mail*, "Taking [bin Laden] out didn't really change anything as far as the war on terror is concerned and using it as a political attack is a cheap shot."[23]

Obama and the "Tough Guy" Election

The bin Laden raid was not the only instance of Obama politicizing foreign policy. In fact, in the Obama administration, intelligence has routinely been placed in the service of politics; America's national security has been the main casualty. Daniel Klaidman reports in his book *Kill or Capture* that Rahm Emanuel "pushed the CIA to publicize its kinetic successes" to portray the administration in a good light.[24]

In late May, Judicial Watch, a government watchdog group, obtained documents revealing that national secrets were provided for a film on the mission to get bin Laden. The filmmakers got access to high-ranking officials involved in the commando operation that killed the terrorist.

Judicial Watch also discovered that the filmmakers had access to top White House officials, including White House National Security Council official Denis McDonough and chief counterterrorism adviser John Brennan. They were also given the identity of a SEAL team member involved in the raid and taken to the top-secret "vault" where the raid was planned.

Soon after the raid, Defense Secretary Robert Gates publicly complained that the White House had breached an agreement not to disclose details about the mission. "[W]e all agreed that we would not release any operational details from the effort to take out bin Laden," he said. "That all fell apart on Monday—the next day."[25]

It soon became clear why the filmmakers got such unprecedented access: the film's initial release date was October 12, 2012—perfectly timed to bolster Obama's foreign policy credentials ahead of the election.

Also, in the spring of 2012, news stories began to appear that included classified national security information. The *New York Times* ran a piece about the United States' involvement in a disrupted bomb plot in Yemen. It involved a Saudi double agent who had infiltrated al-Qaeda in the Arabian Peninsula (AQAP) and prevented an attack on an American jetliner. The agent provided information that made possible a U.S. drone strike in Yemen that took out a key AQAP commander.

The White House subsequently held a conference call about the thwarted attack that included former counterterrorism officials who are now paid commentators on cable TV news shows. That call involved Brennan, and it angered some on Capitol Hill because the administration had failed to inform key committees, including the Senate's intelligence panel, about the bomb plot until after it had been reported in the news media.

In May, the *New York Times* ran a story detailing Obama's weekly "kill list" meetings.[26] The story made it clear that White House officials routinely gave reporters classified information on drone strikes in Pakistan and Yemen, usually on the condition of anonymity.

All of these stories placed Obama in a positive, tough guy light in the lead-up to his crucial re-election bid. As the *Washington Post's* Richard Cohen wrote: "What is remarkable about the recent leaks is the coincidence—it can only be that—that they all made the president look good, heroic, decisive, strong, and even a touch cruel—born, as the birthers long suspected, not in Hawaii but possibly on the lost planet Krypton."[27]

Republican senator Lindsey Graham of South Carolina said, "I don't think you have to be Sherlock Holmes to figure out what is going on here. You've had three leaks of intelligence that paint the president as a strong leader."[28]

Arizona Republican senator John McCain told CBS, "This is the most highly classified information and it's now been leaked by the administration at the highest levels at the White House and that's not acceptable."[29]

Republican representative Peter King of New York said about the leaks, "It has to be for [Obama's] reelection. They can deny it all they want. But it would require a suspension of disbelief to believe it's not being done for political purposes."[30]

The administration strongly denied that politics had anything to do with the leaks. "Any suggestion that this administration has authorized intentional leaks of classified information for political gain is grossly irresponsible," White House Spokesman Jay Carney said.[31]

Obama himself pushed back in a June 8, 2012, press conference. "The notion that my White House would purposely release classified national security information is offensive," he said. "It's wrong."[32]

But it's hard not to come to the conclusion that the information was leaked intentionally given the access reporters had. The *New York Times'* drone kill list article, for instance, included interviews with "three dozen of [Obama's] current and former advisors."[33] Cohen wrote that this "suggests the sort of mass law-breaking not seen since Richard Nixon took out after commies, liberals, conservationists, anti-war protesters, Jews and, of course, leakers."[34]

McCain said all the leaked information "makes the president look very decisive… [it] enhances President Obama's image as a tough guy for the elections."[35] One thing is for sure: it makes the president look far more concerned about his re-election than about America's national security secrets and military personnel. After news of the leaks began to dominate the headlines, Attorney General Eric Holder appointed two prosecutors to lead an investigation into how the classified information was leaked. Don't hold your breath for any findings, much less any prosecutions, before the election.

CHAPTER FOUR

The Out-of-Touch President

President Obama is strikingly out of touch with the middle class, a group of Americans he likes to invoke as a political prop—pitting them against the "rich"—but seems unwilling to get to know.

In actuality, Obama's governing coalition is made up of the very rich and those dependent on the government in some way. For the less well-off, Obama promises to "spread the wealth around." For America's elite, he offers aggressive secularism, worldly sophistication, and a smug satisfaction that they know best.

But for the middle class, he offers only economic incompetence, a foreign policy of apology and retreat that offends against middle class patriotism, and a not-too-well-hidden contempt for middle class mores, culture, and aspirations.

The first major indication that Obama was out of touch with the middle class occurred on the 2008 primary campaign trail. At a high-dollar fundraiser in San Francisco, Obama tried to explain the trouble he was having winning over voters in middle America by claiming that they "get bitter, they cling to guns or religion or antipathy to people who aren't like them or anti-immigrant sentiment or anti-trade sentiment as a way to explain their frustrations."[1]

It tells us everything we need to know about how out of touch Obama is with the middle class that in the 2008 Democratic nominating campaign, Hillary Clinton was seen as the middle class candidate. At $31 million, Clinton's net worth was more than four times as high as Obama's $7.3 million.[2]

But Clinton's policy platform was regarded as more friendly to middle income Americans, including her support for Walmart. She constantly stressed that she was the "candidate of, from, and for the middle class."[3]

But Obama was unable to speak the language of working or middle class voters. Whereas Hillary would throw back a shot of whiskey at a bar in rural Indiana,[4] Obama would ask perplexed Iowans, "Anybody gone into Whole Foods lately and see what they charge for arugula?"[5]

Obama's inability to win over middle class voters was the primary reason Clinton was able to compete until June. And part of the reason for selecting Senator Joe Biden as his running mate was that Middle Class Joe would help Obama to attract the voters who eluded him during the primaries.

It didn't work. The only income group Obama lost in the general election was those with household incomes between $50,000 and $75,000—the middle class.

Part of the reason Obama cannot connect with middle class Americans is that he has spent very little time around them. He was formed by elite schools in urban centers: Punahou School in Honolulu, Hawaii, Occidental College in Los Angeles, Columbia University in New York City, Harvard Law School in Cambridge, Massachusetts, and the University of Chicago Law School.

One would expect Obama to try to compensate for his lack of connectedness to middle class Americans by reaching out to them. But that's not his personality; condescension is.

Obama's Achilles' Heel

Obama has been compared to the Star Trek character Mr. Spock because he appears distant, aloof, unemotional, and very different from the average person.[6] Even some of his top aides concede, as Jonathan Alter relates in *The Promise*, that there is "a hardness beneath" the surface of Obama.[7] "Not cold, but serious and often impatient. One aide described him as 'the most unsentimental man I've ever met.'"[8]

Alter quotes Obama's close friend and senior political adviser Valerie Jarrett making the positive case for his standoffishness. "He has an ability to emotionally detach in order to think clearly."[9] Senior adviser Pete Rouse referred to him as "a step removed from most people."[10]

A longtime White House staffer told the *Atlantic*'s James Fallows, "Surprisingly for someone who led such an inspirational campaign, [Obama] does not seem to have the ability to connect with people."[11]

In his book *Obama's War*, Bob Woodward quotes Obama aide John Podesta saying that he "was not sure that Obama felt anything, especially in his gut. He intellectualized and then charted the path forward, essentially picking up the emotions of others and translating them into ideas."[12] This lack of empathy, Podesta claimed, was Obama's "Achilles' heel."[13]

Granted, the bar for presidential empathy and connectedness was set high by Obama's predecessors. Bill Clinton thrived around other people and had a natural ability to convince people he could feel their pain. George W. Bush seemed to enjoy spending time with ordinary Americans. He was often named as the politician voters would most want to sit down and have a beer with.

Barack Obama is viewed differently by the public. Dee Dee Myers, a White House press secretary under Bill Clinton, captured it perfectly when she wrote that while people would enjoy having a beer with Obama, "they're just not sure he wants to have a beer with them."[14]

In March 2010, Myers wrote an "open letter" to Obama, encouraging him to "get back in touch" with Americans. She argued that, unlike Clinton, who "never tired" of interacting with the American people and demonstrating that he could "feel their pain," Obama projected too much self-reliance. "If people believe you're on their side, they will trust your decision," she wrote, arguing that "too often" Obama sends the signal "that he stands alone—and likes it that way."[15]

Obama seems to have gotten more out of touch over time. At least when he was younger, Obama spent time with people at political events, shaking every hand and answering every question. But Obama's approachability changed quickly as he gained national prominence.

"Now fame and demand drew him deeper within himself," Jodi Kantor writes in *The Obamas* about Obama during his time in the U.S. Senate.[16] "His time and patience were shrinking, his desire for self-protection and privacy increasing. Some staffers had a word to describe the moments when he seemed unable or unwilling to connect: Barackward, a combination of 'Barack' and 'awkward.'"[17]

In *The Operators*, Michael Hastings portrays Obama as unhappy about having to pose for photos with American troops in Iraq. "He didn't want to take pictures with any more soldiers," a State Department official told Hastings. "He was complaining about it."[18]

Jonathan Alters tells a story about Obama meeting in the West Wing with dozens of veterans' groups, including several amputees: "The vets didn't appreciate it when the president told them, 'No one in Washington ever tells you guys no.' They had just been through plenty of no under Bush. Then, speaking of their sacrifice, Obama said, 'Nobody feels this more than I do.' The veterans looked at one another in amazement. 'Our jaws dropped,' remembered one. '*Nobody feels this more than I do?* How about us?'"[19]

When he was elected, Obama told interviewers that his greatest concern about the presidency was "living in the bubble." David Axelrod, Obama's closest adviser, told journalist Ron Suskind that Obama's "greatest fear" was "that he'll lose touch with the people."[20] But that's exactly what he's done (if he was ever "in touch" with them to begin with). The *New*

York Times reported in December 2011 that Obama is increasingly isolated, spending "his down time with a small—and shrinking—inner circle of aides and old friends."[21]

Some critics have charged that Obama has spent an inordinate amount of time on the golf course. The president has played more than 100 rounds of golf during his first term.[22] Others were willing to give Obama a pass—even presidents need to relax. But that was a concession Obama's closest adviser wasn't willing to extend to George H. W. Bush. In June 2012, a 1994 video surfaced of David Axelrod calling former President George H. W. Bush "out of touch" for playing golf while trying to convince voters that the economy is improving. "Bush tastelessly did it, often from the ninth hole, and from the cigar boat and other places," Axelrod said, adding, "The impression you got was that he was out of touch."[23]

Obama's isolation from regular, working Americans shows. When Obama said in June 2012 that the private sector was "doing fine," it was yet more evidence of how out of touch the president had become.[24]

It brought to mind an earlier incident in which Obama was pressed by a woman at a townhall event to explain why he was extending visas for foreigners to come to the United States and take engineering jobs when her husband, an unemployed semiconductor engineer, was unable to find work. Obama responded that he found it "interesting" that her husband could not find work, because "the word that we're getting is that somebody in that type of high-tech field, that kind of engineer, should be able to find something right away."[25]

Checks and the City

The image of Obama as a president out of touch with the middle class is reinforced by his celebrity lifestyle. In May 2009, the Obamas flew to New York City for a "date night" consisting of dinner and a Broadway show. The trip included two helicopter rides, a flight on Air Force One, and a motorcade procession through streets closed to traffic.[26]

The pricey trip was ill-timed. The Republican National Conference released a press statement ahead of the trip stating: "As President Obama prepares to wing into Manhattan's theater district on Air Force One to take in a Broadway show, GM is preparing to file bankruptcy and families across America continue to struggle to pay their bills."[27] The trip reinforced the notion that Obama was too eager to waste other people's money and too out of touch to judge the mood of the country.

The Obamas have spent an unprecedented amount of time hosting elaborate state dinners, appearing on comedy talk shows, and attending White House parties with A-list celebrities. According to one estimate, they have taken seventeen taxpayer-funded vacations, including a 2009 trip to Spain that cost the taxpayers nearly half a million dollars.[28]

President Obama has also spent an inordinate amount of time raising money for his re-election campaign. By one count, Obama held 124 fundraisers in his first three and a half years, more than the ninety-four held by the previous five U.S. presidents combined.[29] Most Americans will never hear about Obama's fundraising prowess. Instead, they'll continue to hear Obama rail against the money in politics. As the *Daily Mail*'s Toby Harnden wrote in 2012: "In his State of the Union speech in January, Obama bemoaned the 'corrosive influence of money in politics.' The following month, he reversed course and announced he was allowing cabinet members and top advisors to speak at big money events for so-called super PACs—unaccountable outside groups raising money for his re-election."[30]

Obama seems to enjoy the company of celebrities much more than that of ordinary Americans or wounded warriors. The list of A-list actors, athletes, comedians, and musicians Obama hasn't spent time with is probably shorter than the one of those he has. He's flown in Lebron James and Tobey Maguire for basketball and held private chats in Los Angeles with Jessica Alba and George Clooney. He's had Alicia Keys, Mick Jagger, and Cee Lo Green over to perform and given Jon Bon Jovi a ride on Air Force One.

Obama has partnered with Hollywood elites to host numerous fundraisers. In June 2012 the Obama campaign launched a political ad with

Vogue editor-in-chief Anna Wintour making a pitch to ordinary Americans to ante up to win a "New York Night" with the president, first lady, Wintour, and actress Sarah Jessica Parker, who hosted a $40,000-per-person fundraiser at her multi-million-dollar West Village home. Actress Meryl Streep and fashion designer Michael Kors also attended the event, which banked about $2 million for the campaign. The fundraiser was announced the same day as reports that the unemployment rate had risen to 8.2 percent.[31] On the same evening as the Parker event, Obama attended a fundraiser hosted by singers Mariah Carey and Alicia Keys. The 250-person dinner yielded the Obama campaign at least $2.5 million.

Obama has traveled so often to Los Angeles to raise money that California-based Democratic consultant Bill Carrick told Fox News in June 2010, "There's a reason it feels like he's been here every two weeks for the last two years. Every time we turn around, there's someone on the radio telling you that you have to drive around the motorcade traffic."[32]

In his campaign to divide and conquer America's electoral map, Obama will continue to invoke his support for the middle class. But in reality, he thinks of the middle class as the L.A. drivers who need to pull over to let his motorcade through so he can wine and dine with the elite and flatter them with all they do for the poor. Of course, what they celebrate is not their own charitable donations, but tax dollars taken from the hardworking private sector employees and small businessmen who are allegedly doing just "fine."

CHAPTER FIVE

Obama's Crass Class Warfare

A June 2012 Gallup poll showed Mitt Romney leading President Obama 49 percent to 45 percent among voters with household incomes between $36,000 and $89,000.[1]

If Obama loses middle class voters in 2012, it won't be because he hasn't talked about them enough. Obama casts himself as a warrior from and for the middle class. He constantly reminds the public that he is "struggling to defend" a middle class that is "under assault" by conservatives and others who care only about the rich.

As evidence of this commitment to the middle class, Obama established a "Middle Class Task Force" a few days into his term, chaired by Vice President Biden. "The strength of our economy can be measured by the strength of our middle class. That is why I have signed a memorandum to create the Task Force on Middle-Class Working Families—and why I have asked my Vice President to lead it,"[2] Obama said in announcing the task force. "This is a difficult moment. But I believe, if we act boldly and swiftly, it can be an American moment—when we work through our differences and overcome our divisions to face this crisis."[3]

It was ironic that Obama mentioned "overcom[ing] our divisions" as the key to reviving the middle class, because to Obama, rebuilding the middle class means tearing down successful Americans and stoking class resentment. It means dividing America by class.

Obama has always been extremely class conscious. His first job out of college in 1983 was working for a publishing and consulting group that collected data on international business and finance. Working in the financial services industry bothered Obama, and it left him feeling contempt for the worlds of finance and commerce.

"Sometimes, coming out of an interview with Japanese financiers or German bond traders, I would catch my reflection in the elevator doors— see myself in a suit and tie, a briefcase in my hand," Obama wrote in *Dreams from My Father*, "and for a brief second I would imagine myself as a captain of industry, barking orders, closing the deal, before I remembered who it was that I had told myself I wanted to be and felt pangs of guilt for my lack of resolve."[4]

Obama's mother wrote that Obama called his job "working for the enemy."[5]

Obama often tries to create solidarity with his middle class audiences by telling them that it took him years to pay off his student loans. He'll also say things like "I wasn't born with a silver spoon in my mouth," to contrast his childhood experience from that of Mitt Romney.[6] In a speech in Osawatomie, Kansas, in December 2011, Obama referred to the "middle class" more than two dozen times as he drew a distinct line between what he refers to as "the wealthy" and the working class.[7] He said that the economic downturn had created a "make-or-break moment" for the middle class and touted more government as an answer to the "you're on your own economics" of Republicans.

Obama's answer to the troubles of the middle class has been to call for a soak-the-rich policy of high tax rates for the wealthy, a policy that's founded on his conception of "fairness." The rich must pay their "fair share," Obama insists, because the "breathtaking greed of a few" is crushing the middle class.

Obama's Fairness Doctrine

Other than "I," "me," and "mine," few words are uttered more frequently by Barack Obama than "empathy" and "fairness." In *The Audacity of Hope*, Obama writes:

> [A] sense of empathy is one that I find myself appreciating more and more as I get older. It is at the heart of my moral code, and it is how I understand the Golden Rule—not simply as a call to sympathy or charity, but as something more demanding, a call to stand in somebody else's shoes and see through their eyes.... I believe a stronger sense of empathy would tilt the balance of our current politics in favor of those people who are struggling in this society. After all, if they are like us, then their struggles are our own. If we fail to help, we diminish ourselves.[8]

The rhetoric of empathy—the ability to understand and be sensitive to the feelings and experiences of others—drives Obama's policy agenda; unfortunately, the practice of empathy does not.

Obama seems to believe that just by declaring that he values empathy he will automatically be able to employ it properly. But Obama practices his empathy very selectively, and has often chosen to "see through the eyes" only of people who will aid his ideological agenda or election prospects.

Obama touted the ability to empathize as a major consideration in selecting federal judges. As a presidential candidate, he said that he would appoint justices to the Supreme Court who have the "empathy... to understand what it's like to be poor, or African-American, or gay, or disabled, or old."[9] While searching for a replacement for retiring Justice David Souter in 2009, Obama said he would "seek someone who understands that justice isn't about some abstract legal theory or footnote in a case book." He added, "I view that quality of empathy, of understanding and identifying with people's hopes and struggles as an essential ingredient for arriving at just decisions and outcomes."[10]

That's why Obama nominated Sonia Sotomayor, who had, Obama claimed, "experience being tested by obstacles and barriers, by hardship and misfortune; experience insisting, persisting, and ultimately overcoming those barriers. It is experience that can give a person a common touch of compassion; an understanding of how the world works and how ordinary people live. And that is why it is a necessary ingredient in the kind of Justice we need on the Supreme Court."[11]

Empathy and fairness are important values, but they are not meant to take the place of constitutional law. Our liberties are secured by our being a nation of laws, not a nation of feelings where judges make decisions based on emotional whim. Obama's empathy talk is another means by which he divides the country, pitting empathetic, fair, liberal Americans against allegedly unfeeling, unfair conservatives.

For instance, Obama has framed the debate over Obamacare as fundamentally about fairness and empathy. Solicitor General Donald Verrilli, defending Obamacare, ended the administration's oral arguments before the Supreme Court with a plea to empathy, citing the millions of Americans suffering from injury or ailment who would receive insurance coverage under Obama's plan.

The president, too, touted empathy, urging the public not to neglect the "human element" of the debate. He said that if the law were overturned, millions of children and adults with pre-existing conditions would be left without care.

Obama's calls to fairness and empathy ignore large segments of people with whom Obama cannot seem to empathize. How fair is it for the government to compel citizens, many of whom simply cannot afford it, to buy health insurance? How fair is it for the government to force some Americans to pay higher insurance premiums? How fair is it to impose, de facto, an onerous tax on employers who might otherwise use the money to hire more workers?

What is fairer: letting people make their own health care decisions or having the government decide for them? How fair is it to force religious institutions, or religious individuals or business owners, to pay for abortion-inducing drugs or contraceptives or sterilizations that they believe are morally wrong, forcing them to violate their consciences and perhaps, in their view, risk their souls?

The limits of Obama's empathy are interesting. He can empathize with the feminist lobby that wants abortion-on-demand, and comment that he wouldn't want his daughters "punished with a baby." But Obama has, obviously, little empathy for the unborn baby in the womb. This is not surprising given that he has displayed shockingly little empathy for babies born alive after botched abortions. As an Illinois state senator, Obama voted against a law to give those babies life-saving care.[12] He can empathize with Muslim victims of intolerance on the rare occasion that such intolerance occurs in America. But he apparently has little empathy for the female victims of Islam's Sharia law around the world. He has empathy for homosexuals suffering persecution abroad, but not for persecuted Christians in other countries.

The president sold the "stimulus" by asking Americans to try and understand what it's like to be unemployed. But Obama's incontinent spending ignores future generations, which will pay for today's record-breaking deficits with higher taxes, a lower standard of living, and an economy whose future is mortgaged and whose prospects are limited by crushing debt.

Obama has often mentioned fairness in his various pushes for immigration reform. When announcing his June 2012 executive order to stop deportations of young illegal immigrants, Obama said, "This morning, Secretary Napolitano announced new actions my administration will take to mend our nation's immigration policy, to make it more fair, more efficient and more just, specifically for certain young people sometimes called

DREAMers."[13] But immigration amnesty can be profoundly unfair to American workers unable to find jobs, because illegal immigrants work for less pay. Amnesty also penalizes immigrants who did things the right way, waiting years and paying a fortune in legal fees to have a shot at citizenship.

Obama clearly lacks empathy for the views of conservatives, who represent a plurality of the American people. Instead, he accuses them of being "hostage-takers."[14] He calls them members of the "Flat Earth Society."[15] And he charges them with embracing "social Darwinism."[16]

Obama is not the only Democrat who uses incendiary rhetoric against Republicans. When congressional Republicans unveiled their energy bill in June 2012, California House Democrat Henry Waxman accused Republicans of "getting away—literally—with murder" because of their record on the environment.[17]

Obama has made "fairness" a focal point of his 2012 campaign. He works the concept into almost every speech, especially as a way to contrast his economic program from Mitt Romney's. "When Americans talk about folks like me paying my fair share of taxes, it's not because they envy the rich," Obama told a joint session of Congress. "It's because they understand that when I get a tax break I don't need and the country can't afford, it either adds to the deficit, or somebody else has to make up the difference."[18]

While both liberals and conservatives may have an easier time being empathetic toward those of like mind, empirical research has shown that liberals in particular have a difficult time understanding conservative values.

In 2011, Jesse Graham of the University of Southern California and Brian A. Nosek and Jonathan Haidt of the University of Virginia published a study called "The Moral Stereotypes of Liberals and Conservatives: Exaggeration of Differences across the Political Divide." They concluded that: "The largest inaccuracies were in liberals' underestimations of conservatives' harm and fairness concerns, and liberals further exaggerated the political differences by overestimating their own such concerns."[19]

The essential divide between the left and the right in America is not, as Obama would have us believe, between empathetic liberals who value fairness and uncompassionate conservatives who care only about the rich and powerful. The divide is rooted in distinct definitions of fairness. Liberals define fairness as equality of outcomes, while conservatives define it as equality of opportunity and equality under the law.

Most Americans don't see their country as inherently unfair. In a 2005 Syracuse University poll, researchers asked a cross section of Americans if they believed that "everyone in American society has an opportunity to succeed, most do, or only some have this opportunity." Seventy-one percent said that all or most Americans can get ahead.[20]

Unlike most Americans, Obama believes he needs to force fairness on an otherwise unfair country. He believes in his moral values but seems unwilling to grant that those who oppose him have moral values equally worthy of consideration and respect. When it comes to fairness, Obama is decidedly unfair in judging his opponents.

Obama vs. the Rich

On April 30, 2012, Obama delivered one of his classic class warfare speeches. He warned union members that Republicans would rather give "rich folks" more tax breaks than invest in the American worker.[21]

"Republicans in Congress would rather put fewer of you to work rebuilding America than ask millionaires and billionaires to live without massive new tax cuts on top of the ones they've already gotten," Obama told union workers.[22] Obama added that the Republicans' economic plan depended on tax cuts for the rich and "dismantling your unions."[23] He added, "After all you've done to build and protect the middle class, they make the argument you're responsible for the problems facing the middle class."[24]

Obama's deficit reduction plan would hurt not only the oft-targeted "millionaires and billionaires." It includes letting the Bush tax cuts expire for couples earning $250,000 a year, a de facto tax hike for many small business owners. And it is not the rich but the middle class and the poor who will suffer most when Obama's taxes on the most successful Americans divert money that would otherwise be invested in jobs to filling the coffers of the government.

The wealthy already pay more than their fair share in taxes. The top 1 percent of earners pays nearly 40 percent of income taxes. The effective tax rate of the well-off is about twice that of middle income earners. Half the country pays no federal income tax at all. The *Weekly Standard*'s Jeffrey Anderson put things in stark relief: "[T]he top 0.1% paid more toward the workings of government than the bottom 80% did," he wrote in 2011. "That's despite the fact that the bottom 80% collectively made more than six times as much money as the top 0.1% did."[25]

These and other statistics show that Obama's rhetoric and policies aren't really about fairness. The sad truth is that, thanks in part to Obama and his media allies, millions of voters believe the wealthy pay not just a lower rate on their taxes, but less in net taxes than do middle-income earners. Polls show that most Americans support raising taxes on the wealthiest Americans. But a Resurgent Republic poll found that 65 percent of American voters say that "the maximum percentage that the federal government should take from any individual's income should be 20 percent or lower."[26] It would then surely be news to many Americans that the average federal income tax rate of those earning between $1 million and $10 million was nearly 30 percent in 2009. Add in state and local taxes, and many are giving more than 40 percent, with new tax hikes scheduled just after the election, on January 1, 2013.

Many of Obama's liberal allies have taken the anti-success rhetoric a step further, predicting, and perhaps even encouraging, violence against wealthy Americans. Filmmaker Michael Moore said:

> The smart rich know they can only build the gate so high. And sooner or later history proves that people, when they've had enough, aren't going to take it anymore. And much better to

deal with it nonviolently now, through the political system, than what could possibly happen in the future, which nobody wants to see.[27]

In February 2012, President Obama released his 2013 budget. A White House press release stated:

> We now face a make-or-break moment for the middle class and those trying to reach it. After decades of eroding middle-class security as those at the very top saw their incomes rise as never before and after a historic recession that plunged our economy into a crisis from which we are still fighting to recover, it is time to construct an economy that is built to last.[28]

The budget itself is an exercise in divisive class warfare. The budget included numerous layers of tax hikes on successful investors and small business owners. It raised the capital gains tax from 15 percent to 24 percent, and the dividends tax from 15 percent to nearly 40 percent. It repealed the Bush tax cuts for top earners and included a 30 percent "Buffett-rule" minimum tax on millionaires. The carried-interest tax for private equity, hedge funds, and other investment partnerships was more than doubled, from 15 percent to 40 percent. The death tax jumped to 45 percent.[29]

A press statement released from Representative Paul Ryan called the budget a $1.9 trillion tax hike, with $47 trillion in government spending over the next decade and the fourth straight year of trillion-dollar deficits.[30]

In March, Obama's budget was voted on in the Senate, where it failed 99 to 0.[31]

Americans Aren't Buying Obama's Class Warfare

A December 2011 Gallup poll found that "Americans are now less likely to see U.S. society as divided into the 'haves' and 'have nots' than they were in 2008, returning to their views prior to that point. A clear majority, 58%, say they do not think of America in this way, after Americans were divided 49% to 49% in the summer of 2008."[32]

One reason Obama's class warfare rhetoric is a bust is that Americans have never seen themselves as being divided by class. We are a fluid society, inherently open to the ability of individuals to move up or down the income and wealth scale.

Even self-identified Democrats were less likely (by three percentage points) in 2011 to see America as divided between "haves" and "have nots" than three years earlier.[33] Most Americans do not buy into Obama's divisive rhetoric pitting economic classes against one another. And they have enough empathy to know that "fairness" is often in the eye of the beholder.

CHAPTER SIX

Obama's Socialism and Crony Capitalism versus the Middle Class

The story of Barack Obama's first term is the story of a president whose preoccupation with the government takeover of large segments of the American economy has come at the expense of America's average, hard-working people.

America's economic troubles have many causes that can't be blamed on President Obama, including globalization, an aging population, and the bursting of the housing bubble. But the president certainly can be blamed for deepening the economic crisis, slowing the recovery, and laying the groundwork for the decline of the middle class for years if not decades to come.

As an indication of how far the middle class has fallen in recent years, consider these two statistics. A 2011 report by Pew Charitable Trusts found that nearly one in three Americans who grew up in the middle class has moved downward.[1] And a Federal Reserve report released in June 2012 revealed that between 2007 and 2010, the median net worth of American families dropped by an astonishing $50,000, from $126,400 to $77,300—a

39 percent decline that brought the median figure all the way back to where it was in 1992.[2]

Obama has spent three years pushing policies that either ignore or aggravate the structural problems in the economy.

Obama supports allowing Bush-era tax cuts to expire for those making more than $200,000 a year, a policy that would raise tax rates from 35 percent to 40 percent on thousands of small business owners who are taxed as individuals. From the start of Obama's presidency until December 2012, 2.5 million homes were lost to foreclosure, and millions of others were in the foreclosure process or seriously delinquent. Home values continue to plummet.[3] Obama has not helped make things better. "'Every [federal housing] program has fallen far short of goals. I can't think of one that's been largely successful,' John Dodds, director of the Philadelphia Unemployment Project, a non-profit that's been involved in foreclosure prevention for decades," told USA Today in December 2011.[4]

Obamacare over the Recovery

In The Escape Artists: How Obama's Team Fumbled the Recovery, Noam Scheiber describes how Obama chose to pursue nationalized health care instead of concentrating on the economic recovery. Obama saw health care as a greater long-term accomplishment, according to Scheiber, who wrote: "There was a strain of messianism in Barack Obama, a determination to change the course of history. And it was this determination that explained his reluctance to abandon his presidential vision."[5]

Former Obama economic adviser Larry Summers told Scheiber, "I always admired the president's courage for recognizing that fifty years from now people would remember that all Americans had health care. And even if pursuing health care affected the pace of the recovery, which was unlikely in my view, people wouldn't remember how fast the recovery from this recession was."[6]

Perhaps that's true. Perhaps fifty years from now people will remember Obama's takeover of the health care industry more than the slow recovery. But Obama wasn't elected to be president of the America of 2062. Long-term vision is fine, but Obama was voted to be president of America today. And for the moment, Americans want a president who will address the slow pace of the so-called recovery.

Obamacare has hurt the economy in myriad ways, including by creating an entirely new entitlement in a nation already suffering from unsustainable entitlements and introducing new levels of uncertainty into the weak economy.

A November 2011 study by the National Federation of Independent Business (NFIB) noted that Obamacare will "impose a cumulative cost of nearly $5,000 per family by 2020" through increased health insurance costs as well as "reduc[ing] private sector employment by 125,000 to 249,000 jobs in 2021, with 59 percent of those losses falling on small business."[7] If these count as "benefits" of the new health care system that Obama wants to see as his legacy, most Americans would demur: this is not the hope and change they voted for.

The incomes of middle class Americans have stagnated over the last ten years, in part because increases in health premiums have absorbed wage growth. While running for president, Obama repeatedly promised that if elected he would reduce premiums by $2,500 a year. But insurance premiums have increased more than $2,000 since Obama became president.[8]

Obamacare was presented as a way to contain costs. But the Centers for Medicare and Medicaid Services Office of the Actuary says Obamacare will increase, not decrease, health care spending by hundreds of billions of dollars.[9] The nonpartisan Congressional Budget Office predicts that Obamacare will reduce the labor force by 800,000 over the next ten years.[10] It also estimates that Obamacare will cost American businesses that do not comply with its dictates $52 billion.[11] As businessman Steve Zelnak has written in *U.S. News & World Report*:

For a small-to-medium sized business, the prospect of having to comb through the 2,700 pages of Obamacare to figure out which of the $525 billion in taxes, or $26 billion in penalties, or hundreds of new regulations and mandates apply to them is daunting, to say the least. Is it any surprise that healthcare costs have risen already? Fifty-seven percent of employers nationwide say that healthcare costs have risen due to Obamacare, and in my home state of North Carolina, premium costs are projected to increase by 5.2 percent over last year's costs.[12]

America's greatest problem is job creation, and Obamacare, the great legacy for which Obama was willing to sacrifice the economy, only aggravates that problem.

Cap and Tax

The president began his term by promising in his inaugural address, "We will harness the sun and the winds and the soil to fuel our cars and run our factories."[13] Obama's pledge was characteristically fantastic. But it was one promise Obama has tried very hard to keep, and the economy has suffered for it.

As was the case with Obamacare, the president has pursued an environmental agenda that places the priorities of a leftwing constituency (in this case, the "green" lobby) ahead of the interests of America's middle class. The president began his term pursuing "cap and trade" legislation—aptly named "cap and tax" by conservatives—to limit greenhouse gas emissions. The point of cap and trade was to hike the price of electricity and gas so that Americans would use less.

Who would have paid for Obama's ambitious legislation, which came to be known as the American Clean Energy and Security Act? Consumers, of course, in the form of higher prices for a variety of goods and services. As

Peter Orszag, Obama's former budget director, told Congress in 2008, "Those price increases are essential to the success of a cap and trade program."[14]

Cap and trade would have hurt low and middle income Americans most, because those households spend more of their income on gas, groceries, and home heating. The Congressional Budget Office estimated that the price increases resulting from the cap and trade scheme would have cost the average household 3.3 percent of their after-tax income every year; middle class workers could have lost up to $1,500 of income annually.[15]

Similar analyses came from the Heritage Foundation and Obama's own Treasury Department. Heritage predicted that cap and trade would have cost the economy $161 billion in 2020, which is $1,870 for a family of four.[16] That number would rise to $6,800 for a family of four by 2035 when further cap and trade restrictions kicked in. Obama's Treasury Department estimated a yearly cost of up to $1,761 per household.[17]

Besides driving up prices, cap and trade promised to drive down jobs. The *Wall Street Journal* explained how the bill would have affected employment: "These higher prices will show up not just in electricity bills or at the gas station but in every manufactured good, from food to cars. Consumers will cut back on spending, which in turn will cut back on production, which results in fewer jobs created or higher unemployment. Some companies will instead move their operations overseas, with the same result."[18]

The *Wall Street Journal* called cap and trade "likely to be the biggest tax in American history."[19] Even some Democrats conceded the same. Representative John Dingell, a Michigan Democrat and former chairman of the Energy and Commerce Committee, said in a hearing, "Nobody in this country realizes that cap and trade is a tax, and it's a great big one."[20]

Ben Lieberman of the Heritage Foundation predicted that the bill would usher in a permanent recession. "We might never really have a full recovery if we have to live with these tremendous constraints on affordable energy use," he wrote, adding, "so we would be talking about exactly the kind of thing that we are worried about now—job losses, high energy costs—these things being exacerbated and staying that way for years and years."[21]

Obama's pursuit of cap and trade belied his campaign promise not to increase taxes on the middle class. "I pledge to you that under my plan, no one making less than $250,000 a year will see any form of tax increase. Not income tax, not capital gains taxes, not any kind of tax," Candidate Obama said in 2008.[22] It didn't take long for President Obama to break that promise.

Democrats made clear that they weren't concerned with the legislation's impact on working Americans by voting down three amendments offered by Republicans—one to suspend the program if gas hit $5 a gallon; one to suspend the program if electricity prices rose 10 percent over 2009; and one to suspend the program if unemployment rates hit 15 percent.

High energy prices weren't simply a negative byproduct of cap and trade; they were the main goal of the scheme. As Obama told the *San Francisco Chronicle* in 2008, "Under my plan of a cap and trade system, electricity rates would necessarily skyrocket.... That will cost money... the [utilities] will pass that money on to the consumers."[23] To Obama, higher energy prices were a good thing, because it would discourage energy use. Congressional Democrats agreed with him, but it is fairly certain that middle income Americans, already wincing at their energy bills, did not.

Cap and tax passed the Democratic-controlled House in June 2009 but failed to garner enough support to pass in the Senate.

Cap and Tax by Executive Fiat

When cap and trade failed in Congress, Obama ordered the Environmental Protection Agency (EPA) to enforce many of its provisions by bureaucratic fiat—part of an alarming trend of ignoring Congress when it would not do his bidding.

In a statement posted on its website in late 2010, the EPA announced it would move unilaterally to clamp down on power plant and oil refinery greenhouse emissions, announcing plans for developing new standards over the next year.[24] EPA administrator Lisa Jackson said the aim was to better cope with pollution contributing to climate change.[25]

In 2011, the EPA issued regulations on coal plants, announcing that it was finalizing new rules to curb pollution from coal-fired power plants. Mercury, smog, ozone, greenhouse gases, water intake, and coal ash were all getting regulated.[26]

The Edison Electric Institute, an association of electric power companies, and the American Legislative Exchange Council, a conservative educational organization, dubbed the new rules the "EPA's Regulatory Train Wreck."[27] They estimated that the new regulations would cost utilities as much as $129 billion and force them to retire one-fifth of coal capacity.[28] Coal provides nearly half of the country's power, so these new rules will mean higher electric bills, more blackouts, and fewer jobs.

Obama decided to bypass Congress to implement cap and trade after the 2010 mid-term election (an election in which more than two dozen members of Congress who voted for cap and trade lost their seats). He made no apologies about his end-run around Congress. "Cap and trade was just one way of skinning the cat; it was not the only way," he said at a press conference. "I'm going to be looking for other means to address this problem."[29]

Obama's "war on coal," while winning kudos from environmental leftists, has taken a toll on Obama in many coal-producing states, including West Virginia, the country's second-largest coal-producing state. In the state's Democratic presidential primary on May 8, 2012, prison inmate Keith Judd received 41 percent of the vote.[30] Two leading West Virginia Democrats, Governor Earl Ray Tomblin[31] and Senator Joe Manchin,[32] declined to say whether they'd vote for Obama in the general election, and both of them and Democratic Representative Nick Rahal announced in June that they'd be skipping the Democratic National Convention in September. Later, Pennsylvania Democratic Representative Mark Critz announced he wouldn't be attending the convention either.[33]

All these developments were widely regarded as proof of the depth of resentment in West Virginia and the mining communities of Pennsylvania over the administration's "war on coal."

Gas Prices

"I think you see a lot and you hear a lot about it being a very stressed relationship, and that's real. We should just be honest about the fact that that's real."[34] So said Shell Oil Company President Marvin Odum in an interview with Platts Energy Week TV, broadcast on June 16, 2012. Odum's candor reinforced the conventional wisdom about the oil industry's adversarial relationship with the Obama administration.

Obama has spent his first term railing against oil companies. "Right now, the biggest oil companies are raking in record profits—profits that go up every time folks like these pull up into a gas station," Obama said during a press conference in March 2012.[35] He signaled his contempt for oil by selecting Dr. Steven Chu as his energy secretary. Chu told the *Wall Street Journal* in September 2008, "Somehow, we have to figure out how to boost the price of gasoline to the levels in Europe."[36]

That remark has dogged Chu (who rides a bicycle to work) during his entire tenure in the Obama administration—and for good reason. Europeans pay about $9 a gallon. Prices haven't gotten that high in America yet, but they have doubled during Obama's term.

Even liberal NBC reporter Chuck Todd conceded about Obama in February 2012, "There is no issue that has been a, I guess, a bigger bust for the president than energy policy in general. There's a lot of, we can come up with a lot of excuses as to why, but boy, it's just like you can't—he's made no progress."[37]

Global markets largely determine oil prices, but Obama's assault on oil drilling has not helped matters.

Obama has consistently opposed exploration for gas and oil in Alaska, including in the Alaska National Wildlife Refuge (ANWR). The federal government leases only 3 percent of federal lands for energy production. If ANWR were opened, it could become the largest oil-producing field in the United States.

The Pipeline to Nowhere

The $7 billion, 1,700-mile Keystone pipeline would connect the tar sands of Alberta, Canada, with American refineries on the Gulf Coast. In 2011, Obama postponed until 2013 a decision by federal agencies about whether an extension of the pipeline, called Keystone XL, would be built.[38]

That looked likely until the EPA intervened in 2010 and said that a draft environmental impact study found that Keystone XL was inadequate and that it should be revised. In August 2011, a new impact report was issued that concluded that the pipeline would pose "no significant impacts" to most resources if environmental protection measures were followed.[39] But protests by environmental groups convinced Obama to postpone the decision until 2013.

On November 6, 2011, thousands of environmental activists formed a human chain around the White House to try to convince Obama to block the project because the pipeline would transport what they consider "dirty oil." They claim it would aggravate climate change, lead to oil spills, and pollute air, water, and wildlife. Organizer Bill McKibben said, "This has become not only the biggest environmental flash point in many, many years, but maybe the issue in recent times in the Obama administration when he's been most directly confronted by people in the street. In this case, people willing, hopeful, almost dying for him to be the Barack Obama of 2008."[40]

Republicans pressed Obama, and in December 2011 Congress voted to give him a 60-day deadline to make a decision on an application for the construction of the pipeline. They noted that the project would create an estimated 20,000 jobs.[41] But in January 2012, Obama rejected the application.

Later in 2012, Obama reversed course, sort of. Obama's rejection of Keystone XL provoked a strong backlash from unions, pro-business groups, and the public. A March Gallup poll found nearly twice as many Americans supported the pipeline (57 percent) as opposed it (29 percent).[42] Canadian Prime Minister Stephen Harper said Canada would look elsewhere, particularly to China, to sell its oil if the United States didn't want it. But rather than green light the critical infrastructure project linking Canadian oil with American refineries, Obama struck a compromise that pleased no one: a pipeline to nowhere. Obama's literal half measure involves constructing a pipeline from the Gulf Coast to Oklahoma—nearly 2,000 miles short of the Canadian oil fields. On June 15, 2012, the U.S. State Department announced it will conduct another environmental review of the proposed pipeline with the goal of making a decision on the project's permit next year.[43]

North Dakota Republican senator John Hoeven said an environmental review of the entire route was "unwarranted and unjustified in light of an already exhaustive four-year review."[44] He added: "Today's notice from the Department of State seems to be yet another obstructive tactic designed to appease a narrow constituency. With rising unemployment, a stagnant economy, and continued instability in the Middle East, the need for Congress to approve the project has never been greater."

The Keystone pipeline would bring in more than 700,000 barrels of oil a day. According to Mario Loyola, a senior analyst at the Armstrong Center for Energy and the Environment, "Obama will soon be personally responsible for preventing some two million barrels per day of possible North American crude oil production from reaching the American economy. The U.S. currently produces only about six million barrels of domestic crude oil, so that would be more than a 30 percent increase in domestic production."[45] The president, Loyola notes, "is preventing the U.S. from increasing oil production by an amount nearly equivalent to Iran's total oil exports.... We are once again entering a period of scarcity, where slight fluctuations in demand or supply will have a disproportionate impact on gas prices—but this time the scarcity is largely the product of Obama's policies."[46]

Obama's energy policies hurt middle class American families most. Energy companies raise their prices when the government sets up bureaucratic roadblocks and higher taxes. Most of the costs are ultimately passed down to consumers.

Solyndra

The story of Solyndra again illustrates how the Obama administration has placed election politics and narrow ideological and political interests ahead of the interests of the American people, particularly middle income Americans.

Solyndra was a California-based manufacturer of solar panels. George W. Bush's Energy Department first considered making a loan to Solyndra, but its review panel unanimously recommended against doing so. President Obama took up the cause as a centerpiece of his "green energy" initiative. In March 2009, the Energy Department made a "conditional commitment" to a $535 million loan guarantee to support Solyndra's construction of a commercial-scale manufacturing plant for its solar panels, with the promise that it would create 4,000 new jobs.[47] The money came from Obama's $859 billion stimulus program.

After securing the loan guarantee, the Federal Financing Bank, part of the Department of the Treasury, loaned Solyndra $527 million.[48] But career employees at the Office of Management and Budget cautioned against proffering the loan. One even predicted Solyndra would run out of money and head for bankruptcy court by September 2011.[49] A Government Accountability Office report said the Energy Department had circumvented its own rules in order to make loan guarantees to at least five firms, including Solyndra.[50]

In March 2010 an independent audit by Price Waterhouse Coopers questioned whether Solyndra could survive as a business, and, according to internal administration emails, even administration staff and close Obama allies in the venture capital world warned the White House that the company was a bad bet.[51] Undeterred, Obama visited the company in a high-profile media event in May 2010, declaring, "The true engine of economic growth will always be companies like Solyndra."[52]

Solyndra executives were privately warning administration officials that they were at risk of going under, and that the company needed to lay off employees. But, according to internal emails, the Energy Department persuaded the firm to delay layoffs until after the 2010 mid-term elections.[53] Solyndra was in dire economic shape, and in February 2011, the Energy Department restructured the loan, providing Solyndra $75 million more in taxpayer financing.[54]

On September 1, 2011, Solyndra filed for Chapter 11 bankruptcy and fired all 1,100 of its employees. The company is now being sued by some employees who were abruptly let go.[55]

Emails between Solyndra and the Obama administration made public by the House Energy and Commerce Subcommittee on Oversight and Investigations made clear that political considerations, as the *Washington Post* put it, "infused almost every level of the decision-making on granting the Solyndra loan and later administration efforts to keep the company afloat."[56]

It was also revealed that the company's shareholders and executives had made numerous substantial donations to Obama's campaign, that Solyndra executives had held meetings with White House officials, and that the company had spent large sums of money on lobbying.[57] In fact, during the period when Solyndra's loan guarantee was under review, the company had spent nearly $1.8 million on lobbying.

In September 2011, the *Washington Post* reported that not only had the Obama administration continued to give Solyndra taxpayer money even after it had defaulted on its $535 million loan, but the Energy Department restructured the loans even after being warned that such action might be illegal.[58]

The Solyndra scandal won't dissuade the Obama administration from continuing to pursue its "green energy" agenda, and from placing narrow ideological interests ahead of the American taxpayers' interests. In 2012, Obama senior adviser David Axelrod said the administration won't "back off" its commitment to alternative and, as it turns out, often ineffective energy production. "This is going to continue being a thrust for us."

In a campaign speech in Cleveland in June 2012, Obama said, "My plan would end the government subsidies to oil companies that have rarely been more profitable—let's double down on a clean-energy industry that has never been more promising."[59]

But a June paper by scholars at the Brookings Institution, a left-leaning Washington, D.C., think tank, found that clean energy subsidies have been a waste. The paper claims they don't reduce dependence to foreign sources of energy, because many technologies favored by current policy—wind, solar, geothermal—replace coal and natural gas, in which the United States is already self-sufficient.

The paper also found that clean energy subsidies don't create jobs; they merely shift them around from one company to another. As Charles Lane of the *Washington Post* wrote about the Obama administration's green obsession: "If government does double down on clean energy, it's the federal budget that will end up busted."[60] Just another bill Obama is prepared to stick to taxpayers.

CHAPTER SEVEN

Obama's Generational Theft

Not so long ago, young Americans swooned for Barack Obama. Obama's support among America's youth derived in part from his perceived coolness. He was young and biracial. He played basketball and listened to Jay-Z. He offered inclusive and uncomplicated slogans like "Yes We Can!" "Change You Can Believe In," and "We are the ones we've been waiting for." But there was something more. Obama appealed to that natural optimism and hopefulness of the young. His soaring rhetoric promised them something better: unity, transparency, no more finger-pointing. And he promised them, and all of us, a fundamental transformation.

Four years after Senator John Kerry won voters twenty-nine and younger by nine percentage points, Obama won them by thirty-four points—66 percent to 32 percent. What's more, 2008 saw two million more young Americans under age thirty vote than in 2004.

Obama didn't just win the youth vote. As Jonathan Alter puts it in *The Promise*, he "carried the future in a landslide.... All the canvassing and college organizing and cool new web videos had paid off. The headline for those who followed politics closely was *generational realignment.*"[1]

Almost as soon as Obama became president, the veneer began to wear. Young people noticed the "I won, you lost" rhetoric. They noticed the backroom dealing over Obamacare, and the harsh partisan rhetoric out of the White House. They also noticed the world apology tour. And they certainly noticed economic conditions, far from improving as had been promised, careening downward.

More subtle, but still noticed, was Obama's attack on the American dream—their American dream. Obama's policies were attacking industry, hard work, ambition—the very characteristics they had seen in their parents and grandparents, and grew up respecting and emulating.

Early in his administration, Barack Obama addressed the graduating class of Arizona State University. It was May 2009, and he told the graduates:

> Now, in the face of these challenges, it may be tempting to fall back on the formulas for success that have been pedaled so frequently in recent years. It goes something like this: You're taught to chase after all the usual brass rings; you try to be on this "who's who" list or that top 100 list; you chase after the big money and you figure out how big your corner office is; you worry about whether you have a fancy enough title or a fancy enough car. That's the message that's sent each and every day, or has been in our culture for far too long—that through material possessions, through a ruthless competition pursued only on your own behalf—that's how you will measure success.
>
> Now, you can take that road—and it may work for some. But at this critical juncture in our nation's history, at this difficult time, let me suggest that such an approach won't get you where you want to go; it displays a poverty of ambition—that in fact, the elevation of appearance over substance, of celebrity over character, of short-term gain over lasting achievement is precisely what your generation needs to help end.[2]

Barack Obama was telling young Americans that striving for success, having ambition, reveals a "poverty of ambition." Here Obama was doing what he does best: denigrating a group in order to create hostility and discontent. He was fostering a distrust of the ambitious and the successful, something we have seen the president do repeatedly—by encouraging the Occupy Wall Street movement and by attacking business. Obama was looking to rob young people of pride in success, and the honor of a hard day's work that is as American as apple pie.

Instead, he was hoping to make a different way of life more attractive—one where there is equality of outcomes, where government determines what is fair, and indeed where the most important jobs are not in the private sector but in the government or non-profit sector. In short, Obama was driving a wedge between young people and what has made America great.

All the while, President Obama has tried his best to maintain young Americans' enthusiasm for him and his presidency. Trying to prolong the rock star fascination he inspired among young people, he has appeared on high school and college campuses with astonishing regularity. He has promised young people free contraceptives; he's promised that "children" can stay on their parents' health insurance until they are twenty-six (although their parents have to pay for it); and he's pledged to forgive their student loan debt if they go into government-approved fields after graduating.

But neither Obama's "coolness" nor his handouts can compensate for the devastating impact his economy has had on young Americans.

The Boomerang Generation

The Obama economy has spawned a new term: the Boomerang Generation. It describes the millions of young people who have graduated from college in the last few years only to find themselves saddled with debt, unable to find work, and having to move back home with their parents. According to the liberal *Huffington Post*, 85 percent of 2011 college graduates had to move home because they were unable to support themselves.[3]

It is difficult to exaggerate the impact of the Obama economy on young people's job prospects. To convey just how bad it really is, Young America's Foundation developed the Youth Misery Index, combining youth unemployment, average graduating college debt, and national debt per capita. The Youth Misery Index under Obama has risen 20 percent, and it's only getting worse.

A 2011 Rutgers University study found that only about half—53 percent—of college graduates between 2006 and 2011 were employed full time.[4] Twenty-one percent were un- or underemployed. Many others, frustrated after months or years of trying to find suitable work, had dropped out of the economy altogether.

According to a study by the Associated Press, in April 2012 more than half of recent college graduates were either unemployed or working in a job that doesn't require a bachelor's degree. The survey was conducted with the help of researchers from Northeastern University, Drexel University, and the Economic Policy Institute, based on data from the Census Bureau's Current Population Survey and the U.S. Department of Labor.[5]

Data from the Bureau of Labor Statistics (BLS) back up these findings. According to the BLS, on June 1, 2012, 12.1 percent of young people had unsuccessfully looked for a job during the last several weeks.[6] The underlying data also showed that 1.7 million people aged eighteen to twenty-nine had given up looking for jobs. And at 15.4 percent, the jobless rate for 18- to 24-year-olds was nearly twice the overall jobless rate.

That news came after a May 9, 2012, Gallup report that showed 13.6 percent of 18- to-29 year-olds were unemployed, and 32 percent were underemployed, in April.[7] That underemployment rate was up from 30.1 percent in April and is more than twice the rate for people aged thirty to sixty-four.

The Obama economy is hurting young people in other ways as well. In April 2012, Obama became the first president since Jimmy Carter to see gas prices double under his watch.[8] (In comparison, during the presidency of Ronald Reagan gas prices dropped 66 percent.) Because young people are more likely than older workers to be un- or under-employed, and to earn less when they do have a job, high gas prices and higher commuter transportation costs hit them harder.

Many young people are postponing marriage and children, not just because of general social trends in that direction but because they believe they can't afford to support a family. And stories are legion about young people with mountains of debt they are unable to pay off. In 2010, for the first time ever, student loan debt exceeded credit card debt. As of late 2011, the average student loan debt was $25,250.[9] In 2012 total student loan debt eclipsed the trillion dollar figure.[10] And nearly six million Americans have a past-due student loan account.[11]

According to the Associated Press, recent graduates are now more likely to work as "waiters, waitresses, bartenders and food-service helpers than as engineers, physicists, chemists and mathematicians combined."[12] All of these statistics explain why more than one-third of young people aged twenty-five to twenty-nine have moved back in with their parents in recent years.[13]

As he does with each of his constituencies, President Obama tries to create solidarity with young people. He tells them he feels their pain. Speaking to students at the University of North Carolina in April 2012, Obama told the crowd he and his wife had "been in your shoes," and that they didn't pay off all their loans until a few years earlier.

"I didn't just read about this," he said. "I didn't just get some talking points about this. I didn't just get a policy briefing on this. We didn't come from wealthy families. When we graduated from college and law school, we had a mountain of debt. When we married, we got poor together."[14]

Loan Forgiveness

President Obama's policies to address America's mounting student debt amount to a government takeover of the student loan industry.

When Obamacare was passed in 2010, it included the Student Aid and Fiscal Responsibility Act (SAFRA), a program that nationalized college student loans. It was a gimmick to increase revenues and make it look like Obamacare reduced the deficit. SAFRA eliminated guaranteed college loans—loans originated through private lenders but completely backed by taxpayer money—and made almost all lending direct from the U.S. Treasury.

As they have on so many other issues, Obama and his Democratic allies removed the intermediary—in this case private lenders—standing between the individual and the federal government. The result is that, today, 85 percent of all student loan debt is owed to the government.

Obama signed a law in March 2010 that expanded Pell grants. It also capped loan repayments at 10 percent of income above the basic living allowance, and forgave loan payments after twenty years of on-time payments, or ten years if the borrower is employed in public service—that is, as a teacher, police officer, or in some other taxpayer-supported job, or in the non-profit sector.

But Obama's plan, imposed by executive order, not passed by Congress, covered only public loans, not private loans, and thus it effectively punishes students who receive loans from outside the federal government.

What's more, as of February 2012, the Obama administration stopped forgiving student loans for public service work if that service is related to religion. The language of the Public Service Loan Forgiveness (PSLF) program is as follows: "Generally, the type or nature of employment with the organization does not matter for PSLF purposes. However, when determining full-time public service employment at a not-for-profit organization you may not include time spent participating in religious instruction, worship services, or any form of proselytizing." So a young person working to help the needy through the Salvation Army, Samaritan's Purse, or Catholic Relief Services would not have his student loans forgiven, but a young person working as a federal bureaucrat at HHS would.

I empathize with those paying off mountains of school debt. But while "forgiving" student loans may sound compassionate, it has to be paid by someone. In this case, it will be paid for by future generations, including those who pay taxes but didn't have the chance or make the choice to go to college.

Generational Theft

Obama's out-of-control borrowing and spending places a huge burden on future generations. The Congressional Budget Office projects that cumulative national debt will increase in the next decade by $9.8 trillion, a sum that will mean lower standards of living for Americans in the future. Some policymakers have labeled the spending "generational theft."[15]

According to statistics from the Obama administration, the actual or projected deficit tallies for the four years in which Obama has submitted budgets are as follows:

2010: $1.29 trillion
2011: $1.3 trillion
2012: $1.3 trillion
2013: $901 billion

The *Weekly Standard*'s Jeffrey Anderson added up all of Obama's spending, (including hundreds of billions of spending in the stimulus package and other spending items) and concluded that deficit spending for Obama's first term will be $5.17 trillion.[16]

"To help put that colossal sum of money into perspective," Anderson writes, "if you take our deficit spending under Obama and divide it evenly among the roughly 300 million American citizens, that works out to just over $17,000 per person—or about $70,000 for a family of four." To put it another way, Obama is on target to increase the national debt in just one term as much as all previous U.S. presidents did combined.[17]

It is not an exaggeration to say that thanks in part to Obama's out-of-control spending, today's young people are the first generation in American history to face a future in which they are less prosperous than their parents.

Obamacare and Young Americans

Obamacare disproportionately hurts young people, because they're the ones who will have to pay for it.

In his Supreme Court opinion upholding Obamacare, which evoked outrage from constitutional conservatives, Chief Justice John Roberts got one point right. He wrote, "If the individual mandate is targeted at a class, it is a class whose commercial inactivity rather than activity is its defining feature."[18] Young people are indeed a "targeted class" under Obamacare.

First, young Americans will be coerced into buying health care—they are needed to make the government scheme feasible, so they will be forced into buying what they may not want or need. If they don't, they will be forced to pay a penalty tax. (Many still won't buy insurance because the tax is less than the insurance, which will only increase the overall cost of Obamacare.)

Second, because of government price controls, Obamacare mandates artificially low premiums for older Americans and artificially high premiums for low-risk young people. Contrary to Obama's promise that premiums would go down, the Heritage Foundation found that Obamacare will result in premium hikes of 45 percent for 18- to 24-year-olds, and 35 percent for 25- to 29-year-olds.[19]

And young people—and the colleges, parents, and employers who might be paying for their premiums—are forbidden under Obamacare from buying affordable and practical "limited-benefit" health insurance, which caps health care expenses for this low-risk pool. Consequently, colleges across the country have dropped their student plans, because Obamacare increases the costs of those plans by upwards of 1,000 percent.[20]

Many young people cannot afford to take on the extra financial burden of health insurance. They are healthy and their health care expenses are relatively low. But Obamacare's individual mandate requires that all adults buy "qualifying health insurance" or face an excise tax penalty of at least 2.5 percent of adjusted gross income. That's a painful expense for a generation that can't find work commensurate with their education and that is already putting off life decisions because of concerns about expenses.

Obamacare also hurts young people's employment prospects. According to a U.S. Chamber of Commerce survey, 74 percent of small businesses said that Obamacare makes it more difficult for them to hire new employees, and 30 percent are not planning to hire at all due to the law.[21]

For some businesses, the costs of hiring new employees are now prohibitive. Moreover, the uncertainty regarding the full implications of the law once implemented in 2014, combined with Obama's determination to let the Bush tax cuts expire, add deterrents to hiring.

Obama's Millennial Challenge

Whether it's the job market, student loan debt, taxes, Obamacare, or the national debt, Obama's policies have made young people poorer and their prospects for prosperity bleaker.

Yet Obama is pulling out all the stops to try and repeat his 2008 performance among young people. A reporter for the *Daily Caller* counted 130 appearances by the president, vice president, their spouses, White House officials, and Cabinet secretaries at colleges and universities between spring 2011 and spring 2012.[22] Young America's Foundation found that the president himself has been on high school or college campuses once every 12 days since his inauguration.[23]

But the slogans young people bought into—"Hope and Change" in particular—are turning out to be a big bust. The administration that pledged to be the most transparent in history is full of secrecy and executive privilege. The petty partisanship that young people despise is at an all-time high. And the economic outlook for them in the near- and long-term is downright bleak.

An April NBC/*Wall Street Journal* poll showed only 45 percent of young people were taking a big interest in the election, compared to

63 percent in 2008.[24] Gallup polling numbers show that more than 80 percent of older Americans say they will definitely vote, while only 56 percent of Americans under thirty say the same.[25]

An April survey by Harvard University's Institute of Politics found that Obama held a 17-point lead over Romney among voters aged eighteen to twenty-nine. But it showed that only 41 percent of white Millennials approved of Obama's job performance—significantly lower than the 54 percent who voted for him in 2008.[26]

The Harvard survey also found that 58 percent of Millennials said the economy was a top issue and that only 41 percent approved Obama's handling of it.[27]

A June 2012 Gallup poll found that 58 percent of Americans are dissatisfied with the opportunity of the next generation to reach the American dream of having a better life than their parents.[28] Meanwhile, according to numerous polls on the RealClearPolitics website, throughout Obama's term, twice as many Americans have thought America is on the "wrong track" as believe it is on the "right track."

Barack Obama has played young people. He reached out to them with soaring speeches championing unity, and they responded to his call to transcend differences and engage in a new kind of politics. In fact, they responded with more enthusiasm, more genuine hope than any other demographic. And the president repaid their trust with betrayal—becoming not the great uniter, but the most divisive president in history. He has robbed them of current and future prosperity, perverted their understanding of the value of hard work, ambition, and the American dream, and poisoned their optimism—the very optimism he used to soar to victory in 2008.

Americans are optimistic by nature. Their current pessimism about the future can't all be blamed on Barack Obama. But he bears a large portion of the responsibility. Obama is doing young people a great injustice by pursuing an agenda that pits them against their future.

CHAPTER EIGHT

The Deceit and Division of Obamacare and the "War on Women"

B arack Obama won the 2008 Democratic nomination for president by defeating the first serious female presidential candidate in U.S. history.

2008 was supposed to be Hillary Clinton's year. She was poised to finally shatter the presidential glass ceiling and become America's first female president. Millions of American women yearned for that outcome, and most Republicans had resigned themselves to the prospect of facing the formidable senator and former first lady. Pundits and pollsters were regularly using the "I" word to describe Clinton's nomination prospects—inevitable.

Obama won instead, of course, and he did so in no small measure due to the support of women. While Hillary edged Obama among female voters overall, Obama won them in many key primary states. In Virginia, for instance, Obama won women by twenty-one percentage points (60 percent to 39 percent), on his way to a 25-point win overall in that state.[1]

Exit polls showed Clinton performed better among older and white working class women but that Obama won younger, minority, and highly educated women. Obama was aided by timely endorsements from prominent female Democratic office-holders, including governors such as Christine Gregoire (Washington), Janet Napolitano (Arizona), and Kathleen Sebelius (Kansas), as well as liberal cultural icons like Oprah Winfrey and Caroline Kennedy.

After Clinton suspended her campaign in early June, Obama's general election opponent, Republican Senator John McCain, initially thought he might be able to lure disgruntled Clinton loyalists to his side.

But that hope quickly vanished, and in the general election Obama captured 56 percent of female voters—more than any Democratic presidential candidate since 1996.[2] He achieved this even though Alaska governor Sarah Palin's name appeared on his opponent's ticket.

Obama's promise of hope and reconciliation drew many women to his side. As Governor Gregoire said in explaining her endorsement, "He is leading us toward a positive feeling of hope in our country and I love seeing that happen."[3] By Inauguration Day, Obama's approval rating among women stood at 71 percent.[4]

But the "positive feeling of hope" that many women felt towards Candidate Obama faded soon after he became president. Less than two years later, in the historic 2010 mid-term congressional elections, female voters abandoned Obama's Democratic Party in droves—a development that was interpreted by most observers as a rebuke of Obama's first two years. According to exit polls, Republicans won female voters for the first time since 1982.[5]

A post-election poll commissioned by EMILY's List, a political action committee dedicated to electing liberal women, explored why so many women abandoned the Democratic Party in 2010.

In "Winning Back the Obama Defectors," pollsters interviewed 608 women who had voted for Obama in 2008 but did not vote for their Democratic congressional candidate in 2010.[6]

Among these "Obama drop-off voters," 66 percent chose not to vote, a third voted for Republicans, while the remainder cast their ballots for a third-party candidate.

Among the "GOP defectors" (women who voted for Obama in 2008 but for the Republican congressional candidate in 2010), 77 percent said they were motivated to switch sides by dissatisfaction with the economy; 57 percent said they voted Republican in part to express dissatisfaction with the Democratic leadership in Congress; and 48 percent said they wanted to express opposition to President Obama.

Among former Obama voters who did not vote in 2010, a majority (51 percent) said they wanted to express their dissatisfaction with the state of the economy.

Also, when "Obama drop-off women" were asked to think about the qualities they saw as most important in deciding which candidates to support in future elections, their clear preference was for candidates willing to work across party lines (36 percent) and those who care about the average person (35 percent).

Aisle-crossing was even more important to former Obama voters who subsequently voted for a Republican congressional candidate, with 40 percent stating that uniting people across party lines was important.

The EMILY's List poll underscored the sense of disillusionment many women felt toward a president who had failed to deliver on his promises of hope and change.

Obama and his party's troubles with women were just beginning. Nearly a year later, in August 2011, Obama's Gallup job approval rating among women hit an all-time low of 41 percent.[7]

Clearly, millions of women had been let down. And it's no secret why. Women have been devastated in the Obama economy. But instead of addressing the real concerns of women and their families, Obama and his Democratic allies advanced the ludicrous notion that Republicans and the Catholic Church were threatening to take away their birth control pills.

Obama Has Failed Women

The facts underscore the painful toll that Obama's policies have taken on women.

- Of women who lead households, 40.7 percent of them are in poverty[8]

- The unemployment rate for women grew from 7 percent in January 2009 to 8 percent in May 2012[9]
- In April 2012, the number of women not in the labor force hit an all-time high of 53,321,000[10]
- Out of all the groups represented in a Pew survey—including blacks, whites, Hispanics, and Asians—women are the only demographic group whose employment growth lagged behind population growth from 2009 to 2011[11]
- From 2009 to 2011, women had job gains of only 600,000, as opposed to men, who gained 2.6 million[12]
- Two million fewer women were employed in the last three months of 2011 than were employed before the recession[13]
- In 2011, the poverty rate among women rose to 14.5 percent—the highest rate in 17 years[14]
- The extreme poverty rate for women (meaning those whose income is below half of the Federal poverty line) is at the highest ever recorded rate. In 2010, more than 7.5 million women were in extreme poverty[15]

Obama is on thin ice when he points his finger at conservatives, suggesting they are engaged in a "war on women."

Obamacare Hurts Women

Obamacare, the president's signature first-term domestic policy achievement, will have a devastating effect on women. It will constrain the choices they can make for themselves and their families. According to the Kaiser Foundation, roughly 80 percent of mothers choose their children's doctors and control their family's health care.[16]

But under Obamacare, millions of families will lose that choice and their employer-based health insurance. According to Dr. Scott W. Atlas, senior fellow at Stanford University's Hoover Institution, 20 million Americans will be moved into Medicaid, where they will have no choice of doctor.[17]

Also, because women see doctors on average more often than men, they will be more bound by Obamacare's decrees defining "essential benefits" coverage, treatment options, and payments to doctors.

More women than men depend on Medicaid. About 9 million nonelderly women and more than a third of all births in the United States are covered by Medicaid. By shifting an additional 20 million people to Medicaid, and consequently overloading the system, Obamacare will make it more difficult for these women and their children to find doctors.

Medicaid outcomes are already bad: there is a shortage of doctors in the Medicaid system, it's more difficult to get a diagnosis and treatment, and Medicaid patients endure longer wait times and suffer more complications from surgery than other patients. Obamacare will make this worse.

Taxing Women's Health

Obamacare also has significant negative tax implications for women. In fact, according to Grover Norquist, president of Americans for Tax Reform, Obamacare contains twenty new taxes or tax increases on American families and employers.[18]

These taxes don't affect just the rich. According to Norquist, there are five that hurt women the most.

First, under Obamacare's highly controversial "individual mandate," all Americans will be forced to purchase "qualifying health insurance" by 2014. Those who do not will face a penalty that will reach at least 2.5 percent of adjusted gross income by 2016.[19]

It won't be enough for women simply to purchase health insurance; it must be a "qualified" plan—approved by the federal government. Obama sold his reform proposal by assuring the public that under his proposal, "if you like your plan, you can keep it." But that's not true. It may not matter if a woman likes her plan. If it is considered by the government to be "not qualified," she will have to find a new one.

Another way Obamacare taxes women is through the so-called "Cadillac plan" excise tax. Starting in 2018, Obamacare will impose a 40 percent excise tax on high-cost health insurance plans (those with premiums over $10,200 for individuals and $27,500 for families).[20]

In essence, this will punish women who might use higher-cost plans because they have larger families or because they have chronic ailments or are older but not yet eligible for Medicare. For women who already have high medical costs but have purchased insurance to help cover them, Obamacare levies an enormously punitive tax.

Another Obamacare tax increase on women is the "medicine cabinet tax," which is a rule within Obamacare that prohibits people from using their flex-spending or health savings account pre-tax dollars to purchase non-prescription, over-the-counter medicines. These are often exactly the types of items busy moms need—from pain relievers to cough medicine. This tax went into effect in January 2011.

A related tax is the cap on flexible spending accounts (FSAs), which begins in 2013. The tax limits to $2,500 per worker the amount of money they can put into their workplace flex accounts. Norquist notes, "For many families, some out-of-pocket health care costs will no longer be pre-tax. This will be particularly cruel for families with special needs children, who have high out-of-pocket medical costs and often use pre-tax flex accounts to ease the burden for them."[21]

Another Obamacare penalty that has already taken effect is the tax on tanning salon sessions. As ridiculous as it sounds, Obamacare has imposed a 10 percent excise tax on tanning bed sessions since July 2010. Most of the headlines these days are about how tanning beds can be abused. But this should not obscure the fact that most tanning bed customers are women and most salon owners are women—and some of these women are not going to be able to afford the tax.

A 10 percent "tanning tax" may not sound all that significant. But according to Joseph Levy, vice president of the International Smart Tan Network, it's going to close some salons (most tanning salons are small businesses) and jeopardize 9,000 jobs. "You can't just pass on a tax like this to customers and not have it hurt your business," Levy told CNN in 2010.[22] The tax is expected to take $2.7 billion out of taxpayers' hands over ten years.

New York City mayor Michael Bloomberg, Michelle Obama, and other nanny-state liberals champion this tax as a "behavior modifier," but free market enthusiasts believe it's not the government's proper role to destroy those businesses the president doesn't like.

I asked Ryan Ellis, tax policy director for Americans for Tax Reform, to sum up Obamacare's tax implications for women and families. "Obamacare raises taxes on families, especially families with children," he said. "There is almost no way in which families interact with the healthcare system which is left untouched by an Obamacare tax hike."[23]

The Contraceptive Mandate and the "War on Women"

Google the term "Republican war on women" and you'll find hundreds of thousands of references to what has become one of the Democrats' primary indictments of the Republican Party. The "war on women" meme is an election year ploy by Obama and his liberal allies to divert attention away from important issues—particularly Obama's poor stewardship of the economy—and toward political stunts meant to pander to and energize women voters, especially Obama's feminist base. It's a gambit Democrats seem intent on playing all the way to Election Day. And it assumes women are gullible enough to fall for it.

It all began with an announcement by Health and Human Services Secretary Kathleen Sebelius. Under Obamacare, all insurance plans will be required to cover "preventive health services" free of charge.

"Preventive health services" include relatively uncontroversial things like immunizations and mammograms (though these became temporarily controversial when it appeared that Obamacare might ration them stingily). But it also includes highly controversial measures such as sterilization, contraception, and abortion-inducing drugs, including emergency contraceptives, or "morning after pills," ella and Plan B.

On January 20, 2012, Sebelius announced that the administration would not exempt religious groups that object to having to cover these more controversial items.[24] The Catholic Church rejects sterilization, artificial contraception, and abortion as gravely immoral, the latter for the taking of a human life, the former for separating sexual activity (possibly) from the confines of marriage and (more certainly) from its reproductive aspect and potential, which in the Church's view violates its meaning and integrity.

Sebelius then offered what she probably thought was a grand concession: religious organizations would have until August 2013, one year later than originally planned, to comply with the new rule.

The one-year delay (after which non-complying organizations would face heavy fines) was offered to give Catholic employers time to incorporate birth control into their plans. "In effect, the president is saying we have a year to figure out how to violate our consciences," said Archbishop Timothy M. Dolan of New York, the president of the United States Conference of Catholic Bishops.[25]

To be clear: the new rule included an exemption for certain "religious employers," including churches and certain houses of worship. But the exemption was so narrow that it was almost meaningless. A religious employer couldn't qualify for the exemption if it employs or serves a large number of non-Catholics, as most Catholic hospitals, universities, charities, and social service agencies do. These religious agencies that do so much good for society were given two alternatives: drop health insurance for their employees or shutter their doors.

The HHS mandate was a direct violation of the First Amendment guarantee of freedom of religion. And it provoked an avalanche of criticism.

The U.S. Catholic bishops did not mince words, vowing to fight the order as "literally unconscionable."[26]

I'll discuss the mandate's religious implications in greater depth in a later chapter. For now, I want to focus on how liberals turned the debate into evidence of a Republican "war on women."

The contraceptive mandate controversy dominated the political headlines throughout the spring. It became a topic of debate in the Republican primary campaign (all the candidates opposed the rule), legislation was drafted to release employers from the mandate on religious grounds (it failed), and parish priests across the country discussed the issue with their congregations. But Democrats and their allies saw an opportunity to portray the pushback not as a response to an unprecedented attack on a constitutional right, but rather as one more front in a larger Republican war on women's health.

Abortion rights groups such as Planned Parenthood, Moveon.org, and NARAL Pro-Choice America launched ad campaigns claiming that Republicans and the Catholic Church wanted to take away women's birth control. "Women are coming out of the woodwork, saying, 'They're attacking birth control? You've got to be kidding!'" Dawn Laguens, executive vice president for policy and communications of Planned Parenthood, told the *New York Times*.[27]

The Democratic Senatorial Campaign Committee began an ad campaign urging voters to fight the GOP's "war on women." The Democratic Congressional Campaign Committee announced, "House Republicans have launched an all-out war on women."[28]

The DCCC later sent a fundraising email accusing Republicans of "waging an unrelenting war on women." The identical phrase was used shortly after in an email blast by EMILY's List.[29]

Hyperbole was the order of the day. New York Democratic Congresswoman Carolyn Maloney said, "I think that we're headed for another year of the woman. The debate has really brought clarity to the fact that women's health needs are under attack by an increasingly conservative Republican party. I think it's much worse than I've ever seen before."[30] Democratic

Congresswoman Sheila Jackson Lee of Texas said, "I think the next act will be dragging women out of patient rooms into the streets and screaming over their bodies as they get dragged out of getting access to women's health care."[31]

Speaking at a NARAL Pro-Choice America luncheon, Secretary Sebelius said that Republicans who oppose the mandate, funding for Planned Parenthood, and other key items on the feminist agenda "don't just want to go after the last 18 months, they want to roll back the last 50 years in progress women have made in comprehensive health care in America. We've come a long way in women's health over the last few decades, but we are in a war."[32]

It wasn't just surrogates for Obama who engaged in the "war" rhetoric. The Obama re-election campaign took full advantage as well. It launched "Women's Week of Action," a major effort to rally women that included phone bank calls, campus activities, house parties, and media events, as well as mailings to one million women in battleground states.

The Democratic National Committee released a web video charging that Mitt Romney is "wrong for women," in part because of his stated opposition to the mandate. But the public saw politics in the controversy. A March public opinion poll by the Henry J. Kaiser Family Foundation found that half of respondents said they believed the mandate debate was "mostly being driven by election-year politics."[33]

The Fluke Affair

In the wake of the mandate announcement, third-year Georgetown University Law School student Sandra Fluke joined students from other universities for a press conference about birth control at Catholic universities. Staff members to Democrats on the House Oversight and Government Reform Committee saw Fluke's appearance at the news conference and recruited her to testify about access to birth control at a congressional hearing on February 16, 2012. But because the congressional hearing focused on religious liberty questions surrounding the mandate, not the availability of birth control, congressional Republicans opposed Fluke's appearance and she did not testify.

So Democrats held an unofficial hearing on February 23, at which Fluke appeared as a witness and spoke at length. Fluke talked about the experiences of her married law school classmates, complaining that they had to pay as much as $1,000 a year in out-of-pocket costs for birth control prescriptions because Georgetown, a Catholic institution, did not cover birth control in its health insurance plans. "We refuse to pick between a quality education and our health," she declared.[34]

The Democrats who invited Fluke to testify tried to cast her as an everywoman whose friends couldn't get the vital health care they needed because of the Catholic Church's outdated views on women and sex. But Fluke had been a student leader in the leftwing feminist and "gender equity" movements as an undergraduate at Cornell University. She received her bachelor's degree in "Feminist, Gender and Sexuality Studies." She was the president of Georgetown Law's abortion advocacy group, and had spent her three years there lobbying the school's administration to change its policy on birth control coverage. In other words, Fluke was no everywoman; she was a dedicated liberal activist.

What's more, Fluke's contention about the onerous costs of birth control was demonstrably false. Birth control pills can be purchased for as little as $9 per month at pharmacies near Georgetown's campus. As one conservative reporter put it, "Nine dollars is less than the price of two beers at a Georgetown bar."[35]

The Fluke story might have ended there. But it got new life when radio talk show host Rush Limbaugh discussed Fluke's testimony on air, calling her a "slut" and a "prostitute." While Limbaugh was doing what he does best—getting people's attention with shock therapy—he had a serious point: it was hardly reasonable to ask a Catholic institution to subsidize a student's sex life. But Democrats made sure that point got lost in the rhetoric.

Limbaugh later apologized,[36] but the Democrats used his comments to further advance the "war on women" narrative for a few more weeks and continue to distract attention away from the contraceptive mandate's gross violation of religious liberty.

Not surprisingly, President Obama entered the fray, publicly condemning Limbaugh's remarks and calling Miss Fluke to offer her his support. At a press conference, Obama explained:

> All decent folks can agree that the remarks that were made don't have any place in the public discourse. The reason I called Ms. Fluke is because I thought about Malia and Sasha and one of the things that I want them to do as they get older is to engage in issues they care about, even ones that I may not agree with them on.... And I don't want them attacked or called horrible names because they're being good citizens.... We want to send a message to all our young people that being part of a democracy involves argument and disagreements and debate. We want you to be engaged. And there's a way to do it that doesn't involve you being demeaned and insulted, particularly when you're a private citizen.[37]

Listen carefully whenever the president talks about abortion or birth control. Very often you'll hear him invoke what would seem to be unlikely sources of inspiration for his radical views: his daughters, Malia and Sasha.

The Obamas have gone to great lengths to make clear that their daughters are off-limits to the media and political opponents. "I have said before and I will repeat again, I think people's families are off limits, and people's children are especially off limits," Obama said in 2008.[38] And well they should be. When Beanie Babies began designing dolls resembling the girls, Michelle Obama complained, calling the dolls "inappropriate," and the company dropped its plans.[39] In March 2012, several liberal news websites published stories about the Obama's elder daughter Malia's planned spring break vacation to Mexico with twelve friends and twenty-five Secret Service agents. But after the White House complained about the coverage, many of the stories were either changed or deleted completely. "From the beginning of the administration, the White House has asked news outlets not to report on or photograph the Obama children when they are not with their parents and there is no vital news interest," Kristina Schake, Michelle Obama's communications director, told *Politico*.[40]

But President Obama often goes out of his way to talk about his daughters to bolster his policy proposals or political objectives. And often it's in the context of abortion. On the campaign trail in 2008, Obama told an audience that he supported sex education that included information about contraception and abortion because, "I don't want [my daughters] punished with a baby."[41]

Obama has talked about his children in explaining his position on other hot-button cultural issues. When he came out for same-sex marriage in May, Obama told ABC's Robin Roberts:

> There have been times where Michelle and I have been sitting around the dinner table and we're talking about their friends and their parents, and Malia and Sasha, it wouldn't dawn on them that somehow their friends' parents would be treated differently. It doesn't make sense to them and frankly, that's the kind of thing that prompts a change in perspective.[42]

I don't doubt that Obama's views on cultural issues are informed in part by his experiences as a father. But I also don't doubt that Obama figures Americans will be more likely to accept his radical positions on those issues if he prefaces his statements of support for them by declaring that they arise from his experiences as a father of two daughters. It's a cynical game Obama plays, on the one hand insisting his kids are "off-limits," and on the other invoking them when political necessity calls.

The Democrats' "Republican War on Women" narrative was driven by more than just the HHS mandate and the Fluke affair. They cited other "attacks," including state and federal efforts to de-fund Planned Parenthood (America's largest abortion provider), and legislation in several states to require that women seeking abortion first be shown ultrasound imaging of their unborn baby.

The conventional wisdom held that all the birth control talk was hurting Republicans (who were, perversely, often accused of making contraception an issue when the real issue was the economy). As many journalists pointed out, most women have used birth control. But polls showed that the left's effort to tarnish the GOP as woman-haters might have backfired.

On March 12, 2012, the *Weekly Standard*'s John McCormick analyzed the polls to see whether the mandate debate had brought any benefit to Obama and the Democrats, and came to the conclusion that, if anything, the mandate debate was hurting them, as Romney's numbers went up and Obama's went down.[43]

Some polls showed that women were moving towards Romney and away from Obama. An April *New York Times*/CBS News poll found that Obama held a 49 percent to 43 percent lead against Romney among women, but by mid-May the poll found that female voters preferred Romney to Obama by two percentage points, 46 percent to 44 percent.[44]

A late May 2012 *Washington Post*-ABC News poll found Romney up thirteen percentage points and Obama down seven points among women since April.[45] After having spent three months advancing the "Republican war on women" narrative, Democrats had achieved little, other than to convince more women to give Romney a second look.

The Left's Abortion Obsession

If President Obama and other Democrats seem preoccupied with abortion and birth control, it's not only because they need to distract the public's attention from their abysmal record on the economy and the general unpopularity of Obamacare. It's also because most of the women's groups that have access to and influence with Obama and the Democrats are preoccupied with those issues. And the reason they have so much access and influence is that they raise so much money for Democrats.

The abortion lobby spends about $40 million each election cycle to elect pro-abortion-rights Democrats to office. In a 2011 column, the *Washington Examiner*'s Tim Carney shed some light on the money link between abortion groups and the Democratic Party, noting that "Everywhere you see Obama and his party raising money, you see an abortion activist playing a lead role."[46]

As the administration searched for an "accommodation" to the mandate after widespread backlash, it was warned by Planned Parenthood and other abortion groups that they would vigorously oppose any compromise that resulted in employees paying even a penny for birth control.

The morning after Mitt Romney officially secured the Republican presidential nomination, Planned Parenthood endorsed Obama and announced the launch of a $1.4 million ad buy slamming Romney.[47]

It is an understatement to say that in the Obama era, the abortion lobby has a lot of influence with the Democratic Party. In fact, in many ways, the abortion lobby *is* the Democratic Party.

Many Obama administration officials once worked for the abortion industry. In April 2012, for example, the Department of Health and Human Services hired Tait Sye as deputy assistant secretary for public affairs. Sye had formerly been Planned Parenthood's media director. The hire prompted Charmaine Yoest, president of Americans United for Life, to tell *Politico*, "Personnel is policy.... This is one more example of how intertwined the Obama administration is with the abortion industry and Planned Parenthood."[48] Other examples included Dawn Johnsen, former legal director of the National Abortion Rights Action League, who was appointed but never confirmed to a position in the Justice Department, and Ellen Moran, former executive director of the pro-abortion group

EMILY's List, who was Obama's White House communications director before moving to the Department of Commerce as chief of staff to Secretary Gary Locke.

The Obama campaign released a web video in May that illustrates the difficulty it will have in reconciling its obsession with abortion and its need to address the economic issues voters care about most. The two-minute video is called "Letters to the President: The Dreams of Our Daughters." In the first half of the video, a mother introduces viewers to her two young daughters, Daisy, six, and Caroline, nine. We learn about their hopes and dreams. "I love that my daughters dream so big," the mother says, "and see no limits to their future."

Then she says, "It is upsetting to me that in 2012 the use of birth control has become controversial." Contraceptives constitute preventive care, she insists, and are necessary for most women. "Beyond that," she continues, "it's a woman's right to make decisions about her own body and her own life. This is just one reason I'm so passionate about getting you reelected this year." The video gives the impression that if Obama doesn't win reelection, Daisy and Caroline's "right to make decisions about [their] own bod[ies] and [their] own [lives]" will be in jeopardy.

That's not the case, of course. Nobody is proposing to outlaw contraceptives. The debate is about whether religious institutions will be forced to provide them to their employees free of charge. It is ludicrous and insulting to women's intelligence for the Obama campaign to advance the fiction that Republicans are trying to take away their birth control pills and devices.

It is difficult to think how contraceptives could be any more accessible than they already are. Democrats often defend the Obama mandate by informing us that 99 percent of sexually active women—including 98 percent of Catholic women—have used contraceptives. Assuming those numbers are correct, they make clear that contraceptives are readily available to most women. The government pays for insurance coverage of contraceptives for millions of its workers and for millions of low-income women through Medicaid, Title X, and other programs. Ninety percent of employer-based health insurance plans cover contraceptives.[49]

So this is really not about contraception. It is about coercing religious groups, in particular the Catholic Church, to follow the dictates of the Obama administration and the abortion lobby. And it is about Alinskyite politics—picking a demagogic fight, which the administration thinks will rally women to its cause.

As politics, this is sheer cynicism. Even abortion rights groups know that women aren't lacking in contraceptive options or information. In 2001, the Guttmacher Institute, a pro-abortion organization affiliated with Planned Parenthood that analyzes reproductive trends, surveyed 10,000 women who had had abortions.[50] Of those who were not using contraception at the time they conceived, 2 percent said they did not know where to obtain contraceptives and 8 percent said they could not afford it.

These facts help explain why, according to Guttmacher, among the 43 million sexually active women who do not want to become pregnant, 89 percent (including 93 percent of teenagers) are practicing contraception.[51]

The most revealing part of the "Letters to the President" ad comes near the end, when the mother/narrator says, "We need a president who will stand up for women's health and stay focused on jobs and the economic recovery."

This one sentence captures the absurdity of the "war on women" meme. "Stand[ing] up for women's health" and "stay[ing] focused on jobs and the economic recovery" are about as mutually exclusive as things get in public policy. If Obama and the Democrats really wanted to stay focused on jobs and an economic recovery, they wouldn't be raising issues such as abortion and birth control. Their preoccupation with the non-existent threat to birth control has come at the expense of dealing with the very real economic threats the country faces.

And perhaps it is time to call the Obama administration out on its condescending assumption that "women's health" issues cover the gamut from "a" (abortion) to "b" (birth control). That's a pretty limiting view of women and their interests, and it speaks volumes about the Obama administration.

CHAPTER NINE

Obama Condescends to Women

"I like hangin' out with women. What can I tell you?"

So said Barack Obama during a May 14, 2012, appearance on *The View*, a daytime talk show hosted by women for a female audience. It was the president's fourth time on the program, and he was clearly in his element as he gabbed about his marriage and his recently announced support for same-sex marriage.

Obama was in the middle of a series of events designed to reassure women that, despite the poor economy, he hadn't forgotten about them. Earlier that day, he had accepted an award from and delivered the commencement address at Barnard College, a prominent women's college.

But for all his feminist talk, there is an unmistakable air of condescension whenever Obama addresses women. As former CNN and NBC News anchor Campbell Brown put it in a May *New York Times* op-ed:

> When I listen to President Obama speak to and about women,
> he sometimes sounds too paternalistic for my taste. In numerous

appearances over the years—most recently at the Barnard graduation—he has made reference to how women are smarter than men. It's all so tired, the kind of fake praise showered upon those one views as easy to impress. As I listen, I am always bracing for the old go-to cliché: "Behind every great man is a great woman."

My bigger concern is that in courting women, Mr. Obama's campaign so far has seemed maddeningly off point. His message to the Barnard graduates was that they should fight for a "seat at the table"—the head seat, he made sure to add. He conceded that it's a tough economy, but he told the grads, "I am convinced you are tougher" and "things will get better—they always do."

But the promise of his campaign four years ago has given way to something else—a failure to connect with tens of millions of Americans, many of them women, who feel economic opportunity is gone and are losing hope. In an effort to win them back, Mr. Obama is trying too hard. He's employing a tone that can come across as grating and even condescending. He really ought to drop it.

Most women don't want to be patted on the head or treated as wards of the state. They simply want to be given a chance to succeed based on their talent and skills. To borrow a phrase from our president's favorite president, Abraham Lincoln, they want "an open field and a fair chance." In the second decade of the twenty-first century, that isn't asking too much.[1]

Polls suggest Brown's view that Obama condescends to women is shared by many Americans. This is especially true when it comes to the work women do. An April 2012 poll of 1,000 likely voters commissioned by *The Hill*, a Capitol Hill newspaper, found that "more voters think Mitt Romney and the Republican Party respect women who work outside the home than think President Obama and the Democrats respect women who stay at home"—and by large margins.[2]

The poll also found that the presidential candidates and their parties were in a statistical tie among likely voters when it came to better understanding women's issues, with Obama and the Democrats taking 42 and 41 percent, respectively, and Romney and the Republicans taking 40 and 42 percent. But here's the kicker: 46 percent of the *women* polled said that Romney better understands women's issues, while 41 percent said Obama. More men than women assumed Obama was the women's candidate.

The working mom versus stay-at-home mom debate was introduced in April when Democratic activist and Obama administration adviser Hilary Rosen claimed during an appearance on CNN that because Mitt Romney's wife, Ann, had been a stay-at-home mom, she "actually never worked a day in her life" and therefore wasn't qualified to speak on women's issues.

Ann Romney shot back on Twitter, writing: "I made a choice to stay home and raise five boys. Believe me, it was hard work."[3]

Under pressure, Rosen later apologized, and the Obama campaign tried to distance itself from Rosen, who, visitor logs revealed, had visited the White House thirty-six times.[4] The episode reinforced the portrait of some liberal women's condescension toward women who choose to stay home. It was reminiscent of Hillary Clinton's remark in 1992 that she could have stayed home to bake cookies but instead decided to focus on her career outside the home. Ann Romney called Rosen's remark "a gift" to her husband's campaign.

The Single/Married Women Divide

Perhaps the starkest political divide among women exists between single and married women. Democrats have always fared better among single women by emphasizing reproductive issues, while Republicans normally win married women by focusing on jobs and championing policies that assist families.

The single/married divide was on full display in *The Hill* poll. While single voters were far likelier than married ones to say that Obama is better on women's issues (54 percent to 35 percent), Romney was chosen by 47 percent of married voters and 26 percent of singles.

A CBS/*New York Times* poll reinforced the disparity. It showed Romney leading Obama among married women, 49 percent to 42 percent, but Obama leading Romney among single women, 62 percent to 34 percent.[5]

So while a divide exists among women, Obama has tried to exploit it by appealing to single women with a two-pronged campaign. One is the big lie that the GOP will try to deny single women contraception for their sex lives. The other is a bribe, telling single women that he has a whole plethora of programs to assist them in all they do.

The (State-Approved) Life of Julia

In early May, the Obama campaign unveiled on its website an interactive (and very creepy) slide show titled "The Life of Julia." It offered tremendous insight into the Obama administration's belittling view of women.

"The Life of Julia" was advertised as an examination of "how President Obama's policies help one woman over her lifetime—and how Mitt Romney would change her story." It employs a timeline to examine the life of Julia, a fictional character who is supposed to represent the average American woman throughout her lifetime. It's pure pandering to young, single women voters, but its principal effect was to outline Obama's cradle-to-grave, government-directed vision for America.

We learn that Julia, at age three, begins the government's Head Start program, which gets her "ready to learn and succeed." Later, with the help of government Pell grants, Julia goes on to college and has a career as a web designer (naturally). She enjoys universal health coverage and taxpayer-funded birth control, which allows her to "focus on her work instead of worrying about her health." Seriously—I'm not making this up.

Tellingly, though no man is ever mentioned (perhaps to allow for the possibility that Julia is a lesbian), we are told that at age thirty-one "Julia decides to have a child." The word choice here is interesting. Rarely does one say, "I decided to have a child" in describing the blessed event. It's usually, "We're having a baby!" The emphasis on Julia's deciding on her own to have a child is no doubt intentional, and revealing of the left's obsession with a woman's needing a man like a fish needs a bicycle.

Julia's son, Zachary, is apparently begotten through immaculate conception (or, since this is Obama's secularist utopia, sperm donation), because there's no mention of a father, husband, or boyfriend. But at age six, Zachary disappears and is never heard from again. Apparently in old age, he has abandoned his mother to be cared for by the almighty Government, which, after all, got her that far.

As far as we know, Julia never marries, and this might be the part of her life that most accurately reflects reality for modern women. Marriage is less likely than ever to anchor the American adult's life. In fact, according to the most recent data, barely half of American adults are married, the lowest share ever recorded.[6] And the decline is continuing. Marriages fell by 5 percent between 2009 and 2010.[7]

From an electoral point of view, this is good news for Obama and the Democrats, who do so well with single women and so badly with married women. Though what's good for the Democratic Party is not necessarily good for America, especially American children, 41 percent of whom are now born out of wedlock, which, as all the research data show, gets children off to a far worse start than, say, life without Head Start.[8]

What's most striking about "The Life of Julia" is not what is included in Julia's life, but rather what—and who—is excluded. The primary institutions of American life—family, church, civil society (aside from the "community garden" she tends in her golden years), and the market—are conspicuously absent or beholden to the government. In Obama's utopia, Julia simply cannot function without the lifelong intervention of the federal government. Julia is completely reliant on the nanny state at every stage of her life.

The Boys' Club

Barack Obama likes to say that, other than the Obama family dog, Bo, he is the only male in his immediate family. Obama presumably thinks that living in a female-dominated household gives him a special window into what women want. But once he moves from the White House's Executive Residence to the West Wing, Obama enters a boys' club.

In his book *Confidence Men*, Ron Suskind provides a detailed account of Obama's first two years in office, including the male-centric culture that pervaded the president's inner circle.

Anita Dunn, who served as the 2008 Obama campaign's communications director, told Suskind that on the campaign trail she was "shocked to find that in spite of Obama's popularity with female voters, his campaign had more to do with frat house antics than third wave feminism."[9]

Former head of the Council of Economic Advisers (CEA) Christina Romer said she "felt like a piece of meat" whenever she visited the president.[10] As president-elect, Obama met with Romer in Chicago to discuss her possible appointment to the CEA.

"But their first meeting would open on an odd note," Suskind recounts. "Before exchanging hellos or even shaking hands, the president-elect delivered what seemed intended as a zinger: 'It's clear monetary policy has shot its wad,' he said."[11] Suskind continues:

> It was a strange break from decorum for a man who had done so outstandingly well with women voters. The two had never met before, and this made the salty, sexual language hard to read. Later it would seem a foreshadowing of something that

came to irk many of the West Wing's women: the president didn't have particularly strong "women skills." The guy's-guy persona, which the message team would use to show Obama's down-to-earth side, failed to account for at least one thing: What if you didn't play basketball or golf?[12]

Suskind noted that by early summer 2009, "There was a nascent gender struggle in the White House."[13]

Many senior-level women complained that they felt invisible during meetings with Obama. They felt dominated by the male personalities in the room and frustrated by Obama's deference to them. The men included Chief of Staff Rahm Emanuel, Director of the National Economic Council Larry Summers, Treasury Secretary Tim Geithner, Office of Management and Budget Director Peter Orszag, Senior Adviser David Axelrod, and Press Secretary Robert Gibbs. Geithner privately conceded to Suskind, "The perception is that women have real power, yet they all feel like shit."[14]

Suskind writes, "The president had hired an array of strong-willed, accomplished women who felt the same way Romer did: ignored."[15]

"'[L]ooking back,' recalled Anita Dunn, when asked about it nearly two years later, 'this place would be in court for a hostile workplace … because it actually fit all of the classic legal requirements for a genuinely hostile workplace to women.'"[16]

Rahm Emanuel and Larry Summers (who had previously been a subject of controversy at Harvard, where he was president, for his comment that men were better than women at the sciences and engineering, and later for the revelation that only four of his thirty-two tenured appointments to the Faculty of Arts and Sciences were women) were the worst offenders. At one point a woman staff member complained directly to the president about Emanuel's rough and chauvinistic demeanor, and indirectly suggested that Obama consider letting Emanuel go. Suskind writes:

Obama paused. "Look," he said, evenly, "I really need Rahm."

"That, to me, was one of the more unsatisfying things. 'They are really important to me. I know they are assholes but I need them,'" the woman said.

Later, when Emanuel was asked in an interview about the women's group and their issues, he was succinct. The concerns of women, he said, were a nonissue, a "blip." As to the fact that the White House's women rather strongly disagreed with him on that point, he said, "I understand," and then laughed uproariously.[17]

"The president has a real woman problem," an unnamed high-ranking female official told Suskind, adding, "The idea of the boys' club being just Larry [Summers] and Rahm [Emanuel] isn't really fair. [Obama] was just as responsible himself."[18]

In *The Obamas*, journalist Jodi Kantor also examined the White House's male/female dynamics. Kantor describes how senior administration officials reacted when they learned that a *New York Times* reporter was writing a story about the hostile work environment for women in the White House.

The *Times* reporter got a call from senior Obama adviser Valerie Jarrett, who defended the president. "Her tone on the phone was defensive, insistent," the reporter told Kantor.[19]

Kantor reveals that the White House opposition to the piece "was being managed behind the scenes by none other than the president, who was personally dictating talking points to the aides who would speak to the reporter."[20]

Once the story was published, Obama responded by inviting Melody Barnes, his chief domestic policy adviser, to join him for a round of golf—the first time a woman had joined his foursome. "The gesture caused a collective cringe among some women in the West Wing, because it was so transparently triggered by the story," Kantor wrote.[21]

When the environment continued to deteriorate for women staffers, Obama hosted a women's-only dinner to discuss their grievances. The meeting began with Obama peeking at his watch and asking, "Are there genuine concerns that I need to know about?"[22]

"It was an awkward, silent dinner where we were given one glass of wine and a piece of fish," one participant told Kantor.[23]

Obama's White House was supposed to be different. Bush was allegedly the towel-snapping ex-fraternity president (though there is no evidence women who worked in the Bush White House were treated with anything but respect). Obama was supposed to be the personification of the progressive ideal of politically correct inclusiveness; but, as with much in the Obama White House, there was a deep disconnect between image and reality.

Obama Stands Up for Women (Unless They Are Conservative)

Inappropriate. Mean. Insulting. These are a few of the words President Obama used in condemning Rush Limbaugh's verbal broadside against Georgetown Law student and abortion activist Sandra Fluke. The president rarely misses an opportunity to ally himself with "aggrieved" women—so long as those women advance the liberal cause, or at least his own re-election chances, as he sees them.

Would that the president displayed as much sympathy for abused women who do not share his political views. But misogynistic attacks against conservative women are almost always met by Obama and the left with deafening silence. It's noteworthy that Obama claims to stand up for women, then abandons them if their ideology differs from his own. Not only does Obama decline to defend conservative women, he implicitly condones those attacks by continuing to associate with the perpetrators.

Soon after the Limbaugh-Fluke flap, Michelle Obama appeared on David Letterman's *Late Show* to plug her new book. Recall that in 2009 Letterman joked that Sarah Palin's then-fourteen-year-old daughter Willow had been "knocked up" by baseball player Alex Rodriguez while attending a Yankees game.[24] More recently, Congresswoman Michele Bachmann was Letterman's target when he bizarrely mocked her physique, suggesting that her "ass" was too large. Rather than challenging Letterman's attacks, the Obamas enjoyed the media spotlight from Michelle Obama's appearance on the show.[25]

An entire book could be written that explores the left's vile attacks on conservative women. But one attacker in particular stands out: comedian Bill Maher, the host of HBO's *Real Time with Bill Maher*. Maher is a well-known liberal and an aggressive atheist. He's also a raging misogynist. Maher regularly insults conservative women in the most degrading terms. Maher has called Palin a "dumb tw*t" and a "c*nt."[26] In September 2011, Maher was discussing Texas Governor Rick Perry's debate performance and then joked about Sarah Palin. "He sounded like a sixth grader who didn't do the reading. Garbled syntax, messing up simple facts, sentences that went nowhere. Sarah Palin was watching and she said, 'If only he was black, I'd f*ck him.'"[27]

He's called Minnesota representative Michele Bachmann "mentally retarded" and compared Newt Gingrich's wife, Callista, to a Martian. He's also theorized about the sexual practices of conservative commentator Michelle Malkin.[28]

But while liberals hyperventilated over Limbaugh's insults against Fluke, they had nothing to say about Maher's hateful and disgusting attacks. The week that Obama spoke up about Fluke, reporters reminded White House spokesman Jay Carney about Maher's prior comments, and asked if the president was prepared to denounce them, too.

Carney said the president would not get involved in the Maher battle, saying that it's not the president's place to be the "arbiter" of every controversial remark. Obama's silence was perhaps explained by the fact that Maher has been a huge donor to Obama. In February, Maher made a million-dollar donation to Obama Super PAC Priorities USA Action.[29]

The left thinks it can be as misogynistic as it wants in attacking conservative women, just as long as it guarantees a "woman's right to choose" an abortion and subsidized access to contraception. And that might be the most misogynistic attitude of all.

CHAPTER TEN

Obama Ignores Real Women's Rights Issues Abroad

The Obama administration takes an extremely limited and divisive view of women's rights. In the Obama administration, "women's rights" is synonymous with free birth control and abortion-on-demand. Nowhere is that more the case than in the administration's policy toward women internationally. Indeed, abortion is at the heart of the Obama administration's diplomatic agenda.

On only his third day in office, Obama rescinded the Mexico City Policy, which prohibited organizations that receive U.S. taxpayer funding from promoting or performing abortions abroad.[1]

Obama's top diplomat, Hillary Clinton, is dedicated to spending billions to spread abortion abroad. Soon after becoming secretary of state, Clinton announced in testimony before the House Foreign Affairs Committee, "We are now an administration that will protect the rights of women, including their rights to reproductive health care."[2]

This was an ironic claim given how little concern the Obama administration has demonstrated for women across the globe, especially those oppressed in the name of Islam.

Clinton added, "We happen to think that family planning is an important part of women's health, and reproductive health includes access to abortion that I believe should be safe, legal and rare."[3]

In 2010, during a Group of Eight (G8) meeting in Ontario, Canada's Prime Minister Stephen Harper discussed an initiative to reduce maternal mortality in poor countries. The plan didn't address abortion, and later, when Hillary Clinton was visiting Quebec, she felt the need to weigh in. "I've worked in this area for many years," she said at a press conference. "And if we're talking about maternal health, you cannot have maternal health without reproductive health. And reproductive health includes contraception and family planning and access to legal, safe abortion." Clinton's meddling was described by the *Toronto Star* as a "grenade in the lap of her shell-shocked Canadian hosts."[4]

Earlier in 2010 Clinton had announced that the United States would engage in a massive funding push over the next five years to promote "reproductive health care and family planning" as a "basic right" around the world. "All governments will make access to reproductive healthcare and family planning services [also known as abortion] a basic right," she declared.[5] Congress appropriated more than $648 million in foreign assistance to family planning and health programs globally, the largest allocation in more than a decade.

These programs were part of the Global Health Initiative (GHI), which Clinton said would commit the United States to spending $63 billion over six years.[6] As if to reinforce the Obama administration's aggressive abortion mission within GHI, in 2011 Obama appointed abortion activist Lois Quam as its executive director.

In 2009, Secretary of State Clinton unsuccessfully lobbied the government of the Dominican Republic to reject a pro-life provision to its constitution.

The Obama administration had greater success in Kenya, where, in 2010, it spent $23 million to promote ratification of a national constitution that radically liberalized the country's abortion laws.[7] Abortion had been illegal in Kenya except to save the life of the mother, a position that reflected the views of the religiously and culturally conservative nation. In August of that year, Kenyans were to vote up or down on a draft constitution that included language that would legalize most abortions, making abortion a constitutional right.

The Obama administration and its abortion advocate allies were very involved in the lead-up to the referendum. The Center for Reproductive Rights pushed the administration, through Secretary Clinton, to "send a message to Kenya expressing support for the Draft Constitution and opposing any amendments to eliminate abortion language."[8]

After the Kenyan Parliament approved the abortion liberalizing draft constitution, the White House released a statement praising the parliament's decision and telling Kenyans that a "united effort to see this important reform element through can help to turn the page to a promising new chapter of Kenyan history."[9]

Vice President Biden was sent to Kenya to lobby for the constitution's passage, at one point telling a crowd of Kenyans that they should adopt the new constitution in order "to allow money to flow" to Kenya from other nations.[10] "The United States strongly supports the process of constitutional reform," Biden said. "Dare to reach for transformative change, the kind of change that might come around only once in a lifetime. If you make these changes, I promise you, new foreign private investment will come in like you've never seen."

President Obama even appeared on the Kenyan Broadcasting Corporation to tell Kenyans that voting for the document was "a singular opportunity to put the government of Kenya on solid footing." He implored Kenyans to "take advantage of the moment."

In the run-up to the vote, American Ambassador Michael Ranneberger was quoted as saying that the U.S. had donated $2 million for "civic education" regarding the proposed constitution, which ended up passing in the August referendum.[11]

The administration's involvement in Kenya prompted a congressional inquiry. Republican congressmen Chris Smith of New Jersey and Darrell Issa of California, and Republican Ileana Ros-Lehtinen of Florida launched an investigation to determine whether the Obama administration violated federal law by using taxpayer money to promote the new Kenyan constitution.

In May of 2011 they wrote to auditors at the State Department, USAID, and the General Accountability Office stating that the administration's advocacy in Kenya may have violated the Siljander Amendment, which prohibits foreign aid from being used to lobby for or against abortion.[12]

A subsequent investigation and report by the Office of the Inspector General of USAID found that the administration gave grants totaling more than $61 million to more than 200 groups working to turn out the "yes" vote in the referendum, and that $12.6 million went to efforts to directly promote the pro-abortion constitution.[13]

"Under no circumstances should the U.S. government take sides," Congressman Smith said during a press conference. "Yet this is precisely what the Obama administration has done."[14]

The federal probe further found that the Kenyan constitution was written partly by "U.S. funded NGOs [non-governmental organizations] working in concert with Planned Parenthood."

A subsequent investigation by the Government Accountability Office (GAO), the investigative arm of Congress, into the Obama administration's use of $18 million in taxpayer funds also found that the administration broke the law. It concluded that at least one Obama grantee openly pushed to expand abortion in Kenya in violation of the Siljander Amendment. The GAO report also revealed that a key Obama official stonewalled investigators and refused to cooperate with the GAO in its investigation.

The group, the International Development Law Organization (IDLO), received $400,000 from USAID to provide advice to the Kenyan government about incorporating abortion into its constitution, specifically language making it clear that the fetus lacks constitutional standing and that a woman's right to abortion should take priority.[15]

Little has happened since the administration's violations became public. The GAO report recommended that Congress and USAID draft clearer guidelines about how to comply with the Siljander Amendment.

"As the GAO points out, it is likely that several other countries will be amending or creating new constitutions in the foreseeable future," Smith said in response to news of the GAO report, "and this U.S. tax-payer funded effort to change Kenya's pro-life laws raises red flags as to how U.S. monies may be used to impose legalized abortion on other countries through their constitutions."

In June 2011, IDLO received another million-dollar USAID grant, this time to support the Kenyan Parliament as it brings its domestic laws into compliance with its pro-abortion constitution.[16]

Obama and Forced Abortion

The Obama administration is often referred to by pro-life advocates as the most pro-abortion administration in history. One of the main reasons is its disregard for human rights violations in China's population control program of forced abortion.

China's one-child policy limits most couples to one child. It was adopted more than thirty years ago during the height of the world over-population craze. Exceptions to the one-child rule are sometimes allowed for rural couples and those whose first child is a girl.

China's Communist government boasts that 400 million births have been prevented through its policy.[17]

Women who become pregnant with a second child face heavy fines, beatings by state police, sterilization, and, sometimes, forced abortion. Blind Chinese pro-life activist Chen Guangcheng was arrested in 2006 for exposing evidence that 130,000 forced abortions and sterilizations were performed one year in a single county in China.

Not only is China's policy galling from a human rights standpoint. It is antithetical to the liberal shibboleth of "choice." Yet the self-described pro-choice advocates in the Obama administration have been complicit in the policy. Obama has restored funding for the United Nations Population Fund (UNFPA), the UN's main population control agency, which has helped implement China's forced abortion regime.[18]

When Secretary Clinton first visited China in 2009, she told Chinese government officials that the Obama administration would not let human rights issues "interfere" with other important matters between the countries, including climate change.[19]

Even the *Washington Post* was prompted to condemn such a cavalier approach, saying:

> [Clinton's] comments understated the significance of what a secretary of state says about such matters, and how those statements might affect the lives of people fighting for freedom of expression, religious rights and other basic liberties in countries such as China.... It will demoralize thousands of democracy advocates in China, and it will cause many others around the world to wonder about the character of the new U.S. administration.[20]

And indeed, the administration has rarely spoken up about human rights issues anywhere, least of all in China.

During a 2011 trip to China, Vice President Biden twice dismissed human rights issues to his Chinese counterparts. During a speech, Biden said, "Maybe the biggest difference in our respective approaches are our approaches to what we refer to as human rights. I recognize that many of you in this auditorium see our advocacy of human rights as at best an intrusion, and at worst an assault on your sovereignty."[21]

Later, Biden let slip that he sympathized with China's one-child policy. In his answer to a question from a Chinese student about the causes of China's emerging demographics crisis, Biden said: "Your policy has been one which I fully understand—I'm not second-guessing—of one child per family."[22]

Biden isn't the only top-tier administration official with sympathy for forced abortion. John Holdren, President Obama's "science czar," was once an advocate of "compulsory sterilization" and forced abortions as solutions to overpopulation.[23]

For all its talk of "choice," "privacy," "women's health," and "women's rights," the Obama administration is, at its foundation, informed by a totalitarian view of reproduction.

Obama Retreats from the Real War on Women

Obama and his abortion-rights allies fight any attempt to limit abortion, even when it is girls who are exclusively being targeted for death. In her book *Unnatural Selection: Choosing Boys Over Girls, and the Consequences of a World Full of Men*, Mara Hvistendahl estimates that at least 160 million females are "missing" in the world because of sex-selective abortion, not only in China but also in India, Malaysia, and other countries.

Because boys are prized more highly than girls in traditional Chinese culture, ultrasound image technology is often employed to detect the sex of the unborn baby and, if it's a girl, to kill her.

Sex-selective abortion is also present in the United States. Researchers at the National Academy of Sciences (NAS) examined the 2000 U.S. Census and found that certain Asian-American families were significantly more likely than other Americans to have a boy if they already had a girl. "This male bias is particularly evident for third children," researchers found. "If there was no previous son, sons outnumbered daughters by 50 percent."[24] A 2008 NAS report found similar results.

New technology could aggravate the problem. Pregnant women can now buy the Intelligender Gender Prediction Test for about $35 at their local chain pharmacy. The test boasts that it can discern the sex of a child with 82 percent accuracy, as early as ten weeks after conception and at home, with no need to visit a doctor's office.

Women who are really serious about giving birth to a child of the desired sex can undergo a procedure called pre-implantation genetic diagnosis. PGD involves examining embryos resulting from in vitro fertilization, testing them for X or Y chromosomes, then implanting the desired embryos into a woman's womb.

A 2002 *Fortune* magazine survey found that 25 to 35 percent of parents and prospective parents said they would use sex selection if it were available.[25]

Legislators concerned about sex-selective abortion in the United States advanced the Susan B. Anthony and Frederick Douglass Prenatal Nondiscrimination Act (PRENDA), which seeks to criminalize the practice of sex-selective and race-selective abortion. In May 2012, Congress considered PRENDA. It was voted down, because most Democrats voted against the bill.[26] President Obama, through a spokesman, said he opposed the legislation.

Revealingly, many self-described women's groups, including Planned Parenthood and NARAL (National Abortion Rights Action League) Pro-Choice America, oppose banning the systematic targeting of unborn girls and testified against the bill.

Many of these groups even have ties to China's one-child policy. When China first adopted the policy in the late 1970s, the International Planned Parenthood Federation (IPPF) worked with the United Nations, devoting millions of dollars to assist its implementation. IPPF's Benjamin Viel supported the coercive population control policies, writing, "Persuasion and motivation [are] very effective in a society in which social sanctions can be applied against those who fail to cooperate in the construction of the socialist state."[27]

The admiration continues. Former Planned Parenthood director Norman Fleishman, among others, has said that the one-child policy should be implemented worldwide.[28]

Abortion was legalized under the guise of privacy, equality, and choice for women. But far from empowering women, abortion has become the greatest act of violence against them. By refusing to condemn sex-selective abortion, the president, his administration, and self-proclaimed women's groups help to ensure that one of the most dangerous places on earth for a baby girl is her mother's womb. There is not much "hope" in that.

Women under the Taliban

While the Obama administration trumpets a fictitious war on women at home, it is abandoning a real fight for women's lives in Afghanistan, where the women-hating Taliban are preparing to regain power once American forces withdraw.

The Taliban, a Wahhabi Islam-inspired and Saudi-funded political group, ruled Afghanistan before the 2001 U.S.-led invasion. Under the Taliban, women were treated like chattel. They were forced to cover themselves from head to foot when in public, allowed in public only with a male "chaperone," prevented from attending school, and barred from voting. They were victims of brutal rape, honor killings, and public stonings.

Not surprisingly, the Taliban couldn't govern or provide for its people. When U.S. Armed Forces invaded in 2001, they discovered a humanitarian crisis. Seventy percent of Afghanistan's people were malnourished, and 25 percent of children died before age five.[29] The infrastructure was in shambles, and clean water, electricity, and other major resources were hard to come by in many places.

After the U.S. drove the Taliban from power, many American leaders were committed to assisting women in the new Afghanistan. In December 2001, President Bush signed the Afghan Women and Children Relief Act, which had been sponsored by then-New York Senator Hillary Clinton, who proclaimed, "We cannot simply drop our bombs and depart with our best wishes, lest we find ourselves returning some years down the road to root out another terrorist."[30]

Not long after, Afghan girls were attending school, and women were returning to work. In the decade since, 4,000 schools have been built and more than 100,000 new teachers have begun teaching. Today, girls make up 37 percent of the seven million Afghan students in primary and secondary schools. Women make up a quarter of the Afghan parliament. Women's life expectancy has jumped from forty-two years to sixty-four years.[31]

During his time in the Senate, and while he campaigned for president, Barack Obama regularly insisted that the U.S.-led war in Afghanistan was the "good war"—the conflict America should focus its resources on, the one it needed to win.

But Obama has done an about face on Afghanistan, and Afghan women are the ones who will suffer most for it. In May, at a G8 Summit in Chicago, Obama announced that the U.S. will end combat operations in 2013—whether or not Afghan forces are prepared to take over. Many experts believe that once American troops leave, the U.S.-backed Karzai government in Kabul will form an alliance with the resurgent Taliban.[32] In fact, the Obama administration supports reconciliation between the Karzai government and the Taliban, because Obama views working with the Taliban as the best option for ending the war.

In January 2012 it was revealed that the State Department had obtained office space for the Taliban in Qatar and intended to start negotiations with them.[33]

The Obama administration has chosen to negotiate with the Taliban in anticipation of its resurgence. There are many signs of the Taliban's ascendancy. Numerous Afghan school girls have been poisoned[34] or attacked with acid,[35] and prominent female political leaders have been killed, according to Amnesty International.[36]

In February, the country's top religious body, the Ulema Council, issued a decree that men are "fundamental" and women "secondary" and barred women from mingling with men in schools or the workplace.[37] Afghan President Hamid Karzai embraced the ruling.

The Obama administration has taken the position that in its rush to leave Afghanistan, women's rights don't matter. Nora Bensahel of the Center for a New American Security told U.S. *News & World Report* that the president "is saying we don't care about what kind of government is formed, or who is in charge, as long as it doesn't allow al Qaeda to return."[38]

Plenty of evidence confirms the lack of regard for the fate of women once the United States leaves Afghanistan. In March 2011, USAID solicited bids for a $140 million land reform program in Afghanistan. But it insisted that the winning contract fulfill specific requirements to promote women's rights. A year later, however, in March 2012, USAID revised its initiative, excluding explicit targets for women.[39]

According to a March *Washington Post* story, these and other changes "reflect a shift in USAID's approach in Afghanistan. Instead of setting ambitious goals to improve the status of Afghan women, the agency is tilting toward more attainable measures."[40] The *Post* story continued:

A senior U.S. official involved in Afghanistan policy said changes to the land program also stem from a desire at the top levels of the Obama administration to triage the war and focus on the overriding goal of ending the conflict.

"Gender issues are going to have to take a back seat to other priorities," said the senior official, who spoke on the condition of anonymity to discuss internal policy deliberations. "There's no way we can be successful if we maintain every special interest and pet project. All those pet rocks in our rucksack were taking us down."

The changes come at a time of growing concern among rights advocates that the modest gains Afghan women have achieved since the fall of the Taliban government in 2001 are being rolled back.

A March 2012 report by the Afghan Human Rights and Democracy Organization concluded that "[m]ost of women's important achievements over the last decade are likely to be reversed" with the departure of U.S. troops. Others involved in supporting Afghan women's rights are similarly worried.[41]

"I am at my wit's end at the lack of discussion by the media, by our government, by our president on the issue of women's rights in Afghanistan," Esther Hyneman of Women for Afghan Women, which runs family centers and safe homes for abused women across Afghanistan, told *Foreign Policy* magazine in November 2011.[42] "I am appalled that [President Obama] has not mentioned Afghan women's rights since his speech on withdrawing U.S. troops."

A senior U.S. official told the *Washington Post*, "Nobody wants to abandon the women of Afghanistan, but most Americans don't want to keep fighting there for years and years. The grim reality is that, despite all of the talk about promoting women's rights, things are going to have to give."

The Obama administration considers the basic rights of women "pet rocks"; meanwhile it regards the "right" of women to abort their children as so fundamental that it's become a cornerstone of the administration's diplomatic agenda. If this is "change," it's certainly not the sort that inspires hope.

CHAPTER ELEVEN

Obama Divides Catholics

On May 28, 2012, Cardinal Timothy Dolan appeared with Bill O'Reilly on his popular Fox News show *The O'Reilly Factor*. As the two discussed the Catholic Church's opposition to artificial birth control and the HHS contraceptive mandate, Dolan made a stunning accusation: the president was trying to divide the Church against itself.

"Our opponents are very shrewd because they have chosen an issue that they know we are not very popular on," Dolan said.

> And I don't want to judge people, but I think there would be a drift in the administration that this is a good issue and if we can divide the Catholic community (because it's already divided) and if one can caricature the bishops as being hopelessly out of touch—these bullies who are trying to achieve judicially and legislatively what they've been unable to achieve because their moral integrity was compromised recently. There is the force out there trying to caricature us, alright? But we

can't back down from this fight because it's about religious freedom—it's close to the heart of the democratic enterprise that we know and love and the United States of America is all about.[1]

Obama had always enjoyed a cordial relationship with the American Catholic Church. He received funding and other resources from the church during his days as a community organizer in Chicago.

Obama won over many Catholic voters during his political rise by downplaying his positions on abortion and gay rights and instead talking broadly about empathy, social justice, and religious pluralism. He charmed many Catholics during his 2008 campaign. Obama was invited to the Alfred E. Smith Memorial Foundation Dinner, a white tie charity fundraiser for Catholic Charities held every third Thursday of October at the Waldorf-Astoria Hotel in New York City.[2] The dinner is held in honor of former New York Governor Al Smith, the first Catholic presidential candidate. Since 1960, almost every presidential nominee has attended and given a speech.

What made Obama's speech notable, however, was that abortion politics had prevented President Bill Clinton from being invited to the dinner in 1996, because he had vetoed a bill that would have outlawed partial-birth abortion;[3] and in 2004 John Kerry, himself a Catholic, was shunned because of his effectively pro-abortion stance (personally opposed, but in favor of legal abortion).[4] Yet Barack Obama's radical pro-abortion views didn't stop the Archdiocese of New York from inviting him in 2008. Obama was welcomed by, and yucked it up with, the East Coast's most prominent Catholics, helping to raise nearly $4 million for Catholic Charities.[5]

It was no surprise then that Catholic voters, blessed in a sense by the Catholic hierarchy, cast their lot with Obama in the 2008 election. Obama won Catholic voters by nine percentage points over John McCain (54 percent to 45 percent).[6] But while Obama won Catholics as a whole in 2008, he performed poorly among the most devout Christians, including faithful Catholics. He lost among voters who attend church at least weekly by twelve percentage points, 55 percent to 43 percent.[7]

This is where the deepest divide exists in the Catholic Church, between observant Catholics and less observant Catholics. And Obama has spent his term in office exploiting that divide at almost every opportunity. He has done so by attacking the church's teachings on moral issues such as birth control, abortion, and same-sex marriage, and even more, by attempting to conscript Catholic and other religious organizations to advance his radical agenda.

The Backlash

When Secretary Sebelius announced that religious organizations would not be exempt from having to pay for their employees' birth control, she assured the public that she had given concerns about religious freedom "very careful consideration" and claimed that the final rule struck "the appropriate balance between respecting religious freedom and increasing access to important preventive services."[8]

Despite Sebelius's assurances, the response from the Catholic Church was immediate, strong, and almost unanimously negative.

Cardinal Dolan felt personally betrayed by Obama, with whom he had met to discuss the mandate the previous fall. At that time, the two men shared what Dolan called a productive and "extraordinarily friendly" meeting. Dolan later recalled that Obama "seemed very earnest, he said he considered the protection of conscience sacred, that he didn't want anything his administration would do to impede the work of the church that he claimed he held in high regard. So I did leave a little buoyant."[9]

After the mandate announcement, Dolan said he felt "terribly let down, disappointed and disturbed, and it seemed the news he had given me was difficult to square with the confidence I had felt in November."

In a March interview with the *Wall Street Journal,* Dolan said that Obama had reneged on assurances to "take the protection of the rights of conscience with the utmost seriousness."[10]

But Dolan couldn't have been completely surprised. He knew Obama's record of abortion extremism. He had to have known that Obama and Sebelius had crafted the mandate policy while in regular contact with pro-abortion and feminist groups, in particular Planned Parenthood and its president, Cecile Richards. Dolan had to have known that these groups would not allow their president, the man in whom they had invested so much, to betray them.

The administration no doubt expected a strong backlash by the U.S. Catholic bishops. But it apparently did not anticipate a strong negative reaction from its liberal Catholic allies.

That, however, is exactly what it got. Liberal Catholic *Washington Post* columnist E. J. Dionne accused the administration of having "utterly botched" the mandate decision and of committing a "breach of faith" with Obama's Catholic supporters. MSNBC *Hardball* host Chris Matthews called the rule "frightening."[11]

Then there was Sister Carol Keehan, president and CEO of the Catholic Health Association (CHA). Sister Keehan, a member of the Daughters of Charity, has led the CHA since 2005. The CHA is a network of more than 600 Catholic hospitals and 1,400 long-term care and other health facilities across the country. It is the largest group of non-profit health care providers in the country. Keehan is arguably the most powerful female American Catholic, and she went out on a limb for Obama in defying the Catholic bishops in her support for Obamacare. She had taken Obama at his word that abortion would not be funded by taxpayers under his reform plan and that conscience protections would be included.

Her support for Obamacare invited criticism from the bishops and others. Thomas Joseph Tobin, bishop of the Diocese of Providence, withdrew his diocese's hospitals from membership in the CHA, telling Keehan, "Your enthusiastic support of the legislation, in contradiction of the bishops of the United States, provided an excuse for members of Congress, misled the public and caused a serious scandal for many members of the church."[12]

Archbishop Joseph Naumann of Kansas City said Keehan had been "incredibly naïve or disingenuous" for claiming that Obamacare precluded taxpayer funding of abortions.[13] United States Conference of Catholic Bishops (USCCB) then-president Cardinal Francis George said Keehan had chosen Obama over the church when she backed Obamacare. "She had weakened the moral voice of the bishops in the U.S.," he said.[14]

But Keehan endorsed Obamacare anyway, and her support was seen as so integral to its passage that the president gave her one of the pens used to sign the bill as a gesture of gratitude.

Keehan had gone all in for Obama. And she got burned. With the administration's mandate announcement, she was exposed as having been precisely what Archbishop Naumann accused her of: either "incredibly naïve or disingenuous." When the mandate was announced, Keehan immediately issued an opposing statement, which said that the mandate had "real potential for serious problems" and that it had "jolted" her organization. Keehan further pledged to use the one-year grace period the administration had provided to "pursue a correction."[15]

A House Divided

As the backlash to the mandate intensified, Obama announced an "accommodation" for religious organizations that objected to covering birth control. In these cases, the insurer, not the employer, would be required to provide contraceptive coverage to women free of charge. The administration later proposed a similar requirement for group health plans sponsored by religious organizations that insure themselves.

But the "accommodation" was unacceptable. After scrutinizing the proposed changes, the USCCB rejected the compromise, because religious employers and other stakeholders would still be required to have their employee health insurance plans and premiums "used for services they find morally objectionable."

"We believe that this mandate is unjust and unlawful—it is bad health policy, and because it entails an element of government coercion against conscience, it creates a religious freedom problem," Anthony Picarello, USCCB associate general secretary and general counsel, and Michael Moses, associate general counsel, wrote in a joint statement.[16]

If the accommodation seemed flimsy, it quickly became clear why: it wasn't meant to accommodate the Catholic bishops' concerns but rather those of the administration's liberal Catholic allies. As a *New York Times* article stated, the accommodation was "never really driven by a desire to mollify Roman Catholic bishops, who were strongly opposed to the plan." Instead, the "rule shift on birth control is [a] concession to Obama['s] allies."[17]

At this point, it seems the administration had given up trying to satisfy the church hierarchy. In fact, as it deliberated with outside groups over the compromise, the White House shut out the USCCB while allowing in and giving regular updates to liberal Catholic critics, including Sister Keehan.

Richard Doerflinger, the U.S. bishops' chief lobbyist on life issues, confirmed that the conference had not received the relevant documents regarding the accommodation until after it had been publicly announced.

By shutting out the bishops, Obama made crystal clear who was a friend and who was foe.

The *New York Times'* Laurie Goodstein wrote that the contraceptive accommodation "threatens to embroil the Catholic Church in a bitter election-year political battle while deepening internal rifts within the church. On the one side are traditionalists who believe in upholding Catholic doctrine to the letter, and on the other, modernists who believe the church must respond to changing times and a pluralistic society."[18]

Goodstein's main point was correct: the contraceptive mandate debate was dividing the church.

Numerous polls, however, also showed that the HHS mandate hurt Obama with Catholics and women. A poll commissioned by the Catholic Association and carried out by the Washington-based polling firm QEV Analytics found that 58 percent of Catholics surveyed believed that it was fair to suggest that Obama was creating divisions and conflicts with the HHS mandate.[19]

Paul Danello, an expert on civil and canon law issues in Catholic health care, told the *National Catholic Register* regarding the split between the CHA and USCCB: "It's the right hand fighting against the left hand. Who is speaking for the Church here? The Church needs to get its house in order."[20]

In June 2012, Carol Keehan and CHA announced in a letter to HHS that they could not support Obama's contraceptive "compromise." Keehan criticized the plan as "unduly cumbersome" to carry out and "unlikely to adequately meet the religious liberty concerns" of all CHA's members.[21]

Catholics Take Obama to Court

In late May, forty-three Catholic entities filed twelve lawsuits challenging the HHS mandate under the First Amendment and the Religious Freedom Restoration Act. Among the plaintiffs suing the Obama administration were the Archdioceses of Washington and New York, Notre Dame University, the Michigan Catholic Conference, Catholic Charities in Illinois, Mississippi, Missouri, and Indiana, and Catholic health care agencies in New York and two dioceses in Texas.

The Catholic institutions filing lawsuits were careful to keep the focus on the essential issue. "This lawsuit is about one of America's most cherished freedoms: the freedom to practice one's religion without government interference," opens the Notre Dame suit. "It is not about whether people have the right to abortion-inducing drugs, sterilization and contraception."[22]

Notre Dame's Turnabout

It was ironic that Notre Dame was among the Catholic entities suing the Obama administration over the contraceptive mandate. In 2009, President Obama had received an honorary law degree from, and gave the commencement speech at, Notre Dame, where he insisted, "I am a believer in conscience clauses" and "Let's honor the conscience of those who disagree with abortion."[23]

But he qualified those statements by saying that he wanted to "draft a sensible conscience clause, and make sure that all of our health care policies are grounded in clear ethics and sound science, as well as respect for the equality of women."[24]

The controversy surrounding Notre Dame's invitation to Obama, and the uproar created by the new president's appearance, was the first major sign of just how deeply Obama could divide Catholics, and a foreshadowing of things to come. A Pew Forum poll released a few days before Obama's speech found "a deep division on this issue between the most-observant Catholics and those who are less observant."[25]

On graduation day, thousands of protestors descended on the Notre Dame campus in South Bend, Indiana. With the protestors outside thumbing their rosaries and getting hauled away by police, Obama walked onto the commencement stage, where he was met, first with a chorus of boos, then with cheers and chants of "Yes, we can!" and "We are N.D.!"

Obama's appearance had drawn strong opposition from many Catholic groups, including the Cardinal Newman Society, which gathered 358,000 signatures for a petition condemning Obama's invitation.[26] More than seventy American bishops—including local Bishop John D'Arcy, who boycotted the commencement—voiced their disapproval.

It had also prompted former Vatican ambassador Mary Ann Glendon, a pro-life advocate and Harvard law professor, to announce she would not speak at the university on the same day as Obama, when she was slated to receive the Laetare Medal—an annual award given in recognition for outstanding service to the Roman Catholic Church and to society. Glendon submitted a letter to university president John Jenkins. It stated, in part:

The task that once seemed so delightful has been complicated. I could not help but be dismayed by the news that Notre Dame also planned to award the president an honorary degree … in disregard of the U.S. bishops' express request that Catholic colleges should not give abortion advocates a platform to speak to students or be honored with special awards and degrees.[27]

In the wake of Obama's appearance, Notre Dame lost more than $8 million in donations from disgruntled alumni.[28]

Beyond the Catholic Church

The Catholic Church wasn't the only religious denomination fighting the mandate. Before Sebelius's January announcement, a group of more than sixty evangelical, Baptist, and Jewish leaders voiced their objection to the mandate in a letter to President Obama. They noted that "religious organizations beyond the Catholic community have deep moral objections" to the proposed mandate.[29]

And in April, three private, evangelical colleges became the first entities to sue. Colorado Christian University, Geneva College, and Louisiana College filed suit in federal court against Obama's mandate. In a *Wall Street Journal* op-ed explaining their decision, the colleges' presidents wrote that they filed suit because they too felt it was wrong that their schools "would be forced to offer abortion-inducing drugs as a part of our insurance benefits, and that is a line we cannot cross."[30]

They noted that exemptions for religious entities with objections to contraceptives and abortion-inducing drugs would not be unprecedented.

> [T]he act is already riddled with exemptions, except to respect our consciences….
>
>   It exempts the Amish, offers thousands of waivers to small businesses, grandfathers certain plans, and exempts churches if they only serve their own members. But the religious schools

we represent are somehow not religious enough, according to the government. We trust that such an obviously bad argument will not succeed in court.[31]

And in June a coalition of 150 religious leaders, led by conservative Protestants, sent a petition to the Obama administration to broaden the contraceptive mandate exception to include them.

For its part, the Catholic Church is poised to fight the mandate with everything it has—including, if necessary, civil disobedience. Citing Martin Luther King Jr. and the civil rights movement, the U.S. bishops issued a nationwide bulletin in June 2012 called "Protecting Consciences: Why Conscience Is Important." It states, in part:

> Some unjust laws impose such injustices on individuals and organizations that disobeying the laws may be justified. Every effort must be made to repeal them. When fundamental human goods, such as the right of conscience, are at stake, we may need to witness to the truth by resisting the law and incurring its penalties.[32]

The USCCB also launched a campaign called the Fortnight for Freedom in late June and early July 2012. Its goal was to alert Catholics and others who believe in the right of conscience to the danger of the HHS mandate, which took effect on August 1, 2012. There are areas of disagreement among the bishops, but on the question of protecting religious freedom there is unanimity.

On the day the Catholic lawsuits were filed, Cardinal Donald Wuerl, Archbishop of Washington, D.C., wrote a *Washington Post* op-ed explaining his church's decision to file suit:

> The Catholic Church has not picked this fight. We are simply trying to defend our—and other faith groups'—long-standing

rights. While the administration wants to regulate religion, we are not trying to force anything on anyone. Allowing religious organizations to serve the public does not violate the separation of church and state. Conscripting us into advancing government objectives against our conscience does.[33]

Wuerl's last two sentences capture the essence of how the Obama administration operates. The common view is that liberals attempt to banish displays and recognition of faith in the public square in order to enforce a strict separation of church and state that denies the inherently religious founding principles of our nation.

But radical leftists (particularly champions of the Saul Alinsky worldview) use the opposite means to achieve a more sinister end. Rather than erecting a wall to keep religion out of the public square, they favor using the brute force of the state to control all that the church does. Obama and his allies would like nothing more than to turn religious groups into instruments of the federal government.

This type of church-state relationship is common in places like China and Cuba, where churches exist but derive any power they have from the state, which exploits the church's influence and means for its own ends.

Obama views civil society, including the church, as an obstacle that interferes with the only important relationship, that between citizens and the state. For that relationship to flourish, civil society must be destroyed or dominated. Radical leftists would prefer the former, but they'll settle for the latter.

With the HHS mandate, Obama is attempting to dominate the church—in order to, as Wuerl wrote, "conscript us into advancing government objectives against [Catholics'] conscience."

CHAPTER TWELVE

Obama Attacks
Religious Freedom

The HHS mandate is a departure from America's tradition of respecting rights of conscience. In 1973, after the U.S. Supreme Court's *Roe* v. *Wade* decision legalizing abortion nationwide, Congress passed the Church Amendment, which exempts private entities that receive public funds from having to provide abortions or sterilizations. It also protects health care workers from being compelled to assist in those practices if they work for fund recipients.

Laws passed in the subsequent forty years have reaffirmed the federal government's commitment to protecting the conscience rights of American citizens, and extended those rights to outlaw discrimination at the state and local government levels.

Despite the vast body of law protecting conscience rights, however, there have been numerous recent attempts to weaken them through legislation, the courts, and medical licensing boards. In 1995, the Accreditation Council for Graduate Medical Education passed a regulation requiring medical schools to offer abortion training in order to receive accreditation. Only a federal law prevented its enforcement.

In 2007, the American College of Obstetricians and Gynecologists (ACOG) issued a statement that health care providers may not exercise their right of conscience if it might "constitute an imposition of religious or moral beliefs on patients."[1]

Not long after, the American Board of Obstetrics and Gynecology (ABOG) issued a policy stating that board certification can be withdrawn from providers "if there is a violation of ABOG or ACOG rules and or ethics principles or felony convictions."[2]

Michael Leavitt, secretary of health and human services under President George W. Bush, summed up the emerging position of the medical community: "[I]f a person goes to medical school, they lose their right of conscience."[3]

President Bush responded to attacks on conscience rights by reinforcing conscience protections. Shortly before leaving office, Bush issued the Provider Conscience Regulation through HHS.[4] It strengthened existing federal conscience laws by requiring recipients of federal funds to certify compliance and specified a mechanism for investigating complaints of conscience violations.

Barack Obama once claimed to support "robust" conscience protections for those with religious or moral objections to participating in life-destroying procedures. But in 2011, Obama, through HHS, released a directive to rescind the Bush order.[5] The Obama administration claimed, without evidence, that the conscience protections could endanger some people's access to medical care.

To understand why the administration would attack conscience rights, one must first understand the mindset of the abortion absolutist. Obama and his allies consider "reproductive care," including abortion, to be "preventive care" and thus "fundamental care." As Obama himself has said, "reproductive justice" is "one of the most fundamental rights we possess."[6]

Since they are "essential" and "fundamental" to health care, birth control and abortion-on-demand must be covered in all health plans free of charge. To abortion advocates, then, whenever First Amendment conscience rights collide with access to abortion or birth control, "reproductive rights" must triumph.

This mindset helps to explain why Obama attacks religious liberty so vigorously. Last October, HHS ceased funding successful Catholic programs that help victims of human trafficking because the Catholic services don't refer them to abortion facilities if they are pregnant.[7] For a time, Catholic Relief Services faced a similar threat to its international relief programs.

Here's a list of other Obama administration attacks on religion and religious freedom:[8]

- Pledged to sign the Employment Non-Discrimination Act (ENDA) into law—interfering with the right for religious employers to choose their employees.
- Appointed radical homosexual activist Chai Feldblum to commissioner on the Equal Employment Opportunity Commission (EEOC). Feldblum is on record saying: "We should ... not tolerate private beliefs about sexual orientation and gender.... Protecting one group's identity may, at times, require that we burden others' belief liberty ... it is essential that we not privilege moral beliefs that are religiously based over other sincerely held, core, moral beliefs."
- Announced that the Attorney General will no longer defend the federal Defense of Marriage Act (DOMA), signed into law by President Clinton in 1996.
- Signed the so-called "Hate Crimes" law, which opens the door to silencing freedom of speech, including religious-based criticism of some sexual behavior.
- Repealed the military "Don't Ask, Don't Tell" policy with no religious liberty protections for military chaplains and servicemen and women of faith.

- Modified Department of Housing and Urban Development (HUD) guidelines—forcing landlords to violate their consciences if they have objections to renting their properties to people they believe are engaged in immoral behavior.
- Removed "religious public service"—the only public service excluded—from being counted as payment towards student loans.
- Repealed President Ronald Reagan's "Mexico City Policy," which denied federal funding to organizations that perform abortions overseas.
- Changed "freedom of religion" to "freedom to worship" in public documents, a lexicon shift that could limit religious freedom outside the four walls of a church or similar facility.
- Ordered the removal of a monogram symbolizing Jesus before speaking at Georgetown University.[9]
- Refused to host the National Day of Prayer at the White House.
- Nominated three pro-abortion ambassadors to the Vatican, which rejected all three.
- Omitted, on at least seven occasions, the mention of the Creator in the Declaration of Independence.
- Misquoted the national motto "In God We Trust," saying it was "E pluribus unum."
- Neglected to fill the position of religious freedom ambassador for almost two years. Finally relented after public and congressional pressure.
- Opposed inclusion of President Franklin Roosevelt's "D-Day Prayer" as part of the World War II Memorial, saying it would "dilute" the memorial.
- Declined to make any religious references in the president's annual Thanksgiving speech.

- As a matter of foreign policy, promoted the demands of homosexual activists over the religious beliefs of other nations, calling those beliefs an "obstacle" to homosexual "rights."
- Ignored a U.S. Supreme Court decision ordering that the Mojave World War I Memorial cross be re-erected.

These are only some of the more obvious instances of the anti-religious bias of the administration. In the now notorious Hosanna-Tabor case, the Obama administration's Equal Employment Opportunity Commission tried to bully a Lutheran church about its hiring practices, arguing that the church didn't have the right to control who it employs according to its religious beliefs. The case started in 1999, when Cheryl Perich began teaching at Hosanna-Tabor Evangelical Lutheran Church and School in Michigan. In 2004, Perich left on disability after being diagnosed with narcolepsy.

When she tried to get her job back, the school told her that they had already hired a replacement. Perich threatened to take the school to court, prompting the school to fire her because using secular courts to solve an interchurch issue violated its teaching on resolving such disputes. With backing from the Equal Employment Opportunity Commission (EEOC) and the Obama administration, Perich filed a lawsuit against the school, arguing that the decision threatened equal protection under the law.

The case made its way to the Supreme Court, where, in January 2012, it ruled unanimously in favor of the school. In *Hosanna-Tabor Evangelical Lutheran Church and School* v. *EEOC*, the court ruled that "the Establishment Clause prevents the Government from appointing ministers, and the Free Exercise Clause prevents it from interfering with the freedom of religious groups to select their own."[10]

The case was seen by many legal analysts as an embarrassment to the Obama administration. Obama court appointee Justice Elena Kagan came close to openly mocking the rationale of her successor as Obama's solicitor general during oral arguments.[11]

The ruling was a landmark victory for religious freedom. Richard W. Garnett, director of Notre Dame Law School's program in Church, State, and Society, told the *Washington Post* that the ruling was the court's most important decision on religious freedom in decades. "The government doesn't get to second-guess religious communities' decisions about who should be their teachers, leaders, and ministers," he said.[12]

When I asked Matt Bowman, legal counsel for the Alliance Defending Freedom, to sum up the Obama administration's actions on religious freedom, he didn't pull any punches. He said, "President Obama is not only the most fervent opponent of religious freedom ever to reside in the White House. He has pursued his agenda by making villains of Americans who have traditional religious values, to divide them from other citizens so he can aggressively promote abortion, same-sex so-called 'marriage,' and the marginalization of religion itself."[13]

Obama's Catholic Apologists

The Catholic Church is the largest religious denomination in the United States, and Barack Obama has always had a line-up of prominent Catholics willing to go to bat for him. For his inner circle, the president chose Catholics who dissent fully from their church on moral matters. Five of his original cabinet secretaries are Catholics who disown the church's teaching on human life. Two in particular stand out: HHS Secretary Kathleen Sebelius and Vice President Joe Biden.

Sebelius is the flagrantly pro-abortion former governor of Kansas. In her current post as secretary of HHS, Sebelius is the Obama official most responsible for crafting the contraceptive mandate. As governor of Kansas from 2003 to 2009, Sebelius aggressively promoted abortion. She vetoed legislation that would have limited abortions in her state on at least four occasions.[14] In 2008, she vetoed the Comprehensive Abortion Reform Act, which would have strengthened late-term abortion laws and prevented coerced abortions.[15] It's no wonder why Sebelius opposed limiting late-term abortions: their principle practitioner was a huge contributor to her campaigns.

George Tiller was notorious for being one of the only abortionists in the country who would regularly perform late-term abortions for almost any reason. Based in Wichita, "Tiller the baby killer," as some of his opponents referred to him, was also a huge contributor to Sebelius and her allies in Kansas. He spent millions funding the Democratic Party through his ProKanDo political action committee. He spent $1.2 million in the 2006 election cycle alone.[16] Sebelius and Tiller were so tight that Sebelius once held a party at the governor's mansion honoring Tiller. Only Tiller, his wife, and clinic staff were present at the event.[17]

Sebelius's promotion of abortion prompted her bishop, Kansas City Archbishop Joseph Naumann, to ask that she no longer receive Holy Communion.[18] In 2009, Archbishop Raymond Burke, prefect for the Apostolic Signatura, the Holy See's highest court, proclaimed that Sebelius should not receive communion. "Whether Governor Sebelius is in the Archdiocese of Kansas City in Kansas, or in any other diocese, she should not present herself for Holy Communion because, after pastoral admonition, she obstinately persists in serious sin," Burke said.[19] (All this negative attention is said to have knocked Sebelius out of the running to be Barack Obama's running mate in 2008.)

With Sebelius at the helm at HHS, nobody should be surprised at the Obama administration's attacks on religious liberty and conscience rights and promotion of controversial abortion laws—these have always been her forte.

In 2012, Sebelius accepted an invitation to deliver the commencement address at the Georgetown Public Policy Institute (GPPI). Georgetown is not Notre Dame. It often seems to downplay its Catholicism, preferring to stress its research and academic credentials rather than its Jesuit tradition. It routinely hires professors and invites speakers, Catholic and non-Catholic, who publicly support abortion and other policies that contradict Catholic moral theology. Bill Clinton[20] and Barack Obama[21] have both spoken there. In 2008, the Georgetown faculty gave $179,000 to candidate Obama. The *Chronicle of Higher Education* ranked Georgetown among the top ten of Obama's academic donors.[22]

GPPI had always been full of liberal Catholics. Its faculty included E. J. Dionne, the liberal Catholic columnist, and Tom Daschle, the former Democratic senator and the man Obama initially tapped to lead HHS before tax problems got in the way. Many of GPPI's previous commencement speakers were liberal Catholics who publicly endorsed abortion. But Sebelius provoked a special kind of negative response even at nominally Catholic Georgetown, and her appearance drew strong criticism.

More than 27,000 Catholics signed a letter opposing her appearance. The Archdiocese of Washington released a statement condemning it.[23]

Prominent Georgetown professor Patrick Deneen wrote a letter to University president John DeGioia signed by eight other GU faculty members asking him to rescind the invitation. According to the letter, Deneen believed that hosting Sebelius at a commencement ceremony signified Georgetown's endorsement of the HHS mandate.[24]

DeGioia responded that the invitation to speak had been made in January, before the mandate announcement, and that it in no way meant that the school endorsed the administration's policy.[25] It was a measure of just how deeply the mandate decision had cut that Sebelius's speech drew any criticism at all.

Then there's Vice President Joe Biden. Unlike other dissenting Catholics, Biden likes to play up his Catholicism whenever he can. He enjoys meeting with the pope when he travels to Rome and glad-handing prominent Catholic officials at every opportunity here at home. But he has had a difficult relationship with the Catholic Church because of his positions on cultural issues, chiefly abortion. Biden once supported some limits on abortion, including limits on public funding of abortion. But as vice president, Biden cannot dissent from Obama's radical abortion policies. Still, that hasn't stopped him from continuing to invoke his faith.

In January 2012, Biden told the *Delaware News Journal* he thinks Catholics may support abortion. "It's very difficult," Biden said. "I was raised as a Catholic, I'm a practicing Catholic, and I'm totally at home with the Catholicism that I was raised in and this whole culture of social responsibility."[26] Biden then misrepresented Catholic teaching on abortion, saying, "Throughout the church's history, we've argued between whether or not it is wrong in every circumstance and the degree of wrong. Catholics have this notion, it's almost a gradation."

In 2008, then-senator Biden invited the ire of the church by claiming that the beginning of human life is a "personal and private" matter of religious faith, and that one's view on the matter cannot be imposed on others. That statement earned swift rebukes from a number of Catholic bishops.[27]

Catholics Abandon Obama

Many alienated Catholics are abandoning Obama. During the Notre Dame commencement speech controversy in 2009, polls showed two in three Catholics approved of Obama's job performance.[28] But even then the seeds of Obama's troubles with Catholics were being planted. In May 2009, political science professor John Green told *Politico*, "It's possible that [Obama] could alienate [pro-life Catholics who voted for him] if the abortion issue becomes salient."[29]

And that's exactly what's happened. Obama will probably always have significant support among some groups of American Catholics—Hispanics, for instance, who make up more than a third of American Catholics.

But Obama lost white Catholics in 2008—the first candidate to do so and win the presidency since 1976.[30] He lost them because they tend to be social conservatives ("Reagan Democrats") or conservatives full stop.

An apparently "moderate" Democrat like Bill Clinton can win them over, but a radically liberal Democrat is unlikely to do so.

Just a few months into Obama's term, Notre Dame professor Scott Appleby said, "A lot of [Catholics] held their noses when they voted for Obama. His decision on life issues and the way he has communicated them have been deeply dissatisfying to Catholics who voted for him, including me."[31]

After the HHS mandate controversy, Matthew N. Schmalz, professor of religion and comparative studies at the College of the Holy Cross, said, "This has hurt the case that some Catholics have made that voting for Obama in some ways is a vote for Catholic social teaching."[32]

Kathy Dahlkemper and Bart Stupak are both Catholic Democrats who lost their congressional seats in 2010 after supporting Obamacare. They were both assured by President Obama that the law would not provide abortions. They both now regret voting for the law.

"I would have never voted for the final version of the bill if I expected the Obama administration to force Catholic hospitals and Catholic colleges and universities to pay for contraception," Dahlkemper said in a 2012 press release sent by Democrats for Life.[33]

Stupak, whose support was instrumental in passing Obamacare, told Fox News' Greta Van Susteren in February 2012 that he was "disappointed" with the HHS mandate.[34]

Doug Kmiec was head of the Office of Legal Counsel under presidents Ronald Reagan and George H. W. Bush and a former dean of the Catholic University Law School. Kmiec gave Obama a timely endorsement in 2008. Obama, Kmiec believed, was a "person of integrity, intelligence and genuine goodwill."[35]

Kmiec felt that Obama's books showed how bipartisan he could be. "I'm convinced," he wrote, "based upon his public pronouncements and his personal writing, that on each of these questions [abortion, traditional marriage, constitutional interpretation and religious freedom] he is not closed to understanding opposing points of view, and, as best as it is humanely possible, he will respect and accommodate them."[36]

He later stated, "Beyond life issues, an audaciously hope-filled Democrat like Obama is a Catholic natural." Kmiec even wrote a book ahead of the 2008 election titled *Can a Catholic Support Him?* and concluded, "Barack Obama has my vote."[37] For his support, President Obama named Kmiec ambassador to Malta.

Kmiec continued to be a vocal supporter of the president until he heard news of the contraceptive mandate, at which point he wrote a letter to Obama expressing his disappointment. He suggested that the president had forced him to choose between "friendship" and his "duty to faith and country." He ended with, "The Barack Obama I knew would never have asked me to make that choice." Later, he told *The Hill* newspaper in response to a question about who he would support in 2012, "I am for now (unhappily) without a candidate."[38]

Another example is the case of Jo Ann Nardelli, who, in late May 2012 defected from the Democratic Party to the Republican Party, citing her Catholic faith and Biden's and Obama's embrace of same-sex marriage. Nardelli was an elected member of the Pennsylvania State Democratic Party and a Pennsylvania State Democratic Committee Executive Board member.

She explained in a press conference that, "as the Democratic Party has taken the stand for same-sex marriage, then I must make a stand on my faith that marriage is between a man and a woman. God's principles for life never change. His guidelines, given in Scripture, produce fruitful lives when you follow them."[39]

Nardelli, a pro-life Democrat for more than forty years, explained her decision in greater depth in an interview:

> I always knew that being a pro-life Democrat was a little difficult but doable in our party. The contraceptive mandate bothered me ... but the last straw came a few weeks ago on Sunday, May 6. In the morning before church, my husband and I were eating breakfast watching Vice President Biden on *Meet the*

Press. I respect Joe Biden. I know he is of deep Catholic faith and his Irish Catholic ways remind me very much of my own father of Italian Catholic background. But when I heard Vice President Biden make the statement on same-sex marriage … I was sick, I had a pit in my stomach. But I knew that was only the beginning. Once the president came out with the support of same-sex marriage and the Democratic Party platform was set for us leaders, I knew I had to make the change.[40]

Nardelli went on to explain that she'd been considering changing parties for a while, but that until Biden's and Obama's same-sex marriage announcements, she "really thought I could make a difference and bring back the party I used to know." She added:

I began to receive notices of state meetings and more and more the platform of same-sex marriage was on the table as support-ing our president. Now, I knew that eventually I was going to have to sign on to this agenda. I could not. I was raised in my Catholic faith that marriage is between a man and a woman. I don't have a problem with gays, rights to properties, or whatever those unions bring; however it is not marriage! Marriage is between a man and a woman in the Bible, and I firmly believe that. Therefore I knew I had to resign my positions, dissolve my affiliations, take a stand, and change to the Republican Party.[41]

At the press conference announcing her switch, Nardelli, one-time member of the Tri County Women for Obama Steering Committee, said, "I thought I could make a difference to change our party. It didn't work." She continued, "I noticed that it's been going more and more to the left. This is not my father's party. I did not leave the party; the party left me."

Obama's Catholic support has plummeted as a result of his attempts to attack the church. According to a March Pew Research Center poll,

31 percent of white Catholics described the Obama administration as unfriendly to religion, compared to 17 percent in August 2009.[42] And from early March to mid-April 2012, Obama's Catholic support dropped from 53 percent to 45 percent. A recent Gallup poll found a similar result, with Obama's Catholic support dipping to 46 percent.[43]

A May 2012 Pew poll found that among Catholic voters with a preference, 47 percent would vote for President Obama, and 52 percent for former Massachusetts Governor Mitt Romney.[44] If that margin were to hold on Election Day, it would mark a swing of 18 million voters *away* from Obama.

At least one poll has linked Catholics' abandonment of Obama with the HHS mandate. A Catholic Association poll conducted by QEV Analytics found that 29 percent of Catholics said they were less likely to vote to re-elect Obama because of the mandate, while 13 percent said they were more likely to do so.[45] Religiously active white females were a stunning 38 percent less likely to vote for Obama (against 12 percent more likely), and independent voters were 28 percent less likely (against 15 percent more likely).[46]

Barack Obama's abortion stridency has provided the Catholic Church with a powerful opportunity to practice one of its most important missions: to educate the faithful. Each of Obama's forays into debates over moral issues has prompted Catholic leaders to reassert the church's position on those issues.

Priests read statements clarifying what the church believes; Catholic leaders appear on popular television shows to do the same; and the Obama administration is put on the defensive as many Catholics ask themselves: I've got my own issues with the church, but do I want the federal government telling us what to do?

With his efforts to divide the Catholic Church, Obama is making more than a political calculation. He's making a high-stakes bet that the bishops and the church teachings they are entrusted to uphold no longer have the respect of the faithful—but that he, the self-proclaimed chosen one, has.

CHAPTER THIRTEEN

Obama's Politicized Faith

All effective action requires the passport of morality.[1]

—Saul Alinsky, *Rules for Radicals*

In *The Audacity of Hope,* Barack Obama states that it's important for liberal politicians to talk about faith. "I think we [liberals] make a mistake when we fail to acknowledge the power of faith in the lives of the American people, and so avoid joining a serious debate about how to reconcile faith with our modern, pluralistic democracy."[2]

Then Obama offers an openly cynical reason why he thinks it's wrong for liberals to dismiss faith: "It's bad politics."[3]

"There are a whole lot of religious people in America, including the majority of Democrats," he explains: "When we abandon the field of religious discourse—when we ignore the debate about what it means to be a good Christian or Muslim or Jew; when we discuss religion only in the negative sense … others will fill the vacuum."[4]

It is fitting that Obama mentions politics first in explaining why Democrats should engage with religion: Obama's faith is overtly political.

The Conversion

Biographies about Obama shed light on the politicized environment in which he embraced Christianity and practiced his faith under the guidance of the Reverend Jeremiah Wright, senior pastor at Trinity United Church of Christ in Chicago.

In his book *The Bridge: The Life and Rise of Barack Obama*, David Remnick interviewed many of Obama's friends and family members about Obama's decision to attend Trinity. He writes:

> Obama's black and white friends say that his motives for joining Trinity were complicated, yet Trinity was undeniably a "power church" in town. Obama "saw it as a power base," Mike Kruglik said. "You can't interpret what Obama does without thinking of the power factor. Even then. For a long time, I wouldn't talk about this, but he told me way back then that he was intrigued by the possibility of becoming mayor of Chicago. His analysis was that the mayor in this town is extremely powerful and all the problems he was dealing with then could be solved if the mayor was focused on them."[5]

Politically, joining Trinity seems to have been the right move for Obama, at least initially. Obama formed a deep bond with the Reverend Wright at a time when Obama was just getting to know the lay of the political land in Chicago.

In *The Amateur*, Edward Klein interviews many of Obama's past friends and colleagues about Obama's faith, including Wright. From these interviews, Klein concludes:

> Jeremiah Wright became far more than a religious and spiritual guide to Obama; he was his substitute father, life coach, and political inspiration wrapped in one package. At each step of Obama's career, Wright was there with practical advice and counsel. Wright

encouraged Obama to make a career of politics, and he offered to hook up Obama with members of Trinity United Church of Christ who had money and important connections.[6]

Wright told Klein, in a 2011 interview, that he believes Obama attended Trinity for political, not spiritual, reasons. "What I remember," Wright said about his first meeting with Obama, "is that he came to talk to me as a community organizer, not in search of Christ."[7]

"[E]ven after Barack and Michelle came to the church, their kids weren't raised in the church like you raise other kids in Sunday school. No. Church is not their thing. It never was their thing.... So the Church was not an integral part of their spiritual lives after they got married."

"But," Wright says, "the church *was* an integral part of Barack's *politics*—because he needed that black base."[8]

It would be easy to dismiss Wright's comments as personal pique. When the contents of some of Wright's more provocative sermons came to light in 2008, Obama gave a speech denouncing them and distancing himself from his former mentor. Wright clearly felt stung by this and is perhaps bitter. In 2010, Wright claimed Obama "threw me under the bus" during the 2008 campaign.[9] But it is still hard to dismiss what he says about Obama's motives for joining his church, especially given the way Obama has politicized his faith as president.

Taking God's Name in Vain

President Obama talks about God—a lot. In fact, a *Politico* story six months into his presidency claimed Obama had cited the Almighty even more often than the evangelist president George W. Bush. And the God-talk seems to have increased since then.[10]

But Obama employs his religious rhetoric in a way that is unusual for liberals. Most liberals confine their religious references to public statements about welfare for the poor, minimum wage increases, and foreign aid programs—all about generosity and charity. But Obama goes much further.

He tends to invoke God at the most implausible times—often in support of policies outlawed or condemned by the Bible and most major religions.

Consider abortion and its related issues. Most pro-choice advocates steer clear of invoking God or their faith to justify the taking of innocent human life. But not Obama. He says he comes about his stance not despite his faith, but in part because of it.

Early in his administration, Obama lifted an executive ban on federal funding of stem cell research, which destroys human embryos. He explained his decision by saying, "As a person of faith, I believe we are called to care for each other and work to ease human suffering. I believe we have been given the capacity and will to pursue this research—and the humanity and conscience to do so responsibly."[11]

At Notre Dame in 2009, he told graduates, "Maybe we won't agree on abortion, but we can still agree that this is a heart-wrenching decision for any woman to make, with both moral and spiritual dimensions."[12]

He's even promoted Obamacare by invoking morality. "We are God's partners in matters of life and death," he told rabbis during a conference call to sell his health care reform proposal.[13]

Obama has also invoked his faith in supporting same-sex marriage and other items on the gay rights agenda. As a presidential candidate in 2008, Obama justified his support for same-sex civil unions. "If people find that controversial," he told people at a town hall event in Ohio, "then I would just refer them to the Sermon on the Mount, which I think is, in my mind, for my faith, more central than an obscure passage in Romans. That's my view. But we can have a respectful disagreement on that."[14]

"When we think about our faith," he said in explaining his decision to support same-sex marriage to ABC's Robin Roberts, "the thing at root that we think about is not only Christ sacrificing himself on our behalf, but it's also the Golden Rule.... Treat others the way you would want to be treated."[15]

This is not to say Obama is always successful in convincing his audience that his policies are faith-based initiatives. A May 15, 2012, CBS News/*New York Times* poll found that 67 percent of respondents said Obama came out for same-sex marriage "mostly for political reasons." Only 24 percent said he made the decision "mostly because he thinks it's right."[16]

Obama isn't alone in citing his faith to justify support for same-sex marriage. In the wake of Obama's announcement, House Minority Leader Nancy Pelosi, who is Catholic, said, "My religion has, compels me—and I love it for it—to be against discrimination of any kind in our country, and I consider [opposition to same-sex marriage] a form of discrimination. I think it's unconstitutional on top of that."[17]

Obama is also more than willing to justify his out-of-control spending with religious talk. At the National Prayer Breakfast in February 2012, Obama broke decorum to talk politics. "I think to myself, if I'm willing to give something up as somebody who's been extraordinarily blessed, and give up some of the tax breaks that I enjoy, I actually think that's going to make economic sense," he said. "But for me as a Christian, it also coincides with Jesus' teaching that 'for unto whom much is given, much shall be required.'"[18]

The left has been on a long crusade to portray Republican budget cuts as antithetical to faith. When it was announced in April 2012 that House Budget Chairman Paul Ryan would deliver a speech at Georgetown University explaining how Catholic teaching shaped his budget proposal, 100 faculty members signed a letter condemning his appearance.[19]

In response to Republican-proposed budget cuts in 2011 and 2012, liberal Christian activist Jim Wallis launched the "What Would Jesus Cut" campaign. Wallis believed the cuts, which included cuts to welfare programs, international aid, and college grants, were "unbiblical."[20]

The premise of Wallis's campaign was that "cutting programs that help those who need them most is morally wrong." Wallis does approve of cutting one item on the budget: military spending, which he says is "the most corrupt government spending."

Obama is in a fortunate position as a believer. He is not a member of an established church with centuries of dogma and doctrines that he must navigate. The Reverend Wright's rantings notwithstanding, Obama doesn't risk provoking the criticism of his church whenever he talks about how his faith guides his public policy. He can articulate it any way he wants, whatever the occasion. So when Obama prefaces support for same-sex marriages with phrases like "I think," "in my mind," and "for my faith," it's hard to argue. This makes it easier for him than for someone like Joe Biden.

During a September 2008 *Meet the Press* interview, moderator Tom Brokaw asked Biden, "When does life begin?" That put Biden in a bind because he had to try to reconcile his pro-abortion views with the pro-life views of his church.[21]

"As a Roman Catholic," Biden started, "I'm prepared to accept the teachings of my church—I'm prepared as a matter of faith to accept that life begins at the moment of conception."[22]

He ran into trouble when he continued:

> But let me tell you. There are an awful lot of people of great confessional faiths—Protestants, Jews, Muslims and others—who have a different view. They believe in God as strongly as I do. They're intensely as religious as I am religious. They believe in their faith and they believe in human life, and they have differing views as to when life—I'm prepared as a matter of faith to accept that life begins at the moment of conception. But that is my judgment. For me to impose that judgment on everyone else who is equally and maybe even more devout than I am seems to me is inappropriate in a pluralistic society. And I know you get the push back, "Well, what about fascism?" Everybody, you know, you going to say fascism's all right? Fascism isn't a matter of faith. No decent religious person thinks fascism is a good idea.[23]

Things only got worse from there, as Biden threw in a reference to Saint Thomas Aquinas's *Summa Theologica* and tied himself in knots trying to reconcile the irreconcilable.

Brokaw then asked Biden about his support for abortion, given what he had just said about his belief that life begins at conception. Biden answered, "I voted against telling everyone else in the country that they have to accept my religiously based view that it's the moment of conception."[24]

Biden's mangling of Catholic moral theology earned him an official rebuke from the bishops and from various Catholic theologians. Father Thomas Reese, senior fellow at the Woodstock Theological Center and a political liberal, said, "Politicians should not do theology. Whenever they start interpreting Catholic teaching, they invite Catholic bishops to jump all over them."[25]

Obama's rhetoric does not invite the Catholic bishops to jump all over him, because he is not a Catholic. Obama is also fortunate because many conservatives are hesitant to criticize his faith. Many religious conservatives are grateful whenever they find anyone on the left willing to talk about God. For others, Obama's faith background is too deeply rooted in race, which makes even raising the issue of Obama's faith complicated. John McCain found Obama's religion and church so potentially hazardous that he refused to bring them up at all in the 2008 campaign.

This leaves Obama free to invoke his faith whenever he wants with little chance that he will be criticized or challenged for it. To Obama, talking about God and faith is a way to shut down debate on controversial issues. As is the case when he invokes his daughters, Obama seems to believe that Americans will accept his extreme views on moral issues so long as those views arise from his deepest religious beliefs.

For others, however, Obama's constant faith invocations may bring to mind his owns words from *The Audacity of Hope*: "Nothing is more transparent than inauthentic expressions of faith—such as the politician who ... sprinkles in a few biblical citations to spice up a thoroughly dry policy speech."[26]

CHAPTER FOURTEEN

Abandoning the Faithful: How Obama Ignores Religious Persecution Abroad

Obama positions himself as a president of deep Christian faith, yet the most powerful man in the world has studiously ignored one of the greatest, if underreported, scandals of our time: the persecution of Christians in the Middle East and other parts of the world.

Part of the reason Obama ignores the plight of beleaguered Christians abroad is his devotion to aggressively advancing a radical social agenda of abortion and, more recently, "LGBT rights" worldwide. (LGBT stands for lesbian, gay, bisexual, and "transgender"—add a couple letters depending on which college campus you visit: "q" for queer or questioning, "I" for intersex, etc.)

To the Obama administration, it is not religious freedom that is a universal right, but rather unrestricted abortion and the gay rights causes.

Obama's policies make clear that he is committed to persecuting Christians in America, denying them their constitutional rights to religious liberty, and to ignoring the violent persecution of Christians abroad—all in the interests of pushing his radical social views on the world.

According to the Universal Declaration of Human Rights, freedom of religion is defined as the freedom of an individual or community, in public or private, to manifest religion or belief in teaching, practice, worship, and observance.

Religious freedom is a right approximately 70 percent of the world does not enjoy, including most of the 12 to 17 million Christians in the Middle East.[1] Throughout that region, Christians are treated as unwelcome intruders at best and mortal enemies at worst. The situation may be worst in Iraq, where, ironically, Christianity predates Islam. Iraqi Christians are mostly Chaldean Catholics and Protestant Assyrians. They face severe, systematic, and ongoing persecution. In fact, the terms "extinction"[2] and "religious cleansing"[3] have been used by those who know the situation best to describe the plight of Iraq's Christians. Pope Benedict XVI has said Iraq's Christians are experiencing an "authentic martyrdom."[4]

Iraq's Christians have seen their churches looted, desecrated, and destroyed, and their leaders kidnapped, murdered, or both. Christians have been forced to pay higher taxes than Muslims and have been barred from voting. "We are seeing another, the umpteenth, attack against Christians," Chaldean Archbishop of Kirkuk Emil Nona said in 2010. "The violence continues without relief."[5]

If liberals want to witness the real war on women, it's happening not in the student pharmacies of elite western private law schools, but in the non-Christian, non-Jewish areas of the Middle East, Asia, and Africa where women are treated as property. Christian women have become a particular target in Iraq, where they are commonly threatened with rape if they don't convert to Islam.

Many Christians are compelled to pay the *jizya*, an Islamic tax levied on non-Muslims for "protection" by local extremist Muslim groups. Attacks and threats against Iraq's Christians constitute what Cardinal Emmanuel III Delly, primate of the Chaldean Catholic Church, has called "open persecution as in the early centuries of the Church."[6]

In 2009, the Reverend Jean Benjamin Sleiman, Catholic archbishop of Baghdad, told the *New York Times*, "I fear the extinction of Christianity in Iraq and the Middle East."[7]

The Iraqi constitution, ratified in 2005, institutionalizes discrimination against non-Muslims. It states, "Islam is the official religion of the state and is a foundation source of legislation," and that "No law can be passed that contradicts the undisputed rules of Islam."[8]

Conditions have gotten so bad that the U.S. Congress recently passed a resolution calling on the Iraqi government to investigate and report on abuses against Iraq's minority communities, including its Christians.

Iraq's Christians aren't alone in facing systematic violent persecution. The "Arab Spring" uprisings have made millions of Christians vulnerable throughout the Middle East. In Egypt, for instance, the transitional government has failed to protect religious minorities, especially Coptic Christians, from deadly attacks at a time when minority communities have been increasingly vulnerable. And Christian converts continue to face death sentences in Iran and Afghanistan.

In December 2011, Catholic Archbishop Dominique Mamberti, the Vatican's secretary for Relations with States, estimated that there are more than 200 million Christians who face persecution around the world.[9]

The essential problem is that many countries with Muslim governments or Muslim majorities do not recognize freedom of conscience, either in principle or in practice. Other problems include state-sponsored extremist ideology and education, and corrupt law enforcement and legal systems that allow crimes against religious minorities to go unpunished.

Every year, the United States Commission on International Religious Freedom (USCIRF) publishes a report. Established by Congress in 1998, the USCIRF is responsible for monitoring and reporting to the president about religious freedom worldwide. Its role is not only to collect facts about religious freedom internationally, but also to suggest how U.S. foreign policy can promote religious freedom.

USCIRF's 2012 report, which runs 337 pages, lays out the scope of the problem in the introduction:

> Over the past year, while economic woes captured world head-lines, an ongoing crisis of equal breadth and scope frequently went unnoticed. Across the global landscape, the pivotal human right of religious freedom was under escalating attack. To an alarming extent, freedom of thought, conscience, and religion or belief was being curtailed, often threatening the safety and survival of innocent persons, including members of religious minorities.[10]

In 2012, the USCIRF designated sixteen countries as CPCs—"countries of particular concern"—with governments that have engaged in or tolerated "particularly severe" violations of religious freedom, including systematic, ongoing, and egregious violations such as torture, prolonged detention without charges, disappearances, or other "flagrant denial of the right to life, liberty, or the security of the person."[11]

After a country is designated a CPC, the president of that country is required by law to implement policies that respond to violations. The 2012 CPCs are: Burma, the Democratic People's Republic of Korea (North Korea), Egypt, Eritrea, Iran, Iraq, Nigeria, Pakistan, the People's Republic of China, Saudi Arabia, Sudan, Tajikistan, Turkey, Turkmenistan, Uzbekistan, and Vietnam.

A majority of these countries are run by Muslim governments that routinely violate the rights of their religious minorities. As Nina Shea, director of the Hudson Institute's Center for Religious Freedom and a USCIRF commissioner, has written:

> Christians are far from the only religious group persecuted in these countries. But, Christians are the only group persecuted in each and every one of them. This pattern has been found by

sources as diverse as the Vatican, Open Doors, Pew Research Center, *Newsweek*, and *The Economist*, all of which recently reported that an overwhelming majority of the religiously persecuted around the world are Christians.[12]

The primary effect of Muslim attacks on religious freedom is that the number of Christians in the Middle East is plummeting. In recent decades, the share of Christians in the Middle East has fallen from 20 percent of the population to less than 5 percent. By one estimate their share of the population may drop more than 50 percent, to 6 million, by the year 2020.[13] An estimated half of Iraq's 1.4 million Christians have left in the last decade.[14]

To be sure, Christians are leaving the region for many reasons, including dwindling economic opportunities. But the most important factor is the ascendance of political Islam. According to a 2010 Vatican document, relations between Christians and Muslims in the Middle East are often difficult "principally because Muslims make no distinction between religion and politics, thereby relegating Christians to the precarious position of being considered noncitizens, despite the fact that they were citizens of their countries long before the rise of Islam."[15]

Obama Abandons Christians

President Obama does the millions of Christians in the Middle East a profound injustice by referring to that region as "the Muslim world," which only serves to reinforce the Islamists' contention that Christians do not belong there.

President Obama signaled early that, despite his professed personal religious fervor, religious freedom for others would not be a priority for his administration. In a profound public demonstration of that, he allowed the position of Ambassador for International Religious Freedom to remain unfilled for more than two years before appointing Susan Johnson Cook late in 2010.

Obama rarely mentions the plight of persecuted Christians. In the rare cases when he is asked to comment, he equivocates, often presenting the slaughter of Christians as "sectarian violence" between two sides of equal strength.

In 2011, when twenty-seven Christian protestors were killed and hundreds injured during a peaceful demonstration against the burning of a Coptic Church in Cairo, Obama urged "restraint on all sides."[16]

In 2010, Leonard Leo, chairman of the USCIRF, noted, "Presidential references to religious freedom have become rare, often replaced at most with references to freedom of worship. The same holds true for many of Secretary of State Hillary Clinton's speeches."[17]

Thomas Farr, director of the Religious Freedom Project at Georgetown University, has been an outspoken critic of the president's record on religious freedom issues. He says that the USCIRF has made many policy recommendations to the State Department that have gone unheeded. In a 2010 op-ed, Farr, who served as the original director of the State Department's Office of International Religious Freedom, wrote, "The Obama administration seems to have decided that other policy initiatives—outreach to Muslim governments, obtaining China's cooperation, advancing gay rights—would be compromised by vigorous advocacy for religious freedom. In fact, such a decision would harm the victims of religious persecution, hamstring key Obama initiatives and undermine U.S. national interests."[18]

When the Democrat-controlled Senate waited until the last minute to reauthorize funding for the USCIRF in late 2011, Farr said that the Senate had made it "reasonably clear to the persecutors ... that advancing religious freedom is not a priority for the United States."[19]

Farr has argued that Ambassador Johnson Cook has not received the resources she needs to succeed in addressing religious freedom issues, and that American diplomats are not adequately trained in religious freedom issues.

In 2012, the State Department purged any mention of religious freedom in its annual report on human rights. The country reports typically include sections on religious freedom, but the 2012 reports, which cover 2011, do not provide details on the status of religious minorities in countries involved in the Arab Spring uprising, in which Islamist movements played a key role.

Besides the basic human rights issues involved, promoting religious freedom is in the United States' interests because freer countries tend to be more pro-American countries, and there is a strong correlation between religious freedom and economic growth, women's rights, and education levels.

Promoting Gay Rights

But instead of standing up for beleaguered religious minorities, Obama and Hillary Clinton's State Department have focused on outreach to Muslims and gays. Promoting Islam is, of course, at odds with securing rights for gays; the only apparent unifying principle is hostility to the Judeo-Christian tradition, and of course winning the votes of Muslims and gays in America.

Late in 2011, the Obama administration made a major announcement: it would use all the tools of American diplomacy, including foreign aid, to promote gay rights around the world.

In a memorandum called "International Initiatives to Advance the Human Rights of Lesbian, Gay, Bisexual and Transgender Persons," Obama said the effort to "end discrimination" against homosexuals is "central to the United States' commitment to promoting human rights."[20]

"Under my Administration, agencies engaged abroad have already begun taking action to promote the fundamental human rights of LGBT persons everywhere," stated Obama. "Our deep commitment to advancing the human rights of all people is strengthened when we as the United States bring our tools to bear to vigorously advance this goal."[21]

The first directive called on embassy officials "to strengthen existing efforts to effectively combat the criminalization by foreign governments of

LGBT status or conduct" and to expand efforts to combat "discrimination, homophobia, and intolerance on the basis of LGBT status or conduct."[22]

Obama also said the Departments of State, Justice, and Homeland Security would "ensure appropriate training is in place" for federal government employees to provide special accommodation for gay and lesbian individuals seeking expedited resettlement.[23]

Obama added that the government will work to raise the profile of gay rights activists in international groups, through efforts such as lobbying government representatives and promoting gay rights activists in various forums. The document calls for all U.S. agencies abroad to prepare a report each year to detail progress implementing the gay rights changes.[24]

In the official roll-out of the new policy at the United Nations Human Rights Council in Geneva, Switzerland, Hillary Clinton said, "Some have suggested that gay rights and human rights are separate and distinct, but in fact they are one and the same."[25] She also said:

> I am also pleased to announce that we are launching a new Global Equality Fund that will support the work of civil society organizations working on these issues around the world. This fund will help them record facts so they can target their advocacy, learn how to use the law as a tool, manage their budgets, train their staffs, and forge partnerships with women's organizations and other human rights groups. We have committed more than $3 million to start this fund, and we have hope that others will join us in supporting it.[26]

The Obama administration's promotion of abortion and gay rights is ironic given that, as journalist George Neumayr has noted, "An administration that came to power calling George W. Bush a bully who sought to impose Western ideology on foreign countries feels entitled to behave imperialistically on [the gay agenda]."[27] It's also ironic because the Obama administration's promotion of gay rights clashes with another of its diplomatic priorities: the appeasement of radical Islam.

It is the height of cynicism and divisiveness for Obama to use American foreign policy to implement the demands of a tiny and radical constituency. It is also a stark double standard to aggressively promote a gay agenda while ignoring the plight of millions of Christians being persecuted around the world. But to the divider-in-chief, gays and Muslims are constituencies to be indulged while the rights of Christians are to be forfeited.

CHAPTER FIFTEEN

The Post-American President

B arack Obama is ambivalent about America. Most American presidents—indeed, most Americans—love their country unconditionally. It's not that they think America is perfect or are delusional about the wrongs America has committed. But most Americans are convinced that their country, despite its flaws, is still the primary force for good in the world, a bulwark against tyranny, a "shining city upon a hill." This is one notion upon which Americans, aside from a radical minority, are united: America is good.

But Obama has said America needs a "fundamental transformation." He wants to root out what he sees as our smug satisfaction as a nation. As America's first "post-American" president, Obama has tried to divide the nation against its most fundamental beliefs about itself. Obama has sought to separate the nation from its founding values, and by doing so to redefine what the great American experiment in liberty means.

In his famous, or infamous, response to a reporter's question about whether he believes in American exceptionalism, Obama said: "I believe in American exceptionalism, just as I suspect that the Brits believe in British exceptionalism and the Greeks believe in Greek exceptionalism."[1] The short answer was: Not really. When Mitt Romney made an issue of this, Obama responded the way he often does: by talking about himself. He said that his career is "testimony to American exceptionalism."[2]

That sounded a lot like what Michelle Obama said on the 2008 campaign trail when she told an audience of admirers that her husband's political rise meant that "for the first time in my adult life I'm really proud of my country."[3]

It also squared with the disgust Obama expressed when he told *Rolling Stone* magazine in 2007 that as a black man he "feels very deeply that this country's exercise of its great inherited wealth and power has been grossly unjust." He added, "I'm somebody who believes in this country and its institutions, but I often think they're broken."[4]

The roots of Obama's ambivalence about America go back to his childhood. In *Dreams from My Father*, he complains that America is a "racial caste system" where "color and money" determine what happens to you in life.

He grumbled that Hawaii, where he grew up, was the result of "ugly conquest of the native Hawaiians... crippling disease brought by missionaries... the indenturing system that kept Japanese, Chinese and Filipino immigrants stooped sunup to sunset in [the fields]."

He complained that Kansas, where his mother and grandparents lived, was the "landlocked center of the country, a place where decency and endurance and the pioneer spirit were joined at the hip with conformity and suspicion and the potential for unblinking cruelty."

Obama feels America has acted with too much bravado abroad, so he reaches out to tyrants and bows to monarchs in an effort to express our national humility. Obama's domestic policies diminish much of what makes America distinct—individual initiative and responsibility, faith in God, the role of civil society.

Obama is perhaps most ambivalent about America's free market economy. Obama's policy agenda seeks to subdue that American free market, to "reform" a system that is inherently broken in its structure. As Michael Gledhill, reviewing *Dreams from My Father,* wrote in National Review Online:

> American affluence offends Obama. The vast upper-middle class lives in a land of isolation and sterility. As a teenager, he envies the white homes in the suburbs but senses that the big pretty houses contain "quiet depression" and "loneliness," represented by "a mother sneaking a tumbler of gin in the afternoon." American consumer culture is comforting but mentally and spiritually numbing, yielding a "long hibernation."
>
> Studying U.S. law at Harvard, Obama concludes it is mainly about "expediency or greed." Working in a large modern corporation, he sees himself as a "spy behind enemy lines." Even science and technology draw his disdain as he warns of "technology that spits out goods from its robot mouth."[5]

As a candidate for president, Obama presented himself as "a citizen of the world." As president it seems as if he feels more at home outside America. This was evident when Obama was awarded the Nobel Peace Prize in 2009, at a point when his public approval ratings began to sag and he was having a hard time working with Congress to pass his agenda.

In *The Obamas,* Jodi Kantor relates what happened when Obama and his entourage traveled to Oslo, Norway, to accept the prize:

> For one day, the Obamas lived the dream version of his presidency instead of the depressing reality. At meals and receptions they mingled with the members of the Royal Academy—government officials, academics. Instead of false rumors or specious charges, the first couple found respectful Scandinavians who were surprisingly well versed in the president's work. "They had read the presidents' books," Susan Sher said later in

amazement. "They knew more about some of his policy ideas than I did." They asked the same question the president had asked Congress: How could a country as rich as the United States not provide health care for its citizens? The president and first lady were deeply touched, proud that they had improved America's reputation abroad, and, in some sense, they felt better understood than they did in Washington. "I was struck by how well read and how knowledgeable every person I met with was," recalled Eric Whitaker, an Obama friend who made the trip. "Americans have no idea what's going on in the rest of the world," he said. "This was a room that represented the better angels of our nature."[6]

The night the Obamas stayed in Oslo, thousands of Norwegians stood outside their hotel room window holding candles. "It's hard to think of a time since the inauguration that the Obamas had received that kind of shower of appreciation," Kantor wrote. "The trip spurred a thought the Obamas and their friends would voice to each other again and again as the president's popularity continued to decline: the American public just did not appreciate their exceptional leader. The president 'could get 70 or 80 percent of the vote anywhere but the U.S.,' a friend said indignantly."[7]

That's right: to the Obamites, and to Obama himself, the only thing exceptional about America is its exceptional president. This might be the most troubling aspect of the divider-in-chief, the fact that he has divided himself from—put himself above—the American people as a whole.

CHAPTER SIXTEEN

Obama's Islamophilia

A Pew Forum on Religion and Public Life survey in August 2010 made news because it found that nearly 20 percent of Americans believed Obama is a Muslim—a significant increase from the share that held that belief at the start of Obama's presidency. It was easy to see why people were confused. Obama has done his best to reach out to Muslims, at home and abroad.

In Cairo, Egypt, in June 2009, Obama said he sought "a new beginning between the United States and Muslims around the world; one based upon mutual interest and mutual respect."[1] Then he said, "I consider it part of my responsibility as President of the United States to fight against negative stereotypes of Islam wherever they appear."[2]

A president has many duties prescribed by the Constitution—to command the Armed Forces, execute federal law, and appoint federal officials, to name a few. "To fight against negative stereotypes of Islam wherever they appear" is not one of them.

But Obama apparently believes it's the responsibility of his entire administration to varnish the image of Islam: to lift it up above other religions, and to ignore offenses committed in the name of Islam against Christians and Jews around the world. Americans are united about the idea that people should be allowed to practice their faith; they express horror and outrage when the inherent freedoms of any religious group or individual are violated. Yet Obama seeks to divide Americans even on the issue of religious freedom.

Obama rarely mentions religious freedom in his remarks. And yet he honors what he sees as his fundamental responsibility to fight against negative stereotypes of Islam.

In June 2010, NASA administrator Charles Bolden gave an interview to Al Jazeera television in which he said that before he accepted his new job, Obama told him that "perhaps" his "foremost" duty was "to find a way to reach out to the Muslim world and engage much more with dominantly Muslim nations to help them feel good about their historic contribution to science... and math and engineering."[3]

So much for Obama's campaign pledge that in his administration "the days of science taking a back seat to ideology are over."[4] Under Obama, Islam guides the mission of one of the federal government's most scientific agencies.

Obama's own Christianity makes way for a deep affinity with Islam. His "Islamophilia" has manifested itself in many ways—in his unflinching mistreatment of Israel, his rhetorical and literal bows to Muslim autocrats, and his repeated labeling of Islam as "a great religion." In 2010, Obama hosted a Ramadan dinner at the White House;[5] five months earlier he had cancelled National Day of Prayer events at the White House.[6]

One way Obama has sought to "fight negative stereotypes of Islam" has been with his administration's efforts to work with Islamic regimes to combat criticism of Islam.

In December 2011 Secretary of State Clinton hosted a summit of international leaders called the "Istanbul Process," which explored steps to fight and criminalize intolerance, discrimination, and violence on the basis of religion or belief. Despite the generalities, the real focus was one form of alleged discrimination—"Islamophobia."

The conference was intended to implement United Nations Human Rights Council Resolution 16/18, also known as "Combating Intolerance, Negative Stereotyping and Stigmatization Of, and Discrimination, Incitement to Violence, and Violence Against Persons Based on Religion or Belief."[7]

The Saudi-based Organization of Islamic Cooperation (OIC) had been pushing laws that criminalize "blasphemy" or "defamation of Islam" for over a decade. Many OIC states that support these laws, including Saudi Arabia, Pakistan, and Iran, routinely imprison or execute those they deem "blasphemers."

To its credit, the State Department made sure that the final resolution didn't limit free speech, but nevertheless it gave voice to states that want to reintroduce anti-defamation laws. The OIC would like the West to punish anti-Islamic speech, cartoons of Mohammed, or books that criticize Islam as inherently violent.

As the OIC reported: "The upcoming [Washington] meetings… [will] help in enacting domestic laws for the countries involved in the issue, as well as formulating international laws preventing inciting hatred resulting from the continued defamation of religions."[8] The conference raised expectations that the United States supports regulation of speech. And why not? Such laws are already in place in Western Europe and Canada.

As Nina Shea, director of the Hudson Institute's Center for Religious Freedom, put it:

U.S. diplomats should stop the "Istanbul Process" and begin to energetically and confidently promote the virtues of our First Amendment freedoms. They should be thoroughly briefed about the OIC's intractable position on blasphemy laws and the extent of atrocities associated with them. They must end signaling that there is common ground on these issues between us and the OIC.[9]

Islam and Violence

In 2010, Rashad Hussain, President Obama's special envoy to the OIC, gave his boss the title of America's "educator-in-chief on Islam."[10] But for all his professed knowledge of Islam, Obama disregards the very real threat that some of Islam's most devout adherents pose. And he fails to recognize that his blame-America-first mindset won't appease violent jihadists.

Obama rarely acknowledges the obvious link between Islam and terrorism. Instead, his Department of Homeland Security has told law enforcement officials to be alert for terrorist acts by violent "Rightwing extremists" and "Christian Identity Organizations."[11]

Modern liberals are at odds with Islamists on many issues. But they find common cause in a common enemy: the Judeo-Christian worldview. The left's list of grievances against America is remarkably similar to that of the Islamists.

"America is unjust, criminal and tyrannical," said Osama bin Laden when asked in a 1997 CNN interview why he had declared war against America.[12] But that indictment could have been uttered by a leftwing college professor or member of Congress. In fact it was similar to Colorado University Professor Ward Churchill's accusation that the victims of 9/11 were "little Eichmanns." Liberal Virginia congressman Jim Moran has accused U.S. troops of having "ethnically cleansed most of Baghdad."[13]

Leftists and Islamists share a totalitarian impulse about the role of the state. Both have as their goal to render their subjects dependent on the state for everything in their lives.

In her book *The World Turned Upside Down*, British journalist Melanie Phillips described the "love affair" among socialists, fascists, radical environmentalists, and Islamists. She writes: "What they all have in common… is a totalitarian mindset in pursuit of the creation of their alternative reality. These are all worldviews that can accommodate no deviation and must therefore be imposed by coercion. Because their end product is a state of perfection, nothing can stand in its way."[14]

There's a reason Obama won more than 90 percent of the Muslim American vote. And I think we can safely assume it wasn't because he promised abortion-on-demand or open homosexuality in the military. It was because Muslim voters believed Obama would treat Israel as the main obstacle to peace in the Middle East, that he would end the war in Iraq (which had begun as a war of liberation but was now portrayed as somehow a war on Muslims), that he would diminish America's stature in the world so that there would be no more such interventions in the Middle East, and that he would protect Muslims from prejudiced Americans.

Obama's outreach to other countries hasn't helped him much. Obama entered office as a global icon, but his status was significantly diminished just three and a half years later. A June 2012 Pew Global Attitudes poll found that global opinion of Obama had plummeted since he became president.[15] Approval of Obama's international policies dropped from 78 percent to 63 percent in Europe; from 34 percent to 15 percent in countries with Muslim majorities; from 40 percent to 22 percent in Russia; and from 57 percent to 27 percent in China.

The "War on Muslims" Farce

Before there was a "war on women," there was a "war on Muslims." The left wants to divide Americans by telling them that Muslims are not welcomed here because of American intolerance, and that only liberals can protect them.

Most journalists take it for granted that Muslims have a hard time in America. "American Muslims ask, 'Will we ever belong?'" ran a *New York Times* headline after public backlash to a proposed mosque near Ground Zero in New York City in 2010.[16]

The proposed mosque's imam, Feisal Abdul Rauf, defended the mosque on ABC's *This Week*, saying, "My major concern with moving it is that the headline in the Muslim world will be, 'Islam is under attack in America.'"[17] But this narrative falls apart under scrutiny.

For starters, tens of thousands of immigrants from Muslim countries flood into the United States each year. And the years of highest immigration from the Middle East have occurred since the September 11, 2001, terrorist attacks. In 2005, for instance, nearly 96,000 people from Muslim countries became legal permanent U.S. residents, the most in any year in the previous twenty years.[18]

Some immigrants from the Middle East are Christians escaping persecution. But the vast majority are Muslims either escaping persecution at the hands of Muslim governments or searching for economic opportunities in a country with a functioning market.

The U.S. Census does not collect information about religion, but estimates about the number of Muslims in the United States range from 1.3 million to 5 million. Every estimate suggests the number of Muslims in America is rising.

According to the American Religious Identification Survey (ARIS), the number of people in America who described themselves as Muslims more than doubled between 1990 and 2008, from 527,000 to 1.35 million.[19]

By virtually every measure, Muslim Americans are flourishing in the United States. According to the ARIS study, 35 percent of American Muslims age twenty-five years and older have college degrees, a share equal to or higher than that of any other religion except Judaism and "Eastern religions."[20]

There are more than 2,100 mosques across the country,[21] and since 9/11 American voters have elected the first two Muslim congressmen in United States history. Zaytuna College, the first accredited Muslim college, opened in 2009.

America has experienced dozens of attacks and foiled plots linked to Islamic radicals since 9/11. But after each, the media conversation centers less on the need to monitor Islamic radicalization and more on the inevitable "backlash" that never materializes.

When Army Major Nidal Malik Hasan, a radicalized Muslim, murdered fourteen people and wounded thirty others at Fort Hood military base in Texas in 2009, government agencies warned that it could provoke violence against Arab and Muslim Americans. A *Christian Science Monitor* story was titled, "Fort Hood Shootings: U.S. Muslims feel new heat."[22]

An Associated Press headline read, "Another attack leaves U.S. Muslims fearing backlash."[23]

U.S. Army Chief of Staff George Casey said, "I'm concerned that this increased speculation [about Hasan's motives] could cause a backlash against some of our Muslim soldiers. And I've asked our Army leaders to be on the lookout for that... [because] as horrific as this tragedy was, if our diversity becomes a casualty, I think that's worse."[24]

That's right. According to the Obama administration, a fictitious backlash that potentially curtails diversity is a greater tragedy than the horrific deaths of fourteen service members.

As former Reagan official Gary L. Bauer wrote in response to the "anti-Muslim backlash" meme, "Our journalistic and political elites have become terrorism's unwitting domestic enablers, perceiving religion-based violence where there is none, while ignoring it where it is widespread and intensifying."[25] He continued:

The misplaced fear of igniting an anti-Muslim backlash is a consequence of the pervasive and stifling political correctness that surrounds Islam in the West. It prevents many of our journalistic and political elites from naming our enemy and compels them to accommodate radical Islam most readily in the very places it can cause the most damage—in our prisons, public schools, and military.

At a time when Swiss voters have banned the nation's Muslims from building minarets, French officials are considering outlawing the burka, and Italian politicians are mulling legislation to prohibit mosque construction, the U.S. is increasingly looking like the most welcome destination for Muslims.[26]

That is undoubtedly true. It is also undoubtedly true that more Muslims will be welcomed as Obama continues his obsessive crusade to eradicate negative stereotypes of Islam.

Americans are more tolerant of differing religions than any other nation. Obama seeks to take that unity on religious freedom—a source of great strength for this nation—and use it to divide us, claiming that there is some sinister internal hostility toward peaceful Muslims, while denying the persecution of Jews and Christians worldwide. He heightens suspicions among Americans and neutralizes decent Americans' ability to point out concerns about the growing influence of Islam in our country.

There *are* reasonable concerns about Islam—such as the growing influence of Sharia law—that should be discussed in a free, open, and intellectually respectful atmosphere. Obama is systematically neutralizing our ability to have those discussions. In ObamaWorld, we have rights, and we are united, only when we agree with our leader's radical perspective.

CHAPTER SEVENTEEN

Obama Divides Americans over Israel

In November 2011, President Obama attended the G20 summit in Cannes, France. Items on the agenda at the two-day conference included coordinating economic policies and strengthening financial regulation.

But it was an embarrassing exchange caught on an open microphone between Obama and French President Nicolas Sarkozy that made the most headlines.

Obama approached Sarkozy and began questioning him about why he had not warned him in advance that France would vote in favor of Palestinian membership in UNESCO. Then the conversation quickly turned to Israeli Prime Minister Benjamin Netanyahu.

Sarkozy said, "I don't want to see him anymore, he's a liar." Obama responded, "You're fed up with him, but I have to deal with him every day!"[1]

Obama's moment of unscripted candor clashes with what he wants America and the Jewish lobby to think he feels about the country Netanyahu leads. Running for president, Obama said, "Peace through security is the only way for Israel,"[2] and "When I am president, the United States will stand shoulder to shoulder with Israel."[3]

He has talked about America's "unshakeable" commitment to Israel's security and about how the "friendship" between the two countries is "rooted deeply in a shared history and shared values."[4] Vice President Biden has said that America has "no better friend than Israel."[5] But if there is one thing we've learned about Obama, it's that words often mean very little.

Anti-Israel Roots

Obama signaled his antipathy toward Israel early on. Before becoming president, he said, "Nobody has suffered more than the Palestinian people"[6]—a profound misstatement by any objective measure—and "the Israeli government must make difficult concessions for the peace process to restart."

Anti-Israel activist Ali Abunimah claimed to have known Obama well when Obama was a state senator in Chicago, and claimed that they met at several pro-Palestinian events. Abunimah said, "Obama used to be very comfortable speaking up for and being associated with Palestinian rights and opposing the Israeli occupation."[7]

Obama's former pastor and mentor Jeremiah Wright is a raging anti-Semite. His church, Trinity United Church of Christ, published many anti-Semitic rants on its website. One letter claimed that Israel committed "genocide" and "ethnic cleansing" of Palestinians and that Israelis "worked on an ethnic bomb that kills blacks and Arabs."[8]

Wright gave anti-Semite Louis Farrakhan an award for being a leader who "truly epitomized greatness."[9] Wright even traveled to meet with Libyan terrorist leader Muammar al-Gaddafi and has compared conditions in Israel to the apartheid of South Africa.[10]

After Obama shunned him, Wright told PBS it was because Obama "can't afford the Jewish support to wane or start questioning his allegiance to Israel."[11]

Before the 2008 elections, some polls suggested Obama was preferred by Israelis over the staunchly pro-Israel John McCain. But by June 2009, a *Jerusalem Post*-sponsored Smith Research poll of 500 Israeli Jewish adults found just 6 percent believed the Obama administration was pro-Israel.[12] A similar poll conducted two months later showed Israelis' support for Obama had declined to 4 percent.

The poll also found that half of Israeli Jews considered the administration's policies to be more pro-Palestinian than pro-Israeli. It's not a stretch to think that, like many Americans, many Israelis initially bought into Obama's rhetoric about hope and change. But also like many Americans, Israelis have been sorely disappointed.

"A Crisis of Historic Proportions"

One of the Obama administration's first offenses against Israel occurred when Vice President Biden visited the Jewish State in early 2010. While Biden was there, the Israeli government announced plans to construct 1,600 housing units in East Jerusalem. The United States does not recognize Israel's sovereignty over East Jerusalem, but it's part of Israel's capital city, and the housing units were needed because of natural population growth.

Israeli Defense Minister Ehud Barak said the settlement area "is an ultra-Orthodox city very close to the green line [dividing Israel from the Palestinian Authority], and these are housing units for people who are struggling and cannot buy elsewhere."[13] The housing expansion had been in the works for three years.

The Obama administration, however, erupted. Biden declared that the announcement from the Israeli district planning committees "is precisely the kind of step that undermines the trust we need right now."[14] Obama senior adviser David Axelrod called the move "an affront, an insult."[15] Secretary of State Hillary Clinton called Israel's behavior "insulting." Obama, the cool, calm, no drama president, was reportedly "seething" over the move. Michael Oren, Israel's ambassador to the United States, said relations with Washington had plummeted to a thirty-five-year low and that relations between the two countries constituted a "crisis of historic proportions."[16] It was a crisis made by Obama's demand that Israel cease building homes for Jews in East Jerusalem; it was he, not the Palestinians, who made it a central condition for Israeli-Palestinian negotiations; the Palestinians merely jumped on his bandwagon.

Two-State Problem

Barack Obama, like most American presidents before him, supports a two-state solution to the Israeli-Palestinian conflict. But Obama's two-state solution always seems to involve Israel making grand concessions before negotiations even begin.

In May 2011, Obama delivered a speech at the State Department in which he endorsed the Palestinians' demand for their own state based on the borders that existed before the 1967 Six-Day War. He said:

> The United States believes that negotiations should result in two states, with permanent Palestinian borders with Israel, Jordan, and Egypt, and permanent Israeli borders with Palestine. The borders of Israel and Palestine should be based on the 1967 lines with mutually agreed swaps, so that secure and recognized borders are established for both states.[17]

Many commentators noted how Obama's speech undermined Israel's negotiating position. Such a scenario would divide Jerusalem and help Israel's enemies get one step closer to their ultimate goal of obliterating the Jewish state. Obama was demanding that Israel go into peace talks having already forfeited one of its only bargaining chips—its claim to the territory won in the 1967 war.

Reacting to Obama's speech, Prime Minister Netanyahu rejected a full withdrawal from the West Bank, calling the 1967 lines "indefensible."[18]

Even if negotiations happen, it is unclear who would represent the Palestinians. One would assume it would be the Palestinian Authority, led by President Mahmoud Abbas. Abbas is a member of the Fatah Party, the more "moderate" of the two main Palestinian political parties. But Fatah may no longer speak for most Palestinians.

Hamas, a terrorist organization funded by Iran, is the elected government of Gaza and holds a majority in the Palestinian parliament. Hamas Prime Minister Ismail Haniyeh has said that Hamas will never recognize the "usurper Zionist government" and will continue its "jihad-like movement until the liberation of Jerusalem."[19] Haniyeh is someone who hailed Osama bin Laden as a "Muslim warrior" after the September 11, 2001, terrorist attacks against America.[20]

Hamas has launched thousands of rockets into Israel over the last decade. Nearly one million Israeli citizens live within range of these rockets. As Gary Bauer has written, "Obama's [two-state] vision cannot be realized when one side is led by a terrorist group whose governing charter calls for the destruction of the other side."[21]

Appeasing Iran

Obama argues that under his leadership, the United States "has Israel's back."[22] But that's not true, especially when it comes to Israel's arch nemesis, Iran. In 2009, when millions of brave Iranian Democrats rose up to protest a stolen election at the hands of Iran's ruling theocracy, Obama was silent.

The sham elections prompted France's Nicolas Sarkozy to denounce the "extent of the fraud" and the "shocking" and "brutal" response by Iran's mullahs to public demonstrations in Tehran and elsewhere.[23]

Even after the murder of a young woman protestor provoked international outrage, Obama said that he didn't want the United States "to be seen meddling" in Iranian affairs. Obama's meager response set the stage for his administration's appeasement of Iran, which has been reflected in the administration's long campaign of public pressure to stop Israel from attacking Iran's nuclear weapons program.

Former U.S. ambassador to the United Nations John Bolton wrote in 2012, "So intense is this effort, and so determined is President Obama to succeed, that administration officials are now leaking highly sensitive information about Israel's intentions and capabilities into the news media."[24] Bolton believes Obama is more opposed to an Israeli attack on Iran than he is to Iran developing nuclear weapons, even though Iran's President Mahmoud Ahmadinejad has promised to "wipe Israel off the map" and could easily sell nuclear weapons to terrorists or anti-American regimes around the world.

Obama might easily have his cake and eat it too in the 2012 election—winning Muslim votes for his appeasement of radical Islam and winning Jewish votes because of Jewish voters' traditional liberalism and adherence to the Democratic Party. But Obama manifestly does not have Israel's best interests at heart; and as Israel is our only reliable ally in the Middle East, Obama does not have America's best interests at heart either.

CHAPTER EIGHTEEN

Playing the
Hispanic Card

The Obama economy has been devastating for Hispanic Americans, whose unemployment rate rose to 11 percent in May 2012, almost three points higher than the national average of 8.2 percent.[1] But instead of addressing these concerns, Obama has spent his term rhetorically attacking and demonizing opponents of amnesty for illegal immigrants.

A few months before winning the 2008 election, Obama gave a speech to the National Council of La Raza, in which he said that federal immigration agents "terrorized" communities during immigration raids.

> The system isn't working when 12 million people live in hiding, and hundreds of thousands cross our borders illegally each year; when companies hire undocumented immigrants instead of legal citizens to avoid paying overtime or to avoid a union; when communities are terrorized by ICE immigration raids; when nursing mothers are torn from their babies; when children come home from school to find their parents missing;

when people are detained without access to legal counsel; when all that is happening, the system just isn't working and we need to change it.[2]

Nearly two years later, in April 2010, Obama sounded similar in demonizing opponents of amnesty. "You can try to make it really tough on people who look like they, quote, unquote look like illegal immigrants," Obama told a crowd in Ottumwa, Iowa.[3] "[N]ow suddenly if you don't have your papers and you took your kid out to get ice cream, you're going to be harassed, that's something that could potentially happen."[4]

Obama was referring to SB 1070, Arizona's immigration law, which was signed into law by Governor Jan Brewer in 2010. Critics, including President Obama, said it encourages racial profiling. But the bill was modified specifically to address those concerns. It allows police only to check the immigration status of someone stopped for other reasons.

Lawsuits were filed challenging the law's constitutionality and compliance with civil rights statutes. Eric Holder's Department of Justice filed suit and also asked for an injunction against enforcement of the law. The Obama administration argued that the law's provisions clash with the federal government's role in setting immigration policy.[5]

In April 2012, the U.S. Supreme Court began considering the constitutionality of SB 1070. During oral argument, the justices did not seem to buy into the administration's contention that the federal government can stop Arizona from enforcing immigration laws, telling government lawyers that the state appeared to want to assist federal officials, not conflict with them.

"It seems to me the federal government just doesn't want to know who's here illegally," Chief Justice John G. Roberts Jr. said at one point.[6] Even some of the liberal justices appeared not to buy the Obama administration's arguments. When the solicitor general argued that Arizona's enforcement of immigration undermined federal authority, the court's first Hispanic justice, Sonia Sotomayor, replied, "You can see it's not selling very well."[7]

Liberals followed Obama's lead and demonized the statute. Ignoring the clear language of the law, news outlets portrayed it as allowing racial profiling. Public protests took place in more than seventy cities. An economic boycott of Arizona was led by the Reverend Al Sharpton (who else?).

Despite the uproar, the law was not controversial among the general public. A Rasmussen Reports poll found that 60 percent of Americans supported the law, while just 31 percent opposed it.[8] A Gallup poll found that of the 75 percent of Americans who had heard of the law, a majority— 51 percent—were in favor of it, compared to just 39 percent who were opposed.[9] Numerous other polls came to similar conclusions.

The law received bipartisan support in Arizona. Democratic Congresswoman Gabrielle Giffords defended some of the motivation for the bill. She said her constituents were "sick and tired" of the federal government failing to protect the border, that the current situation was "completely unacceptable," and that the legislation was a "clear calling that the federal government needs to do a better job."[10]

Twenty House Republicans sent a letter to Holder that stated, "Not only does this lawsuit reveal the Obama administration's contempt for immigration laws and the people of Arizona, it reveals contempt for the majority of the American people who support Arizona's efforts."[11]

President Obama personally weighed in numerous times, repeatedly mischaracterizing the law and demonizing its supporters. He labeled it "misguided" and suggested that it "undermines basic notions of fairness that we cherish as Americans, as well as the trust between police and our communities that is so crucial to keeping us safe."[12]

Obama's immigration fear-mongering reached a low point in a speech at the U.S.-Mexico border in May 2011 when he mocked Republican demands that a border fence be erected as a condition to immigration reform. "Maybe they'll need a moat," he said. "Maybe they'll want alligators in the moat."[13]

Obama even targeted Mitt Romney. "We now have a Republican nominee who said that the Arizona laws are a model for the country," Obama said in an interview with Univision in April 2012.[14] "These are laws that potentially would allow someone to be stopped and picked up and asked where their citizenship papers are based on an assumption."

When the reporter interjected to describe such stops as "racial profiling," Obama didn't disagree. Instead, he reinforced the falsehood, responding, "Very troublesome… this is something that the Republican nominee has said should be a model for the country. So what we need is a change either of Congress or we need Republicans to change their mind, and I think this has to be an important debate… throughout the country."[15] As Obama knows well, he's minimizing the chances for "an important debate" when he denigrates those who support the measure as proponents of racial profiling.

In late June, the U.S. Supreme Court ruled that the most controversial part of SB 1070 was constitutional. In a 5 to 3 decision (Justice Elena Kagan recused herself because she served as President Obama's solicitor general when the federal government filed the original lawsuit against the state), the court upheld the part of the law that requires an officer to make a reasonable attempt to determine the immigration status of a person stopped, detained, or arrested if there's reasonable suspicion that person is in the country illegally.

Three parts of the law were ruled unconstitutional, including a provision that would have made it a state crime for an immigrant not to be carrying papers, another allowing for warrantless arrest in some situations, and another forbidding illegal immigrants from working in Arizona.

Governor Brewer nonetheless called the decision "a victory for the rule of law." She added in a news release, "It is also a victory for the 10th Amendment and all Americans who believe in the inherent right and responsibility of states to defend their citizens. After more than two years of legal challenges, the heart of SB 1070 can now be implemented in accordance with the U.S. Constitution."[16]

It is clear Obama's divisive tactics are not addressing the issues Hispanics care about most. A June 2012 Gallup poll found Hispanic voters

prioritized numerous issues ahead of immigration, including the economy, health care, and economic growth.[17]

But with nothing to offer Hispanics or anyone else on the economy,
Obama continued to pander on immigration. On June 15, 2012, Obama
issued an executive order that allows illegal immigrants under age thirty
who came to the United States as children and who do not pose a risk to
national security to be eligible to stay in the country and apply for work
permits.

"Remember Me in November"

While many immigration groups were happy about the announcement,
it was an overtly political move made for electoral gain. South Carolina
Republican senator Lindsey Graham denounced the rule change as "possibly illegal" because it bypasses Congress.[18] Even Senator Marco Rubio, a
Florida Republican who generally supports the substance of the measure,
said that by going around Congress, Obama had made it "harder to find a
balanced and responsible long-term" solution.[19] Henry Bonilla, a former
Republican House member from Texas, told *Politico* that Hispanics understand that if Obama's true conviction was to legalize young illegal immigrants, he would have done it upon taking the oath of office. "People are
smart and they see through that," he explained.[20]

Even many of Obama's allies who support immigration amnesty saw
cynical politics in the move. "In many ways, President Obama's unilateral
shift in immigration policy was a bluntly political move, a play for a key
voting bloc in the states that will decide whether he gets another term,"
reporters for the *New York Times* wrote.[21] "But as political moves go, it held
the potential for considerable payoff. It sent a clear signal to fast-growing
Hispanic populations in Florida, Colorado, Nevada, Virginia and other
states that he understood their frustration at his lack of progress so far in
addressing problems with the immigration system and reducing the number of deportations."[22]

A writer for the United Kingdom's leftwing *Guardian* newspaper wrote that she was initially "elated" at hearing about the decision. "Yet, as the initial shock wears off, I can't ignore a rising sense of skepticism in response to the president's nakedly political move in an election year."[23]

Or as a *Politico* article put it, the decision was "a loud message to Hispanic voters to remember Obama in November."[24]

A 2011 *Politico* op-ed by Alfonso Aguilar, executive director of the Latino Partnership for Conservative Principles, argued that Hispanics know Obama is pandering to them in his vilification of Republicans and his posturing on immigration issues. Aguilar concluded: "This doesn't mean that the majority of Latinos are going to vote Republican. But it does mean that many will consider voting for the Republican candidate. If the GOP nominee gets at least 40 percent of the Latino vote—and can win states like Colorado, Florida, Nevada and New Mexico—Obama could possibly be defeated in 2012."[25]

There is another factor, too. In his efforts to slice and dice the American voting public, to play the balkanizing game of identity politics, Obama might have failed to recognize that when he emphasizes issues like gay marriage for his well-heeled homosexual constituency, he could be helping to alienate an already restive Hispanic constituency.

And if Obama's war with the Catholic Church and other religious groups continues over issues of freedom of religion, his support among Hispanic voters could erode even further. Though it has worked for him so far, Obama's politics of theatrics over substance, of dividing the electorate into balkanized groups to which he can deliver empty, demagogic messages of hope and change, might just have run its course.

CHAPTER NINETEEN

Obama's Divisive Justice Department

O n February 18, 2009, less than one month after starting his job as Obama's U.S. attorney general, Eric Holder delivered a speech to Justice Department employees marking Black History Month in which he declared, "We are a nation of cowards on race."[1]

Holder—America's first black attorney general—said race "is an issue we have never been at ease with and, given our nation's history, this is in some ways understandable.... [But] if we are to make progress in this area, we must feel comfortable enough with one another and tolerant enough of each other to have frank conversations about the racial matters that continue to divide us."[2]

Holder's words now seem more than a little ironic. For Holder has often used the Justice Department he leads to deepen America's racial divides. Under Holder, the Department of Justice is accused of systematically ignoring civil rights cases in which blacks are the alleged perpetrators, invoking Jim Crow in response to states' attempts to cut down on voter fraud, and suing the state of Arizona for overtly political purposes when the state attempted to enforce the nation's immigration laws.

The New Black Panthers

After the 2008 election, the Bush Justice Department brought a case against two members of the New Black Panther Party who were videotaped in front of a Philadelphia polling place dressed in military-style uniforms and allegedly hurling racial slurs and threats while brandishing night sticks.

The Anti-Defamation League, Southern Poverty Law Center, and U.S. Commission on Civil Rights all consider the New Black Panthers to be a hate group. And the Philadelphia incident was a fairly straightforward case of voter intimidation. The Bush Justice Department filed suit against the New Black Panther Party, accusing it in a civil complaint of violating the Voting Rights Act.

The Obama administration initially pursued the case, but then moved to dismiss the charges after the accused New Black Panther members agreed not to carry deadly weapons near polling places in 2012.

J. Christian Adams, a former lawyer for the Justice Department, quit his job over the agency's failure to pursue the case further. And, in testimony before the Commission on Civil Rights, Adams described the department's unwillingness to pursue cases involving black defendants as "pervasive."[3]

By not pursuing the case, Holder was exhibiting the very cowardice he had just told the country to move beyond.

Voting Wrongs

The 1965 Voting Rights Act outlawed discriminatory voting practices that had been responsible for extensive disenfranchisement of black voters across the country. Today, voter disenfranchisement is almost non-existent. In fact, illegal voter registration and voting is a far greater problem. But Holder and the Obama administration have political reasons to revive fears of discrimination against minority voters.

In a June 2012 speech, Holder told members of the Council of Black Churches that the sacred right to vote faced "the same disparities, divisions, and problems that—nearly five decades ago—so many fought to address."[4]

He said, "In my travels across this country, I've heard a consistent drumbeat of concern from citizens, who—often for the first time in their lives—now have reason to believe that we are failing to live up to one of our nation's most noble ideals; and that some of the achievements that defined the civil rights movement now hang in the balance."[5]

Holder referenced the words of Congressman John Lewis, a civil rights leader who in a 2011 speech on the House floor claimed that voting rights were "under attack… [by] a deliberate and systematic attempt to prevent millions of elderly voters, young voters, students, [and] minority and low-income voters from exercising their constitutional right to engage in the democratic process." Holder said:

> Not only was [Lewis] referring to the all-too-common deceptive practices we've been fighting for years. He was echoing more recent fears and frustrations about some of the state-level voting law changes we've seen this legislative season. Let me assure you: for today's Department of Justice, our commitment to strengthening—and to fulfilling—our nation's promise of equal opportunity and equal justice has never been stronger.[6]

Holder's purpose in speaking to the Council of Black Churches was clear. He was there to plead with black pastors to get their parishioners to the polls on Election Day. According to the Census Bureau, black voter registration is down 7 percent across the country.[7] By invoking Jim Crow and the specter of civil rights violations, Holder was making his point crystal clear: Get your parishioners to vote for Barack Obama or the gains of the civil rights movement could be revoked.

The laws Holder alluded to as threatening voting rights are voter ID laws that have been passed in various states to make sure people are voting legally. Voter ID laws are enacted to prevent ballot box fraud. Such laws have been found by numerous courts not to be an "undue burden" under the Voting Rights Act and the Constitution. Supporters of the laws argue they will ensure that elections are fair and cut down on the potential for voter fraud.

Some states have seen turnout among minorities rise after voter ID laws were passed. Georgia, for instance, began implementing a Voter ID law in 2007 that required voters to show one of six forms of ID. According to data from Georgia Secretary of State Brian Kemp, the black vote increased by 42 percent, or 366,000 votes, in 2008 over 2004.[8]

The Hispanic vote grew by 140 percent, or 25,000 votes, in 2008, while the white vote increased by only 8 percent from four years earlier. The black vote in Georgia also increased, by 44.2 percent during the mid-term congressional races of 2010 from 2006. The Hispanic vote rose by 66.5 percent in 2010 from four years earlier.[9]

These and other data suggest that voter ID laws discriminate only against those for whom it is illegal to vote in the first place. But Holder has made blocking voter ID laws a centerpiece of his tenure at the Department of Justice.

South Carolina passed a law in 2011 that requires voters to display government-issued IDs at polling places. Under the 1965 Voting Rights Act, South Carolina is one of a number of states that are required to receive federal "pre-clearance" on voting changes to ensure that they don't hurt minorities' political power. The Justice Department rejected the law, arguing that it discriminated against minority voters. It was the first time the government had rejected a voter-identification law in nearly twenty years.[10]

The Obama administration struck again in March 2012, blocking a Texas law requiring voters to show photo identification before they can vote. The administration asserted potential harm to Hispanic voters who don't have the necessary documents.[11] The law required voters to show government-issued photo identification, such as a driver's license, passport, military identification card, birth certification with a photo, or concealed handgun permit.

Texas Republican Governor Rick Perry criticized the Obama administration's decision. "The DOJ [Department of Justice] has no valid reason for rejecting this important law, which requires nothing more extensive than the type of photo identification necessary to receive a library card or board an airplane,"[12] he said in a statement.

Texas Senator John Cornyn blasted the political calculation in the lawsuit. He said that the lawsuit "reeks of politics and appears to be an effort by the Department of Justice to carry water for the president's reelection campaign."[13]

The Justice Department has also sued Florida, which is suing the federal government right back, over the state's voter ID law. The left characterizes Florida's efforts to make sure all voters are legal as a campaign to purge Latinos from the voting rolls. But as Florida Senator Marco Rubio has said, "I think there's the goal of ensuring that everyone who votes in Florida is qualified to vote. If you're not a citizen of the United States, you shouldn't be voting. That's the law."[14]

How does opposition to voter ID laws help President Obama? Not only does it allow the president to pretend that he is standing in defense of the voting rights of minority voters—and to imply the Republicans are trying to take these rights away—but it is apparently the presumption of President Obama and the Democratic Party that votes cast illegally will be overwhelmingly in favor of Democrats, whether they be the votes of illegal immigrants or other groups who can be lined up to vote "early and often" without voter ID.

Public opinion polls show strong support for voter ID laws. A 2011 Rasmussen poll found that 75 percent of likely voters "believe voters should be required to show photo identification, such as a driver's license, before being allowed to vote."[15]

Voter ID laws have passed in many states. In 2011, eight states passed voter ID laws, and some states will consider voter ID referenda in 2012. All of this virtually guarantees that the Obama administration will remain preoccupied with battling voter ID laws, and using them to further divide Americans, for the foreseeable future.

CHAPTER TWENTY

Obama's Destructive Race-Baiting

In December 2006, when Barack Obama was weighing whether or not to run for president, he huddled in Chicago with a few close aides, friends, and family members to make a final decision. In *Confidence Men*, Ron Suskind recounted what happened:

> It was Michelle... who stopped the show. "You need to ask yourself *why* you want to do this," she said. "What are you hoping to uniquely accomplish, Barack?" Obama sat quietly for a moment, while everyone waited to hear what he would say.
>
> "This I know," Obama said. "When I raise my hand and take that oath of office, I think the world will look at us differently. And millions of kids across the country will look at themselves differently."
>
> Obama understood, from his own search for identity, how America's struggle with race was part of a larger story—a quest for dignity and hope that defined countless lives across the globe.[1]

The notion that Obama would bring us together is the narrative that helped him become president of the United States. It was one that America embraced. How different the reality has been.

The conventional wisdom holds that Obama shies away from talking about race and is uncomfortable viewing his presidency in racial terms. But make no mistake: race is at the heart of how Obama defines himself and his presidency.

Obama and his allies view most issues through the prism of race. Very often their cries of racism aren't fundamentally about race, however, but rather about exploiting society's most divisive issue to pander to narrow constituencies, smear opponents, or shut down debate. By framing many issues in racial terms, liberals like Obama avoid having to engage their opponents on the substance of debates they can't win.

Race dominated Obama's early life. His first autobiography, *Dreams from My Father*, is subtitled *A Story of Race and Inheritance*. It describes Obama's inner struggle to reconcile the white and black worlds into which he was born and raised. The Obama of *Dreams* is hypersensitive to race and sees an unbridgeable gulf between whites and blacks, a perception that forces him to choose between his white and black identities.

The memoir makes clear that, after a period of uncertainty about his mixed racial identity, Obama decided to craft a black identity for himself.

But Obama never seems to be able to fully reconcile his understanding of race with his circumstances. As the pseudonymous Michael Gledhill has written in National Review Online, "The reader of *Dreams* cannot help being struck by the unexplained contrast between the circumstances of Obama's life—an opportunity to attend a fine school, white grandparents who love him—and his great anger at white society."[2]

In *The Bridge*, David Remnick suggests that Obama exaggerated his racial issues in his early years in Hawaii. He writes:

> Obama's self-portrayal in his memoir as a troubled kid trying
> to cope with race and racism came as a shock to some of his old

teachers and classmates. His teacher Eric Kusunoki was surprised by the book [*Dreams*]. "In Hawaii, ethnicity is blurred.
I like to think of kids not in terms of black and white—it's more
like golden brown," he said. "Everyone is mixed and everyone
is different. So when I read his book it was kind of a surprise to
me." Constance Ramos, whose background is Filipino-Hun-
garian, wrote, "I never once thought of Barry as 'black.' I still
don't." She said she felt "betrayed" by Obama's angst-ridden
self-portrayal.[3]

That wasn't the only time Obama may have distorted his experiences with
race. Obama has talked about coming across a photograph in *Life* magazine
of a black man who had used a chemical treatment to whiten his complex-
ion—an experience that Obama wrote was like an "ambush" on his sensi-
bilities and innocence, but this might have been another dream from his
father rather than an actual event. As Remnick wrote: "During the presidential campaign, a journalist from the *Chicago Tribune* searched for the
article. No such article ran. Obama responded feebly, 'It might have been
Ebony or it might have been.... Who knows what it was?' Archivists at
Ebony could not find anything, either."[4]

   In high school, according to his autobiography, Obama became preoccupied with black literature with themes of anger and alienation. In college,
he eschewed interracial student groups to identify with black students. In
From Promise to Power, former *Chicago Tribune* reporter David Mendell
writes that as a student, "[Obama] consciously chose politically active black
students as his friends because he feared being labeled a 'sellout.' In trying
to convey an image of being a true black, he would sometimes overreach
to gain acceptance among his black peers."[5] Years later, Mendell wrote,
Obama "still had a tendency to overreach in order to fit in with some urban
blacks."[6]

   Obama's tendency to overreach may explain why he joined the Reverend Jeremiah Wright's church. Wright subscribed to black liberation

theology, which is the belief that Jesus came to liberate people of color from the bondage and injustice of a white-dominated world. He preached that the United States was founded on racism and that the U.S. government introduced AIDS into the black community.

Running for president, Obama said that he was shocked when he heard Wright's outrageous remarks about the racism that pervaded American society. But Obama had been a member of Wright's church for over a decade. And Obama's memoir makes it clear he was fully aware that Wright's views were not uncommon in some parts of the black community. In fact, Wright's sermons seem to reinforce some of what Obama wrote in *Dreams*—that America is unsafe for black people and that white people are greedy and exploitative.

Acting Stupidly on Race

The election of our first black president was supposed to signal a milestone in America's pursuit of a post-racial society. Part of the hope and change millions of voters expected involved racial reconciliation. After all, Obama sprang from nowhere with that thrilling 2004 convention speech proclaiming that there is "not a black America and white America and Latino America and Asian America; there's the United States of America."[7]

Interviewed in the wake of Obama's 2008 victory, Martin Luther King III predicted, "Race relations clearly will be advanced... because of President-elect Obama." But instead of marking a new beginning in race relations, Obama's presidency has given new life to the old politics of racial grievance.

Two incidents highlight Obama and his allies' willingness to stir the racial pot. On July 16, 2009, Harvard professor Henry Louis Gates Jr. was arrested in his home in Cambridge, Massachusetts. Gates had returned from an overseas trip to find his front door jammed shut. He and his driver were able to force it open, but a passerby called 911, reporting what looked like a potential burglary in progress. When police arrived, they found Gates (who is black) in his home. Sergeant James Crowley (who is white) of the Cambridge Police Department asked for Gates's identification; Gates refused and became belligerent; Crowley arrested him for disorderly conduct.

The charges were later dropped, but the incident generated a national debate about whether it constituted racial profiling. It was hardly a presidential issue, but Obama weighed in on the case at a news conference. While admitting that he did not know all the facts, Obama declared that Cambridge policemen had "acted stupidly." "There's a long history in this country of African-Americans and Latinos being stopped by law enforcement disproportionately," he added. "That's just a fact."[8]

Obama was criticized by law enforcement groups and many others for wading into a topic he knew little about. Some felt Obama spoke up to appease professional race-baiters like Al Sharpton and Jesse Jackson, both of whom had criticized Obama for not speaking up soon enough or loudly enough in the wake of the 2007 Jena 6 case in Jena, Louisiana. That incident involved what some black leaders and others felt was the unjust punishment of six black teenagers who beat up a white teenage boy. Jackson lashed into Obama for "acting like he's white."[9]

The Cambridge incident established a pattern that Obama and the left have followed at certain times throughout his presidency. They have been willing to thrust race into the forefront of political and social controversies. They've alleged racism without sufficient knowledge of the facts and sometimes in contradiction with the clear facts.

Obama's Son, Trayvon

"If I had a son, he'd look like Trayvon."[10]

Those were Barack Obama's words when asked by a reporter to comment on Trayvon Martin, a black 17-year-old, who was shot dead in February 2012. He was killed by 28-year-old George Zimmerman, a community watchman, in Sanford, Florida. Zimmerman was not initially arrested or charged, and because his father is white and his mother is Hispanic, the growing controversy over the case quickly became racially supercharged.

A few days after the incident began to make headlines, Obama weighed in, making the "If I had a son…" remark, calling Martin's death a "tragedy," and saying, "When I think about this boy, I think about my own kids. And every parent in America should be able to understand why it is absolutely imperative that we investigate every aspect of this."[11]

Michelle Obama also commented. She told NPR, "My heart goes out to the parents, because we all as parents understand the tragedy of that kind of loss, and I think that's really the thing that most people connect to. And it's important for us not to lose sight of the fact that this is a family that's grieving and there's been a tremendous loss. And we all have to rally around that piece of it."[12]

By invoking their own family and creating solidarity with Martin, the Obamas, instead of encouraging calm and restraint, reinforced the racial aspect of the case, and appeared to cast Zimmerman in the role of villain.

Martin's parents attended a Capitol Hill briefing on racial profiling and hate crimes organized by members of the House Judiciary Committee. The twenty-one Democratic congressmen assembled denounced the death as a hate crime. "You have friends in the Congressional Black Caucus," Democratic congressman Andre Carson told Martin's parents. "We have your back."[13]

Jesse Jackson, as usual, took to the incident as an opportunity to advance the idea that "blacks are under attack."[14] That statement had no basis in fact; any racial targeting would appear to be in the other direction. A Justice Department report found that 93 percent of black murder victims are killed by other black people.[15] According to the FBI statistics, whites are more than twice as likely to be killed by blacks as vice versa.[16]

Then there were instances of media malpractice that played into the race-baiting. NBC's *Today* show broadcast a doctored version of Zimmerman's conversation with a police dispatcher moments before the shooting to make it sound as if Zimmerman targeted Martin because he was black.

NBC was forced to apologize for its outrageous behavior.[17] Some instances of media prejudice were subtler, with mainstream media outlets consistently using younger, more innocent-looking pictures of Trayvon Martin rather than more recent photos that reflected a very different youth. The media rarely reported that he had in fact been expelled from school and at a minimum dabbled in illegal drugs.

Still, marches and demonstrations were held, and sweatshirts with hoods—hoodies like the one Martin was wearing at the time he was killed—became a symbol of solidarity for all those who felt justice had not been served.

Zimmerman claimed the shooting death was self-defense, a notion later corroborated by police video and witness testimony. In April, a Special Prosecutor was appointed to take over the investigation. She filed charges of second degree murder against Zimmerman. According to Zimmerman's father, George Zimmerman received death threats after the shooting and was forced to move out of his home. Filmmaker Spike Lee re-tweeted to his 200,000 followers an erroneous address for Zimmerman.[18] Mike Tyson said about Zimmerman, "It's a disgrace he hasn't been shot yet."[19]

The New Black Panther Party offered a $10,000 reward for the "capture" of Zimmerman, and incidents of vandalism and assault were alleged to be acts of revenge for the shooting of Martin.[20] A white man in Mobile, Alabama, was beaten almost to death by a mob of twenty black men. One of them reportedly said as he left the crime scene, "Now that's justice for Trayvon."[21]

Never once did Obama step in to calm the tension or call for restraint. Never once did he call on Americans to rise above racial differences and embrace what brings us together as Americans. No, he talked about how if he had a son, he would look like Trayvon.

No matter how the Trayvon Martin case is resolved, one thing is clear: anyone who thought Barack Obama would usher in post-racial harmony was sorely mistaken.

Playing the Race Canard

Obama and his allies are often quick to attribute bad faith to their opponents when it comes to race. And they are quite open about it. On the 2008 campaign trail, Obama told a crowd of supporters, "We know what kind of campaign they're going to run... they're going to try to make you afraid of me. 'He's young and inexperienced and he's got a funny name. And did I mention he's black?'"[22]

In the age of Obama, race is a convenient cudgel with which to strike anyone who opposes the president's agenda. The Tea Party movement arose early in Obama's term in response to the new president's out-of-control spending and proposals for the government to take over major industries and vast swaths of the economy. The movement was immediately labeled as racist.

At its annual conference, the NAACP adopted a resolution condemning the allegedly "racist elements" of the Tea Party.[23] Comedian Janeane Garofalo called the Tea Partiers "racist rednecks."[24] Of course, had the Tea Partiers been pushing a liberal policy agenda, no one on the left would have noticed that most of them were white. Very few people of color attend Earth Day rallies, for instance, which are filled with liberals. And there was a conspicuous lack of color at the Occupy Wall Street protests in 2011.

Plus, there *were* black Americans at the Tea Party rallies, including some who were Tea Party leaders and speakers. Black Republican presidential candidate Herman Cain called accusations of racism against the Tea Party "ridiculous," and said, referring to his victories in Tea Party straw polls ahead of the GOP presidential nomination campaign, "If the Tea Party organization is racist, why does the black guy keep winning all these straw polls?"[25]

Black people have always been given a hard time in the conservative movement—not from other conservatives but from liberals aghast that blacks could choose conservatism over liberalism's grievance politics. Black Republican politicians have been called Uncle Toms, traitors, and Oreos. Black conservative students on college campuses—those brave enough to admit being conservative—are sometimes mocked and belittled for their beliefs.

Cain also said that a lot of Obama's supporters "use race selectively to try to cover up some of his failures, to try to cover up some of his failed policies."[26] And he suggested that Obama's surrogates "try to play the race card, because there's supposed to be something wrong with criticizing him.... Some people have tried to use [race] to try to give the president a pass on failed policies, bad decisions and the fact that this economy is not doing what it's supposed to do."[27]

Conservatives are often cowed on matters of race. They get so worried about being labeled racists that they shy away from talking about anything that might have racial overtones. Running for president against Obama in 2008, Senator John McCain refused to raise, or allow campaign surrogates to raise, Obama's relationship with Jeremiah Wright because any mention of Wright or the black church would have elicited cries of racism. McCain's silence might have cost him the election. Regarding the Wright situation in 2008, Obama's campaign manager, David Plouffe, wrote, "I felt like the wheels could spin off our whole venture."[28] But Republican reticence ensured that didn't occur.

On college campuses in 2008, conservative students were at a loss for how to mount effective opposition to the first serious black presidential candidate. When they attempted to criticize his leftist ideology, they were labeled racists. It worked. Obama secured the overwhelming support of college students with little opposition.

Something similar happened in 2009 when President Obama nominated Sonia Sotomayor to replace retiring justice David Souter on the U.S. Supreme Court. Given the Democrats' record of attacking Republican presidents' court nominees, it would have been reasonable for Republicans to scrutinize closely Sotomayor's history as a jurist. But, as one press report put it, "The nomination... of Sonia Sotomayor to the high court brought a surprisingly muted response from the Republican senators who will actually vote on it."[29]

Sotomayor was the first Latina Supreme Court nominee. And some liberals and media commentators warned that tough questioning during her confirmation hearings would risk being viewed as ethnically insensitive and would thus risk alienating Hispanic voters. Aside from some principled opposition from a few conservative stalwarts, Sotomayor's hearings became a virtual love-fest, and she won confirmation easily.

What explains the liberal argument that any opposition to Obama is rooted in racism? In some cases, liberals simply equate correlation (conservatives oppose Obama, who happens to be black) with causation (conservatives oppose Obama *because* he's black). But there is often something more sinister at play. As black conservative Ward Connerly has written:

> If I have learned one thing from life, it is that race is the engine that drives the political Left. When all else fails, that segment of America goes to the default position of using race to achieve its objectives. In the courtrooms, on college campuses, and, most especially, in our politics, race is a central theme. Where it does not naturally rise to the surface, there are those who will manufacture and amplify it.
>
> Such is the case with the claims that the "Tea Partiers" are a bunch of racists and that many of them spat upon members of the Congressional Black Caucus and called them "n*****s." I am convinced beyond any doubt that all of this is part of the strategic plan being implemented by the Left in its current campaign to remake America.[30]

But in the current economic climate, even race-baiters are beginning to concede that some opposition to Obama might not be linked to racism. In a June 2012 interview with *GQ* magazine, Spike Lee said, "I can't say to all the people that are unhappy with him that they're racist people. People ain't got jobs, people are hurting. So I don't care what color you are, if people are out of work, it's tough."[31]

Obama Has Failed Black Americans

President Obama talks a lot about empathy, but he seems to employ it very selectively.

In his writing and in his speeches Obama makes it clear that he feels and understands deeply the experiences of black Americans. Unfortunately, Obama often uses empathy to exploit the suspicions of black Americans. He aims to create solidarity with them through hollow gestures and enhancing, not transcending, the racial divide. In the meantime, he has pursued policies that have made the economic circumstances of black America worse rather than better.

Obama is quick to talk about violence when it allows him to pander to segments of the black community who feel the justice system is fundamentally biased against blacks or those who see hate crimes as pervasive. But when it comes to addressing the real problems black Americans face in forming stable families and gaining work experience and jobs, Obama is too often silent and ineffective.

This was not always the case. In *The Audacity of Hope*, Obama wrote candidly about problems in the black community:

> Then there's the collapse of the two-parent black household, a phenomenon that is occurring at such an alarming rate when compared to the rest of American society that what was once a difference in degree has become a difference in kind, a phenomenon that reflects a casualness toward sex and child rearing among black men that renders black children more vulnerable—and for which there is simply no excuse.[32]

He even conceded that government doesn't have all the answers.

> Although government action can help change behavior... a transformation in attitudes has to begin in the home, and in neighborhoods, and in places of worship. Community-based

institutions, particularly the historically black church, have to help families reinvigorate in young people a reverence for educational achievement, encourage healthier lifestyles, and reenergize traditional social norms surrounding the joys and obligations of fatherhood.[33]

Obama is clearly reluctant to say these sorts of things in public these days. In the rare instances when he does, he is often slapped down by professional race-baiters. When Obama gave a 2008 Father's Day speech exhorting black fathers to be more engaged with their children, he was scolded by Jesse Jackson for "talking down to black people." Jackson added, "I want to cut his nuts out."[34]

Obama appears to take the support of black Americans for granted. His public support of same-sex marriage, for example, was clearly meant to attract the support and campaign contributions of homosexual groups. But it was at odds with the majority of black Americans who oppose same-sex marriage.

Pastor Barbara Reynolds wrote in the *Washington Post* that after Obama's same-sex marriage announcement, she received numerous phone calls from other black Christians. One exchange went like this:

> **Caller**: Barbara, what… is going on with Obama? I thought he was a Christian.
>
> **Reynolds**: He is a Christian. Reverends Jesse Jackson, Al Sharpton and NAACP's Julian Bond all agree with the president.
>
> **Caller**: I don't [care] if the Pope said men could marry each other, until my Bible says that, I'm not voting for Obama.
>
> **Reynolds**: You don't have any choice, you certainly couldn't vote for Romney. Robbing the poor and the widows is also a sin which the Romney crowd does well.
>
> **Caller**: I have a choice; I can stay home and… vote for Jesus.[35]

Obama's economic policies have disproportionately hurt black Americans. The black unemployment rate was 13.6 percent in May 2012,[36] a full point higher than when Obama took office in January 2009, and more than 60 percent higher than the 8.2 percent unemployment rate for all Americans.[37] For black men, the unemployment rate was 15 percent in May 2012; the black teen unemployment rate was 36.5 percent.[38] And these numbers would be much higher if they included the hundreds of thousands of black Americans who have dropped out of the job market.

This devastation has not gone unnoticed. Throughout Obama's term, the Congressional Black Caucus has been warning Obama that black voters are frustrated with his economic policies and the impact they are having on the black community.

In September 2011, amid a reported 21 percent unemployment rate for blacks, Democratic representative Emanuel Cleaver II of Missouri, chairman of the Congressional Black Caucus, told the *Wall Street Journal*, "I'm frustrated with the president, I'm frustrated with the Senate, I'm frustrated with the House. The president and his White House team [are] trying to minimize the discussion of race as it relates to job creation.'"[39]

Obama gave a remarkably patronizing speech to the Congressional Black Caucus in September 2011. In the face of their very real concerns about economic conditions, he told them to "take off your bedroom slippers, put on your marching shoes… stop complaining, stop grumbling, stop crying."[40] In other words, if you don't agree with me and my approach, I don't want to hear it.

Stop complaining, stop grumbling, stop crying? Needless to say, those remarks did not go over very well with black leaders in Congress. Democratic representative Maxine Waters of California quipped, "I've never owned a pair of bedroom slippers."[41]

Black leaders called the unemployment epidemic among blacks a "state of emergency" and put pressure on Obama to address the problem. "This is not necessarily President Obama's fault—but right now, this is his watch. He has to address this issue," Robert Johnson, founder of Black Entertainment Television and the first black American billionaire, told *Politico*.[42]

Representative Waters said, "The Congressional Black Caucus loves the president, too. We're supportive of the president, but we're getting tired. We're getting tired. The unemployment is unconscionable. We don't know what the strategy is."[43]

Waters's comments were reminiscent of a 2010 town hall event in which a black supporter of Obama told him:

> I'm one of your middle class Americans. And quite frankly, I'm exhausted. Exhausted of defending you, defending your administration, defending the mantle of change that I voted for.
>
> My husband and I have joked for years that we thought we were well beyond the hot dogs and beans era of our lives, but, quite frankly, it's starting to knock on our door and ring true that that might be where we're headed again, and, quite frankly, Mr. President, I need you to answer this honestly. Is this my new reality?[44]

Obama's relationship with blacks in the private sector has been frayed. In his book *The Amateur,* Edward Klein quotes Harry C. Alford, the president and CEO of the National Black Chamber of Commerce, which represents the nearly two million black businesses in the United States:

> When Obama became president, we were all happy about the symbolism—America's first black president.... We didn't really care about his position or views on anything. We just wanted a black president no matter what. We should have been more careful, as his views on small business, especially black business, are counter to ours.
>
> His view of business is that it should be a few major corporations which are totally unionized and working with the government, which should also be massive and reaching every level of American society. Thus, the first Executive Order was the

reinstatement of Project Labor Agreements in government contracting. PLAs give labor unions an exclusive [option] in construction jobs—all participating firms must use union labor, or, at least, pay union wages and abide by union rules. This activity, in effect, discriminates against blacks, Hispanics, and women per se, as trade unions deliberately under-employ them.

President George W. Bush eliminated PLAs from federal contracting and his main reason was "unions discriminate against small business, women and minorities." So here we were with the first black president who deliberately discriminates against small businesses, women and minorities. How ironic![45]

Ironic indeed. Obama knows he can take black voters for granted. He figures he can use identity politics and the race card to compensate for a policy agenda that has left more blacks without work and with less economic hope than they had before.

CHAPTER TWENTY-ONE

Obama Bullies
the Media

With the possible exception of academia, no segment of American society was more thoroughly won over by Barack Obama in 2008 than the mainstream media. According to one study, Obama enjoyed an 8 to 1 voting advantage over John McCain among journalists.[1]

And that advantage helped Obama win. A Pew study found that the media's coverage of the presidential campaign was skewed 3 to 1 in favor of Barack Obama. (The study found that Fox News provided the most balanced coverage.)[2]

As *New York* magazine political reporter John Heilemann wrote in January 2012, "No person with eyes in his head in 2008 could have failed to see the way that soft coverage helped to propel Obama first to the Democratic nomination and then into the White House."[3] The media malpractice surrounding Obama was summed up best by MSNBC's Chris Matthews, who, in a moment of candor, said, "I want to do everything I can to make this... new presidency work."[4] After Obama won, many journalists abandoned their careers as "objective" journalists to join the new administration.

The relationship between Team Obama and the mainstream media was captured perfectly by former CBS newsman Bernard Goldberg in the title to his bestselling book, *A Slobbering Love Affair: The True (and Pathetic) Story of the Torrid Romance between Barack Obama and the Mainstream Media.*

Obama often acts as though he expects the media to fawn over him. When they don't he gets tetchy and even vindictive. In his first term, President Obama spent an inordinate amount of time threatening and attempting to divide and marginalize the few media outlets that challenged him and his allies.

On the rare occasions during the 2008 campaign when the mainstream media scrutinized Obama, he lashed out. When the *New York Times* ran a front-page article with a poll finding that Obama hadn't closed the racial divide, the administration's press office sent a curt email conveying its displeasure to the *Times*' chief political correspondent, Adam Nagourney. As Gabriel Sherman wrote in the *New Republic*:

> Nagourney responded and thought the matter was resolved, but discovered the next day the Obama campaign had issued a statement slamming the article. Nagourney said, "I've never had an experience like this, with this campaign or others. I thought they crossed the line. If you have a problem with a story I write, call me first. I'm a big boy. I can handle it. But they never called. They attacked me like I'm a political opponent."[5]

Journalist Jodi Kantor wrote that when things were going badly for Obama in 2009, he "took his frustration out on the media, which he largely viewed with condescension bordering on contempt."[6] She writes that "the president was perversely fascinated by cable news—he liked to see 'what the idiots are paying attention to,' in the words of an aide." And early in his administration,

Obama set out to destroy the conservative media, particularly conservative talk radio and Fox News.

In the initial days of his presidency, Obama told congressional Republicans to "quit listening" to Rush Limbaugh if they wanted to work with him. The administration had hired pollster Stanley Greenberg to survey the public about Limbaugh and discovered they might benefit if Rush were linked in the public's mind to the Republican leadership. So that's exactly what they did. The administration launched a campaign to divide Republicans by branding Limbaugh as the de facto leader of the Republican Party. The goal was to force Republican leaders to disassociate from the talk radio icon. The campaign provoked a *Time* magazine story titled "Team Obama's Petty Limbaugh Strategy."[7]

The story noted that Obama "promised to be a different, more substantive, less gimmicky leader" who would not engage in "phony outrage" but would work on solving problems. *Time* quoted *Politico*'s Jonathan Martin saying the entire Limbaugh "controversy" had been "cooked up and force fed to the American people by Obama's advisers."[8]

Obama Targets Fox News

Obama has saved his most vicious treatment for his most effective critic, Fox News, which he's tried to delegitimize and isolate from the rest of the media. Obama had always viewed the popular cable network as illegitimate. He was one of a group of Democratic presidential candidates who pulled out of a debate cosponsored by Fox News in 2007.[9]

As the only political news network not "in the tank" for Obama and the Democratic Party, Fox News attracts a large and loyal audience. Just months into his presidency, Obama began what *Politico* described as working "systematically to marginalize the most powerful forces behind the Republican Party," unleashing "top White House officials to undermine conservatives in the media, business and lobbying world."[10]

As *Time* magazine put it:

[A] new White House strategy has emerged: rather than just giving reporters ammunition to "fact-check" Obama's many critics, the White House decided it would become a player, issuing biting attacks on those pundits, politicians and outlets that make what the White House believes to be misleading or simply false claims....

The take-no-prisoners turn has come as a surprise to some in the press, considering the largely favorable coverage that candidate Obama received last fall and given the President's vows to lower the rhetorical temperature in Washington and not pay attention to cable hyperbole. Instead, the White House blog now issues regular denunciations of the Administration's critics, including a recent post that announced "Fox lies" and suggested that the cable network was unpatriotic for criticizing Obama's 2016 Olympics effort.[11]

White House Press Secretary Robert Gibbs used a baseball analogy to describe how the administration would counter critical media. "The only way to get somebody to stop crowding the plate is to throw a fastball at them," he explained. "They move."[12]

Senior Obama adviser David Axelrod told ABC's George Stephanopoulos that the White House didn't consider Fox News to be a real news organization. Axelrod then advised that ABC and others "ought not to treat them" as if they are a news organization.[13]

White House Chief of Staff Rahm Emanuel echoed Axelrod on CNN, saying, "[Fox News is] not a news organization so much as it has a perspective.... And more importantly is to not have the CNNs and the others in the world basically be led and following Fox."[14]

Interim White House Communications director Anita Dunn scolded Fox News in comments she gave to the *New York Times*, saying, "As they are undertaking a war against Barack Obama and the White House, we don't need to pretend that this is the way that legitimate news organizations behave." She added, "We're going to treat them the way we would treat an opponent." She also called Fox a "wing of the Republican Party."[15]

Things sank to an unprecedented low when the White House tried to bar Fox's White House correspondent, Major Garrett, from the press pool. As Jonathan Alter wrote in *The Promise*: "White House communications aides insisted that the only way to change the network's behavior was to elevate the confrontation. They saw it as 'political malpractice' to treat Fox as a normal media outlet and felt vindicated when Garrett stopped asking them about anti-Obama slurs spread by the network's commentators."[16]

The administration also tried to block a Fox interview with "pay czar" Ken Feinberg. Administration officials denied that it had intervened to block the interview, saying, "There was no plot to exclude Fox News and they had the same interview [opportunity] that their competitors did. Much ado about nothing."[17] But reporters knew otherwise. Four networks rallied to Fox's defense and refused to participate in the interview without Fox. CBS reporter Chip Reid said the administration "crossed the line."[18]

On the campaign trail in Amherst, Ohio, over the fourth of July weekend in 2012, Obama stopped into Ziggy's Pub and Restaurant. When the pub's owner said, "You're in a building that has Fox News on," Obama suggested that he change the channel.

A State-Run Media

The Obama administration seems to have an authoritarian impulse when it comes to news media, which explains why it has used such heavy-handed tactics against the few media outlets that refuse to dutifully push the Obama message.

Anita Dunn once bragged that the Obama campaign had been able to "control" the media.[19] This is the same woman who once identified the Marxist mass murderer Mao Tse-Tung as one of her "favorite political philosophers."[20]

Mark Lloyd, the Obama administration's Federal Communications Committee "Chief Diversity Officer," has voiced admiration for Venezuelan dictator Hugo Chavez, whom Lloyd has called "incredible" and "dramatic." Chavez has imprisoned numerous dissenting journalists and overseen a state takeover of all media.[21]

The Obama administration likes media that it can, in Anita Dunn's word, "control." Any media that it can't control it tries to marginalize, dividing the media into friends and foes, excluding the latter and expecting adulation from the former. If this hallmark behavior of the Obama administration represents the new politics of hope and change, it's not the sort of hope and change a free people is likely to want.

CHAPTER TWENTY-TWO

The Imperial Presidency

While running for president, Barack Obama regularly criticized President George W. Bush for what he claimed was Bush's abuse of executive authority. "These last few years we've seen an unacceptable abuse of power at home," Obama said in Chicago in 2007. "We've paid a heavy price for having a president whose priority is expanding his own power."[1]

By condemning Bush, Obama was assuring voters that he'd show much more restraint. But in his quest to "fundamentally transform America," Obama has displayed a shocking eagerness to flout the Constitution's separation of powers and checks and balances. Obama has eschewed compromise and outreach to Republicans and shown an unmatched willingness to intimidate other branches of government and subvert their constitutional authority.

Calling Out the Court

Obama has trained much of his rhetorical fire on the U.S. Supreme Court. Obama attacked the court for its 2010 decision in *Citizens United*

v. *Federal Election Commission*, which overturned restrictions on corporations' political speech.

A few days after the decision, Obama launched an unprecedented attack on the court during his State of the Union address, accusing the court of judicial activism for striking down campaign finance laws that violate the First Amendment. Obama claimed the justices had "reversed a century of law to open the floodgates for special interests—including foreign corporations—to spend without limit in our elections."[2] Obama then encouraged Congress to pass a law to overturn the court's decision.

Obama's accusation against the court provoked a stunned Justice Samuel Alito to shake his head and mouth the words, "That's not true." The justices attend the State of the Union speech out of respect for the president. Obama showed no similar respect for the court, unfairly attacking the justices at a venue that gave them no chance to respond.

In April 2012, as administration attorneys argued the case for Obamacare before the Supreme Court—saying the mandate both was and was not a tax—Obama made veiled political threats against the justices, telling the media that he was "confident that the Supreme Court will not take what would be an unprecedented, extraordinary step of overturning a law that was passed by a strong majority of a democratically elected Congress."[3]

Obama referred to the Supreme Court derisively as "an unelected group of people,"[4] and he said that striking down the law or the mandate would be an unacceptable act of "judicial activism."[5] He called on justices to show "deference to democratically elected legislatures" by upholding the law, or risk diminishing its "credibility."[6]

Democratic senator Richard Blumenthal of Connecticut declared that the court would damage its reputation if it didn't uphold the law. "The court commands no armies, it has no money; it depends for its power on its credibility," he said. "The only reason people obey it is because it has that credibility. And the court risks grave damage if it strikes down a statute of this magnitude and importance."[7]

Many legal experts criticized the threats against the court, especially those by the president. "Though past presidents have occasionally inveighed against judicial activism," the *Washington Post* reported, "legal analysts and historians said it was difficult to find a historical parallel to match Obama's willingness to directly confront the court."[8] The threats, though, achieved their desired effect, as Chief Justice John Roberts stunningly sided with liberals in a convoluted decision that upheld Obamacare in spite of its glaring constitutional deficiencies.

Pushing the Envelope

When it comes to the law-making branch of government, Obama's slogan is, "If Congress won't act, I will." Obama has uttered a version of this in response to Republican opposition to many key parts of his domestic agenda.

"Now, whenever Congress refuses to act, Joe and I, we're going to act,"[9] Obama promised at a February 2012 event on the payroll tax cut extension. "In the months to come, wherever we have an opportunity, we're going to take steps on our own to keep this economy moving."[10]

"What I'm not gonna do is wait for Congress," Obama declared in an April interview on *60 Minutes*, in which he was asked what he'd do if the Supreme Court overturned Obamacare.[11]

Obama's by-any-means-necessary approach to implementing his agenda involves unconstitutional power grabs, administrative usurpations, and various other forms of executive overreach. He has not only acted without congressional approval but sometimes in direct contradiction to a majority of the people's elected representatives.

Obama started his presidency by appointing dozens of "czars," White House liaison officers who were neither elected nor confirmed by the Senate and were thus accountable only to the president and his senior staff.

Obama has issued an unprecedented number of presidential signing orders and executive orders, which he began issuing right away. In the first few days of his term, Obama issued an order reversing a ban that prohibits taxpayer funding to groups that perform abortions abroad, another to close the prison at Guantanamo Bay in Cuba, and still another to restore funding for research on stem cells derived from human embryos. In the first two years of his administration, Obama worked with a Democratic Congress to pass key parts of his agenda. But after congressional Democrats suffered what Obama referred to as "a shellacking" in the 2010 mid-term elections, Obama quickly discovered that he would have a difficult time advancing his liberal agenda.

Instead of looking for ways to compromise with congressional Republicans, however, Obama searched for other means to enact his policy goals. Then-Chief of Staff Rahm Emanuel promised that Obama would govern through "executive orders and directives to get the job done across a front of issues."[12]

According to the *New York Times*, in fall 2011, Obama interrupted a White House strategy meeting to raise an issue not on the agenda. "He declared, aides recalled, that the administration needed to more aggressively use executive power to govern in the face of Congressional obstructionism."[13]

"'We had been attempting to highlight the inability of Congress to do anything,' recalled William M. Daley, who was the White House chief of staff at the time. 'The president expressed frustration, saying we have got to scour everything and push the envelope in finding things we can do on our own.'"[14] But Obama has done more than push the envelope on executive authority. He's conducted an all-out assault on the constitutional separation of powers.

Obama hasn't tried to hide his executive office imperialism. According to the *New York Times*, "Each time, Mr. Obama has emphasized the fact that he is bypassing lawmakers. When he announced a cut in refinancing fees for federally insured mortgages last month, for example, he said: 'If Congress refuses to act, I've said that I'll continue to do everything in my power to act without them.'"[15]

One of Obama's first decisions after the mid-term elections was to direct the Justice Department to stop defending the Defense of Marriage

Act (DOMA), which bars federal recognition of same-sex marriages against constitutional challenges.[16]

Other efforts include ordering the Environmental Protection Agency to issue regulations on greenhouse gas emissions, after his cap and tax legislation (which was intended to do the same thing through proper legislation) ended up in the dustbin, and granting at least ten states waivers from the strict requirements of the 2002 law No Child Left Behind.[17] And in 2011, Obama issued a signing statement claiming that he could bypass a provision in the budget that prevented him from appointing White House czars on issues such as health care, climate change, and the auto industry.[18]

In July 2011, Obama told a crowd of Hispanic activists that it would be "tempting" to bypass Congress and change immigration laws himself, but "That's not how our democracy functions…. That's not how our Constitution is written."[19] Less than a year later, in June 2012, Obama announced that the Department of Homeland Security would no longer deport certain illegal immigrants who were brought to the country as children. The move was seen as a de facto amnesty for millions of illegal immigrants.

It was also seen as an overtly political move, a desperate lunge for Hispanic votes. Republican senator Marco Rubio of Florida said Obama's decision "exposes the fact that this issue is all about politics for some people."[20] Obama's amnesty by fiat allowed him to exploit the ultimate wedge issue—immigration—to divide Republicans and rally wary Hispanic voters.

One estimate from January 2012 put the number of executive orders issued by Obama at 108.[21] "Obama has amazingly enough gone even further than President Bush in the use, or abuse rather, of executive power," Gene Healy, vice president of the Cato Institute, told the *Washington Examiner*.[22]

Obama has also been willing to go it alone on foreign policy. He has used executive power to target people for death using drone attacks, including American citizens living abroad. Obama provoked criticism from

Congress and elsewhere when he decided to join a NATO military mission in Libya without seeking lawmakers' approval. Challenged on the constitutionality of the operation, Obama argued that the Libyan mission wasn't a declared war but rather a "kinetic military action."

Both of Obama's two major legislative accomplishments are executive branch power grabs. Obamacare granted the Department of Health and Human Services sweeping new powers to determine what the new law meant. As reporter Philip Klein wrote in the *American Spectator*:

> There are more than 2,500 references to the secretary of HHS in the health care law (in most cases she's simply mentioned as "the Secretary"). A further breakdown finds that there are more than 700 instances in which the Secretary is instructed that she "shall" do something, and more than 200 cases in which she "may" take some form of regulatory action if she chooses. On 139 occasions, the law mentions decisions that the "Secretary determines." At times, the frequency of these mentions reaches comic heights. For instance, one section of the law reads: "Each person to whom the Secretary provided information under subsection (d) shall report to the Secretary in such manner as the Secretary determines appropriate."[23]

Due to the ambiguity of the law, Klein wrote, Sebelius will, if she remains in office, have "wide ranging... powers" to determine "what type of insurance coverage every American is required to have... what hospitals can participate in certain plans," and otherwise oversee how billions of dollars in taxpayer money is spent.[24]

Then there's the Consumer Protection Act, otherwise known as the Dodd-Frank Act. The 2010 law puts a great deal of power in the hands of the executive branch. C. Boyden Gray, White House counsel for the George H. W. Bush administration, wrote in 2010 that Dodd-Frank "create[s] a structure of almost unlimited, unreviewable and sometimes secret bureaucratic discretion, with no constraints on concentration—a breakdown of the separation of powers, which were created to guard against the exercise of arbitrary authority."[25]

Recess Appointments

Dodd-Frank also created the Consumer Financial Protection Bureau (CFPB), headed by a five-year presidential appointee. The power of that appointee, law professor Todd Zywicki told author and lawyer David Limbaugh for his book *The Great Destroyer*, is "so significant it may be unconstitutional," adding, "I am not familiar with an institution that gives so much power to one person."

Obama nominated former Ohio attorney general Richard Cordray to direct the bureau in December 2011.[26] Concerned about the amount of power Cordray would wield, the Senate refused to confirm him. This prompted Obama to make a recess appointment—only the Senate was not technically in recess at the time. Asked about his non-recess appointment of Cordray, Obama replied, "I refuse to take no for an answer. When Congress refuses to act and—as a result—hurts our economy and puts people at risk, I have an obligation as president to do what I can without them."[27]

Obama's unconstitutional appointment of Cordray was not his only dubious appointment. Obama also installed three members to the National Labor Relations Board, the government agency charged with investigating and remedying unfair labor practices, without senatorial consent.

Former attorney general Edwin Meese wrote in a *Washington Post* op-ed that the non-recess recess appointments were a "breathtaking violation of the separation of powers and the duty of comity that the executive owes to Congress."[28] Meese also predicted that Obama's "flagrant violation of the Constitution not only will damage relations with Congress for years to come but will ultimately weaken the office of the presidency. There eventually may be litigation over the illegal appointments, but it will be a failure of government if the political branches do not resolve this injustice before a court rules."[29]

Republican senator Chuck Grassley of Iowa accused Obama of acting "more and more like a king that the Constitution was designed to replace." Grassley implored colleagues of both parties to fight against Obama's "power grabs."[30]

A June 2012 *Politico* story's headline summed up the Obama approach: "Obama's policy strategy: ignore laws."[31] Liberal constitutional law scholar Jonathan Turley said:

> The president is using executive power to do things Congress has refused to do, and that does fit a disturbing pattern of expansion of executive power under President Obama. In many ways, President Obama has fulfilled the dream of an imperial presidency that Richard Nixon strived for. On everything from [DOMA] to the gaming laws, this is a president who is now functioning as a super legislator. He is effectively negating parts of the criminal code because he disagrees with them. That does go beyond the pale.[32]

What a transformation! Only four years ago, Obama presented himself as a reformer and a uniter, and as America's first post-partisan president. "I will listen to you, especially when we disagree. Let us resist the temptation to fall back on the same partisanship and pettiness and immaturity that has poisoned our politics for too long," Obama announced just after winning the 2008 presidential election.

But after three and a half years in office, Obama has been exposed as just another self-interested Washington politician, and the most partisan and divisive president in our nation's history.

A Second Term?

What would a second Obama term bring? Some liberals are concerned that Obama would move to the center to try and achieve as much as possible with what is sure to be a fairly evenly divided Congress. But I suspect that, if re-elected, Obama will pursue a more ideological agenda, free from the moderating influence of a looming election.

In a June 2012 *New Yorker* article, Ryan Lizza spoke with many top aides both in the Obama White House and in the re-election campaign and concluded, "Obama has an ambitious second-term agenda."[33] Lizza reports that Obama "has said that the most important policy he could address in his second term is climate change, one of the few issues that he thinks could fundamentally improve the world decades from now."[34]

Lizza speculates that other items on Obama's second-term agenda include addressing nuclear proliferation, foreign aid, and, perhaps foremost, immigration reform.

If Obama wins, he'll be poised to make many critical decisions right away. As Lizza puts it, "His immediate task will be to settle more than a decade's worth of deferred arguments about how big the government should be and who should pay for it."[35] And make no mistake about it: he will settle it.

On January 1, 2013, a number of tax increases—the largest tax increase in American history—are scheduled to take place. A month later there will be a replay of the summer 2011 debate over the federal debt ceiling, as the president and Congress will again debate whether or not to raise the amount of money the federal government can borrow.

If Obama wins re-election, he will have won as a divider, not a uniter. As Lizza acknowledges:

> Obama campaigned from 2004 through 2010 as a bridge between competing orthodoxies.... Now Obama is emphasizing the ideological divide, not the bridge across it.
>
> "A lot of the tussles what we've had over the last three and a half years have had a lot to do with this difference in vision," [Obama] told [an] audience in Minneapolis in June 2012, "and it will be coming to a head in this election."[36]

But whether Obama wins or loses, the country he promised to unite, the nation he pledged to heal, will be far more deeply divided than on the day he took office in 2009. Obama's presidency has exposed the utter fraud of his once inspiring mantra of "hope and change."

Acknowledgments

For her confidence in me, I would like to thank Marjorie Ross—a role model, mentor, and friend. Thank you to all the wonderful professionals at Regnery Publishing, particularly Harry Crocker, Mary Beth Baker, Alberto Rojas, and Karen Woodard.

My great thanks go to Daniel Allott, whose help has been instrumental in making this book a reality. He is a brilliant conservative who is making major contributions to traditional values and freedom in this country. He has been a joy to work with on this project.

I am truly thankful to Ron Robinson, one of the greatest unsung heroes of the conservative movement, and all my friends and colleagues at Young America's Foundation. This group is doing the heavy lifting of passing on a genuine understanding of liberty and free markets to the next generation. After working with this valiant organization in various capacities for the past twenty-two years, I can say without reservation that there is no group of individuals more dedicated to expanding liberty in our nation than the staff and board of Young America's Foundation and the Reagan Ranch. I am thankful to Ron in particular for his wisdom, support, and most especially, his friendship.

Thank you to Michelle Easton and the Clare Boothe Luce Policy Institute for all their support. CBLPI encourages and promotes conservative women in the face of never-ending attacks, and I am the grateful beneficiary of their efforts. It has been a joy to work with Michelle and to witness her courageous work on behalf of women such as myself, enabling us to spread our message—that women can indeed be conservative, traditional, and strong—to young women on college campuses and beyond.

For their encouragement and advice, thank you to Dr. Burt Folsom, Peter Schweizer, Wynton Hall, Tim Phillips, Audrey Jackson, Stephen K. Bannon, Dan Fleuette, Jason Mattera, S. E. Cupp, and Alyssa Cordova.

Thanks to Sean Hannity, Neil Cavuto, and all the great Americans at Fox News who have allowed me a forum.

Thank you to my precious circle of friends and prayer warriors—Leigh Ann, Christine, Allison, Nicole, Elizabeth, Dana, Angie, Nancy, and Andrea. Thank you to Michael for encouraging me to take the plunge.

My warmest thanks go to my family, Mark, Suzanne, Anne, Steve, Dodie, and Jim, and especially, to the quintessential example of gracious strength, Mom—who is forever encouraging me to "say something!" Ok, Mom. I did.

It's impossible to thank my father, since he's not here, but I do. With all my heart.

Finally, if my children didn't give the thumbs up for me to pursue this book, I never would have done it. They knowingly make the sacrifice of not having mom's full attention and time. But they are generous souls, my unwavering encouragers, and, I'm proud to say, emerging stalwarts for freedom. They "get" what's on the line: the future of their liberty. And they believe it is worth fighting for. So to Henry, Paul, Stone, and Lucy: Thank you. I love you.

Notes

Introduction: The Divisive President

1. Rick Klein, "Obama: I Think Same-Sex Couples Should Be Able to Get Married," ABC News, May 9, 2012.
2. Jeff Mason, "Obama Talks Gay Marriage at George Clooney Fundraiser," Reuters, May 11, 2012.
3. "Obama Slams GOP, Calls Tax Deal Politically Realistic," CNN, December 7, 2010.
4. Janie Lorber, "The Early Word: Financial Forays," *New York Times* The Caucus, April 26, 2010.
5. Ben Smith and Jonathan Martin, "Obama Plan: Destroy Romney," *Politico*, August 9, 2011.
6. Ibid.
7. Ibid.
8. Noam Scheiber, "From Hope to Hardball," *New Republic*, April 20, 2012.

Chapter 1: The Community Organizer President

1. President Barack Obama, "Inaugural Address," January 20, 2009.

221

2. Illinois Senator Barack Obama, "Keynote address at the Democratic National Convention," July 27, 2004.

3. Barack Obama, *The Audacity of Hope* (Random House, 2006), 11.

4. "Candidates Tout Their Electability in 2008," Reuters, November 30, 2007.

5. Barack Obama, "Our Time Has Come" speech, *CQ Transcripts Wire*, February 6, 2008.

6. Barack Obama, "Obama's Victory Speech," *New York Times*, November 5, 2008.

7. Lydia Saad, "Obama Starts with 68% Job Approval," Gallup, January 24, 2009.

8. "The 2008 Official Presidential General Election Results," Federal Election Commission, January 22, 2009, http://www.fec.gov/pubrec/fe2008/2008presgeresults.pdf.

9. Ibid.

10. "2008 voter turnout," FactCheck.org, January 8, 2009.

11. "Most Liberal, Most Conservative: 2007 Vote Ratings," *National Journal*, March 8, 2008.

12. WSJ Staff, "Obama: 'If They Bring a Knife to the Fight, We Bring a Gun,'" *Wall Street Journal* Washington Wire, June 14, 2008.

13. Saul Alinsky, *Rules for Radicals* (Vintage Books, 1989), 118–20.

14. Stanley Kurtz, *Radical-in-Chief* (Threshold Editions, 2010), 127.

15. Ibid., 359.

16. Ryan Lizza, "Barack Obama's unlikely political education," *New Republic*, March 19, 2007.

17. David Remnick, *The Bridge* (Knopf, 2010), 294.

18. Jodi Kantor, *The Obamas* (Little, Brown and Company, 2012), 164.

19. Charles Hurt, "PREZ ZINGS GOP FOE IN A $TIMULATING TALK," *New York Post*, January 23, 2009.

20. "Partisan Gap in Obama Job Approval Widest in Modern Era," Pew Research Center, April 2, 2009.

21. "Obama's Approval Most Polarized for First-Year President," Gallup, January 25, 2010.

22. Andrew Rafferty, "Marco Rubio calls Obama most 'divisive figure' in US politics," MSNBC.com *First Read*, May 20, 2012.

23. Artur Davis, "A Response to Political Rumors," ArturDavis.com, May 29, 2012.

24. Kantor, *The Obamas*, 109.

25. Ibid., 110–11.

Chapter 2: The Blame-Shifter-in-Chief

1. David Remnick, *The Bridge* (Knopf, 2010), 207.
2. Ibid., 209.
3. Ibid.
4. Peter Wehner, "The Great Divider," *Weekly Standard*, April 23, 2012.
5. Peter Wehner, "Barack Obama Political Hack," *Commentary*, December 8, 2011.
6. Jonathan Alter, *The Promise* (Simon and Schuster, 2010), 129.
7. Frank James and Ben Meyerson, "Obama, with stimulus underway, warns mayors about waste," *Los Angeles Times*, February 21, 2009.
8. Michael Sluss, "Obama throws political muscle to Deeds," *Roanoke Times*, August 7, 2009.
9. Ibid.
10. Jake Tapper, "President Obama: Tax Cuts for Wealthy Are Republicans' 'Holy Grail,'" ABC News, December 7, 2010.
11. Stephanie Condon, "Obama: Time to 'eat our peas' and pass debt deal," CBS News, July 11, 2011.
12. "Great procrastinators in history," *The Daily Beast*.
13. Perry Bacon, Jr., "Obama's budget speech has partisan tone," *Washington Post*, April 13, 2011.
14. Ibid.
15. Geneva Sands, "Obama: GOP field 'must have been founding members of the Flat Earth Society,'" *The Hill*, March 14, 2012.
16. "Barack Obama's Kansas speech targets 'fend for yourself' stance of Republicans and corporations," *London Guardian*, December 6, 2011.
17. Peter Wehner, "The Great Divider," *Weekly Standard*, April 23, 2012.
18. "Obama: Massachusetts' Anger," ABC News, January 20, 2010.
19. "Press Conference by the President," The White House Office of the Press Secretary, November 3, 2010.
20. David Corn, *Showdown* (William Morrow, 2012).
21. Jodi Kantor, *The Obamas* (Little, Brown and Company, 2012), 278.
22. Ibid.
23. Ibid., 98.
24. Edward Klein, *The Amateur* (Regnery, 2012), 83.
25. In Obama's Words, "Obama delivers weekly radio address," *Washington Post*, June 11, 2011.
26. "Time running out for Obama to turn around the economy," Fox News, June 1, 2012.

27. Bill Thomas, "The United States of Chicago," *San Francisco Chronicle*, June 25, 2012.

28. Jacob Weisberg, "Down with the People: Blame the childish, ignorant American public—not politicians—for our political and economic crisis," Slate.com, February 6, 2010.

29. Ibid.

30. Mark Steyn, "His Genius is Wasted on You," *National Review Online*, January 26, 2010.

31. David Jackson, "Obama's comments about 'scared' voters continue to linger," *USA Today*, October 19, 2010.

32. Lloyd Grove, "Exclusive: President Obama Asks Campaign Donors to Send Him More Money," *The Daily Beast*, June 30, 2012.

33. James W. Ceaser, "The Unpresidential President," *Weekly Standard*, August 2, 2010.

Chapter 3: Spiking the Football

1. Nancy Gibbs, "The Case of Modesty, in an Age of Arrogance," *Time*, November 9, 2012.

2. David Mendell, *From Promise to Power* (Amistad, 2007).

3. Kathy Kiely, "His Diversity a Plus, Obama Says," *USA Today*, October 31, 2008.

4. Jim Geraghty, "Obama: I Can Do Every Job Better Than Those I Hire to Do It," National Review Online *The Campaign Spot*, April 24, 2012.

5. Ibid.

6. Jonathan S. Tobin, "Liberal Lamentations and the Book of Job," *Commentary*, November 23, 2010.

7. Rick Moran, "One more from *Game Change* on Obama," *American Thinker*, January 16, 2010.

8. The Nobel Peace Prize 2009, NobelPrize.org.

9. Peter Wehner, "Obama Gives Up Pose as Nation's 'Healer,'" *Commentary*, October 25, 2011.

10. The White House, Office of the Press Secretary, Press Gaggle by Press Secretary Robert Gibbs, July 23, 2009.

11. Dinesh D'Souza, *Obama's America* (Regnery, 2012), 206–7.

12. Scott Wilson, "Iran Unrest Reveals Split in U.S. on Its Role Abroad," *Washington Post*, June 23, 2009.

13. "Republicans blast Obama's attempt to take credit for Keystone pipeline progress," Fox News, March 21, 2012.

14. E. J. Dionne, Jr., "Numb," *New Republic*, November 5, 2009.

15. Brian Montopoli, "Obama: I won't release bin Laden death photos," CBS News, May 4, 2011.
16. Byron Tau, "Team Obama: Would Mitt Romney have killed bin Laden?" *Politico*, April 27, 2012.
17. Geneva Sands, "Huffington: bin Laden ad 'despicable,'" *The Hill*, April 30, 2012.
18. Toby Harnden, "SEALs slam Obama for using them as 'ammunition' in bid to take credit for bin Laden killing during election campaign," U.K. *Daily Mail*, April 30, 2012.
19. Ibid.
20. Geneva Sands, "Huffington: bin Laden ad 'despicable,'" *The Hill*, April 30, 2012.
21. Philip Rucker, "Romney: 'Even Jimmy Carter' would have ordered Osama bin Laden killing," *Washington Post*, April 30, 2012.
22. Toby Harnden, "SEALs slam Obama for using them as 'ammunition' in bid to take credit for bin Laden killing during election campaign," U.K. *Daily Mail*, April 30, 2012.
23. Ibid.
24. Jack Goldsmith, "Temple of Silence," *New Republic*, July 12, 2012.
25. Devin Dwyer, "Robert Gates: We Had Agreed We Wouldn't Release Details About the Operation Against OBL But 'That All Fell Apart,'" ABC News, May 12, 2011.
26. Jo Becker and Scott Shane, "Secret 'Kill List' Proves a Test of Obama's Principles and Will," *New York Times*, May 29, 2012.
27. Richard Cohen, "What the Obama Leaks Have Wrought," *Washington Post*, June 12, 2012.
28. M. J. Lee, "White House leaks meet growing outrage," *Politico*, June 7, 2012.
29. Ibid.
30. Gary Bauer, "Obama Risks National Security to Secure His Own Re-election," *Human Events*, June 11, 2012, http://www.humanevents.com/2012/06/11/gary-bauer-obama-risks-national-security-to-secure-his-own-re-election/.
31. Ibid.
32. Chris McGreal, "Obama denies White House responsibility in national security leaks," *London Guardian*, June 8, 2012.
33. Jo Becker and Scott Shane, "Secret 'Kill List' Proves a Test of Obama's Principles and Will," *New York Times*, May 29, 2012.
34. Richard Cohen, "What the Obama Leaks Have Wrought," *Washington Post*, June 12, 2012.
35. Meghashyam Mali, "McCain: Security leaks coming from 'highest levels' of White House," *The Hill*, June 6, 2012.

Chapter 4: The Out-of-Touch President

1. Ben Smith, "Obama on small-town Pa: Clinging to religion, guns, xenophobia," *Politico*, April 11, 2008.
2. Tom Shine, "Obama, Clinton and Biden: The Wealthy, Wealthier and... Not So Wealthy," ABC News, December 6, 2011.
3. "Clinton presents her case for the middle class," Associated Press, February 15, 2008.
4. "Hillary's Whiskey Pandering," DailyKos, April 14, 2008.
5. Jeff Zeleny, "Obama's Down on the Farm," *New York Times* The Caucus, July 27, 2007.
6. Seth Borenstein, "Is Obama too much like Mr. Spock?" Associated Press, December 1, 2009.
7. Jonathan Alter, *The Promise* (Simon and Schuster, 2010), 152.
8. Ibid.
9. Ibid.
10. Ibid.
11. James Fallows, "Obama, Explained," *Atlantic*, March 2012.
12. Lynn Sweet, "Bob Woodward's tough takes on David Axelrod, Rahm Emanuel in 'Obama's Wars,'" *Chicago Sun-Times*, September 28, 2010.
13. Tim Rutten, "Book review: 'Obama's Wars,'" *Los Angeles Times*, September 27, 2010.
14. Dee Dee Myers, "Memo to President Obama: Get back in touch," *Politico*, March 12, 2010.
15. Ibid.
16. Jodi Kantor, *The Obamas* (Little, Brown and Company, 2012), 28.
17. Ibid.
18. Tiffany Gabbay, "New Book Claims Obama Complained About Taking Pictures With Troops During Trip to Baghdad," *The Blaze*, January 12, 2012.
19. Alter, *The Promise*, 331.
20. Ron Suskind, *Confidence Men* (Harper, 2011), 620.
21. Helene Cooper, "Bipartisan Agreement: Obama Isn't Schmoozing," *New York Times*, December 28, 2011.
22. Mark Knoller, "President Obama plays 100th round of golf, draws fire from critics," CBS News, June 17, 2012.
23. Matthew Larotonda, "Golfer in Chief? Obama Hits 100th Time on the Links," ABC News, June 17, 2012.
24. Mark LaRochelle, "Private Sector doing fine?" *Human Events*, June 19, 2012.
25. "Obama Tells Woman: 'Interesting' Unemployed Husband Can't Find Job," *RealClearPolitics* video, January 30, 2012.
26. Evan Harris, "Obama's Date Night in New York," ABC News, May 30, 2009.

27. Kenneth T. Walsh, "Republicans Grumble as Obamas Jet to New York and Tax-payers Pick Up Tab," *U.S. News & World Report*, June 1, 2009.

28. "Michelle Obama's Spain vacation cost taxpayers nearly $470 G, watchdog group claims," Fox News, April 26, 2012.

29. Toby Harnden, "Obama has held more re-election fundraisers than previous five Presidents combined as he visits key swing states on 'permanent campaign,'" U.K. *Daily Mail*, April 29, 2012.

30. Ibid.

31. Shushannah Walshe, "RNC Web Video Lampoons Obama's Anna Wintour Fundraising Effort," ABC News, June 4, 2012.

32. "Obama taps celebrity circuit in search for campaign cash," Associated Press, June 14, 2012.

Chapter 5: Obama's Crass Class Warfare

1. Jeffrey M. Jones, "Romney Edges Obama in Battle for Middle-Income Voters," Gallup, June 4, 2012.

2. Macon Phillips, "A strong middle class equals a strong America," The White House Middle Class Task Force, January 30, 2009.

3. Ibid.

4. Barack Obama, *Dreams From My Father* (Canongate Books Ltd., 2009), 136.

5. Jonathan Karl, "The Hidden Obama," *Wall Street Journal*, June 15, 2012.

6. Byron Tau, "Obama: 'I wasn't born with a silver spoon in my mouth,'" *Politico*, April 18, 2012.

7. Barack Obama, "Obama in Osawatomie," speech transcript, *New York Times*, December 6, 2011.

8. Barack Obama, *The Audacity of Hope* (Crown, 2006), 66.

9. Jonah Golberg, "'Empathy': just a code word for bias," *New York Post*, April 14, 2010.

10. Major Garrett, "Obama Pushes for 'Empathetic' Supreme Court Justices," Fox News, May 1, 2009.

11. "Remarks by the President in nominating Judge Sonia Sotomayor to the United States Supreme Court," White House Office of the Press Secretary, May 26, 2009.

12. Joel Mowbray, "Did Obama Lie About Born Alive Bill?" *RealClearPolitics*, August 21, 2008.

13. President Obama, "Remarks by the President on Immigration," The White House Office of the Press Secretary, June 15, 2012.

14. John McCormack, "Obama Compares Republicans to Hostage-Takers," *Weekly Standard*, December 7, 2010.
15. David Nakamura, "White House moves into full reelection mode," *Washington Post*, March 15, 2012.
16. Rachel Weiner, "What Obama meant by 'social Darwinism,'" *Washington Post*, April 4, 2012.
17. Jonathan Strong, "Democrats Rip GOP Energy Package," *Roll Call*, June 18, 2012.
18. Barack Obama, "Remarks by the President in State of the Union Address," White House Office of the Press Secretary, January 24, 2012.
19. Jesse Graham, Brian A. Nosek, and Jonathan Haidt, "The Moral Stereotypes of Liberals and Conservatives: Exaggeration of Differences across the Political Divide," April 5, 2012.
20. Arthur C. Brooks, "True fairness means rewarding merit, not spreading the wealth," *The Blaze*, May 21, 2012.
21. President Barack Obama, "Remarks by the President at the Building and Construction Trades Department Conference," The White House Office of the Press Secretary, April 30, 2012.
22. Ibid.
23. Ibid.
24. Ibid.
25. Jeffrey Anderson, "Top 0.1 Percent Pays More Income Tax than Bottom 80 Percent," *Weekly Standard* The Blog, September 21, 2011.
26. Jon McHenry, "Obama and Voters Define 'Fair Share' Differently," *Western Free Press*, September 20, 2011.
27. Michael Moore, "Michael Moore Threatens The Rich: Let's 'Deal With It Nonviolently Now,'" *RealClearPolitics* video, September 22, 2011.
28. "The President's Budget for Fiscal Year 2013," Office of Management and Budget.
29. Larry Kudlow, "Obama's Class-Warfare, Tax-the-Rich Budget," National Review Online *The Corner*, February 13, 2012.
30. Ibid.
31. Erik Wasson and Daniel Strauss, "Senate rejects Obama budget in 99-0 vote," *The Hill*, May 16, 2012.
32. Lymari Morales, "Fewer Americans See U.S. Divided Into 'Haves,' 'Have Nots,'" Gallup, December 15, 2011.
33. Ibid.

Chapter 6: Obama's Socialism and Crony Capitalism versus the Middle Class

1. Gregory Acs, "Downward Mobility from the Middle Class: Waking up from the American Dream," The Pew Charitable Trusts, September 2011.
2. Steve Kornacki, "Bush Still Boosts Obama," *Salon*, June 14, 2012.
3. "Obama To Announce Housing Program After Three Years In Office And Past Failed Housing Announcements," GOP.com, March 2012.
4. Julie Schmit, "What went wrong with foreclosure aid programs?" *USA Today*, December 12, 2011.
5. Noam Scheiber, *The Escape Artists: How Obama's Team Fumbled the Recovery* (Simon and Schuster, 2012).
6. Ibid.
7. Ross Kaminsky, "No Friend of the Middle Class," *American Spectator*, December 30, 2011.
8. Alyene Senger, "Side Effects: Employees Lose Insurance and Taxpayers get the Bill Under Obamacare," Heritage Foundation *The Foundry*, May 2, 2012.
9. Alyene Senger, "New Report Shows Health Spending Spikes Under Obamacare," Heritage Foundation *The Foundry*, June 15, 2012.
10. Steve Zelnak, "How Obamacare Hurts Job Creation," *U.S. News & World Report*, Economic Intelligence, March 30, 2012.
11. Ibid.
12. Ibid.
13. Barack Obama's Inaugural Address, January 20, 2009.
14. "Who Pays for Cap and Trade?" *Wall Street Journal*, March 9, 2009.
15. Ibid.
16. Richard Burr, "Cap-and-trade bill will cut jobs, not emissions," *The Hill*, July 21, 2009.
17. Declan McCullagh, "Obama Admin: Cap And Trade Could Cost Families $1,761 A Year," CBS News, September 15, 2009.
18. "The Cap and Tax Fiction," *Wall Street Journal*, June 26, 2009.
19. Ibid.
20. "Dingell: Cap and trade a 'great big' tax," *Politico* On Congress, April 24, 2012.
21. Pete Chagnon, "Cap-and-trade—'Largest tax increase of all time,'" *OneNewsNow*, March 30, 2009.
22. Peter Roff, "Obama Considers Middle Class Tax Hikes for Healthcare, 'Cap and Trade,'" *U.S. News & World Report*, June 29, 2009.
23. Garrett Haake, "Romney says Obama 'kept promise' to raise the price of gas," NBC News *First Read*, March 18, 2012.

24. Juliet Eilperin, "EPA announces plans to regulate power plant, oil refinery emissions," *Washington Post*, December 23, 2010.
25. Ibid.
26. John M. Broder, "E.P.A. Issues Tougher Rules for Power Plants," *New York Times*, July 7, 2011.
27. "EPA's Regulatory Train Wreck," American Legislative Exchange Council.
28. Kerry Picket, "EPA imposes Obama's cap and trade regs—energy prices 'skyrocket,'" *Washington Times*, August 20, 2011.
29. "Energy Policy Explored As Cap-And-Trade Dies," NPR, November 5, 2010.
30. Alexandra Petri, "Keith Judd takes 41 percent of West Virginia Democrat votes—for he's a jolly good felon," *Washington Post*, May 9, 2012.
31. Fred Lucas, "WV Democratic Governor Not Backing Obama," CNS News, May 2, 2012.
32. Josh Lederman, "Sen. Manchin might not vote for Obama," *The Hill*, April 20, 2012.
33. Doug McKelway, "Cracks showing in Democratic Party's 'big tent' strategy ahead of convention," Fox News, June 25, 2012.
34. Ben Geman, "Oil executive: 'Very stressed relationship' between industry, Obama White House," *The Hill*, June 17, 2012.
35. Darren Goode, "Obama: Oil companies 'hitting the American people twice,'" *Politico*, March 29, 2012.
36. Neil King Jr. and Stephen Power, "Times Tough for Energy Overhaul," *Wall Street Journal*, December 12, 2008.
37. "They Said It! Biden: 'Our Energy Policy Is The Best It's Ever Been,'" GOP.com, April 2012.
38. Jennifer A. Dlouhy, "Obama postpones final call on Keystone XL pipeline," *Houston Chronicle*, November 11, 2011.
39. David Lerman and Jim Efstathiou Jr., "TransCanada's Keystone Pipeline's Environment Risk Limited, U.S. Finds," Bloomberg.com, August 26, 2011.
40. "Boehner Pushes the XL Pipeline, Obama Gets Soggy," Salem-News.com, February 29, 2012.
41. Steve Hargreaves, "Keystone pipeline: How many jobs it would really create," CNN, December 14, 2011.
42. Elizabeth Mendes, "Keystone pipeline: How many jobs it would really create," Gallup, March 22, 2012.
43. Steve Gelsi, "Keystone Pipeline Environmental Review Re-starts," FoxBusiness.com, June 15, 2012.

44. "Hoeven: State Department's Expanded Keystone Environmental Review Unjustified After Four Years of Exhaustive Study," News Releases, June 15, 2012.
45. Mario Loyola, "How Obama is Choking Off U.S. Oil Production," National Review Online, March 9, 2012.
46. Ibid.
47. Alison Vekshin, "Solyndra's Loan Guarantee 'Was Rushed,' Treasury Audit Says," Bloomberg.com, April 3, 2012.
48. Matthew L. Wald, "Solar Firm Aided by Federal Loans Shuts Doors," *New York Times*, August 31, 2011.
49. Ibid.
50. Ibid.
51. Jim Snyder and Christopher Martin, "Obama Team Backed $535 Million Solyndra Aid as Auditor Warned on Finances," Bloomberg.com, September 12, 2011.
52. Adam Clark Estes, "Obama's Big Bet on Solar Power Is Backfiring," *National Journal*, September 2, 2011.
53. Matthew L. Wald, "Solyndra Was Asked to Delay Layoff News Till After Midterms, Memo Says," *New York Times*, November 15, 2011.
54. "Solyndra Bankruptcy Confirms $535 Million Loan Guarantee Was a Bad Bet for Taxpayers from the Beginning," Press Release, House Energy and Commerce Committee, August 31, 2011.
55. Ibid.
56. Rachel Weiner, "Solyndra, Explained," *Washington Post*, June 1, 2012.
57. C. J. Ciaramella, "Bankrupt solar company with fed backing has cozy ties to Obama admin," *Daily Caller*, September 1, 2011.
58. Carol D. Leonnig and Joe Stephens, "E-mails show Energy Department was moving toward second loan for Solyndra," *Washington Post*, October 5, 2011.
59. Charles Lane, "Doubling down on 'green energy' bad bet," *Washington Post*, June 19, 2012.
60. Ibid.

Chapter 7: Obama's Generational Theft

1. Jonathan Alter, *The Promise* (Simon and Schuster, 2010), 43.
2. "Obama's Commencement Address at Arizona State University," *New York Times*, May 14, 2009, http://www.nytimes.com/2009/05/13/us/politics/13obama.text.html?pagewanted=all.
3. Amanda M. Fairbanks, "2011 College Grads Moving Home, Saddled With Historic Levels Of Student Loan Debt," *Huffington Post*, May 13, 2011.

4. Jessica Godofsky, M.P.P., Cliff Zukin, Ph.D., Carl Van Horn, *Work Trends, Unfulfilled Expectations: Recent College Graduates struggle in a Troubled Economy*, May 2011.

5. Jordan Weissmann, "53% of Recent College Grads Are Jobless or Underemployed—How," *Atlantic*, April 23, 2012.

6. "Unemployment Among Young Adults Is 12.1 Percent in May, Signals More Bad News for a Generation Whose Careers and Dreams Are Delayed Due to the Lack of Jobs and Economic Opportunity," *PR Newswire*, June 1, 2012.

7. Dennis Jacobe, "One in Three Young U.S. Workers Are Underemployed," Gallup, May 9, 2012.

8. Lauren Fox, "Gas Prices Grow More Under Obama than Carter," *U.S. News & World Report*, April 9, 2012.

9. Blake Ellis, "Average student loan debt tops $25,000," CNN *Money*, November 3, 2012.

10. "Student Loan Debt Exceeds One Trillion Dollars," NPR, April 24, 2012.

11. Don Lee, "Report on college loan delinquency rate raises alarms," *Los Angeles Times*, March 5, 2012.

12. Aimee Groth, "Actually, College Grads Are More Likely To Be Bartenders Than Engineers," *Business Insider*, April 23, 2012.

13. Pew Research Center, "Young, Underemployed and Optimistic," February 9, 2012.

14. Ben Feller, "Candidates back effort to combat college debt," *USA Today*, April 25, 2012.

15. Vicki Needham, "CBO estimates $9.8 trillion in deficits over 10 years," *The Hill*, March 24, 2010.

16. Jeffrey Anderson, "The Cost of Obama," *Weekly Standard*, February 14, 2012.

17. Ibid.

18. *National Federation of Independent Business, et al. v. Sebelius, Secretary of Health And Human Services, et al.*, No. 11-393, June 28, 2012.

19. Alyene Senger, "Obamacare's 2nd Anniversary: No Gift for Young Americans," Heritage Foundation *The Foundry*, March 21, 2012, http://blog.heritage.org/2012/03/21/obamacares-2nd-anniversary-no-gift-for-young-americans/.

20. Avik Roy, "Obamacare Increases Costs of College Health Plans by as Much as 1,112%," *Forbes*, June 5, 2012.

21. "The Uncertainty Of ObamaCare Is Causing Small Business To Flat-Line," GOP.com, February 2012.

22. Neil Munro, "Obama, White House officials visit more than 130 universities, schools in massive campaign for young voters," *Daily Caller*, April 27, 2012.

23. Joshua Gilder, "Obama's Student Loan Proposal Won't Lower College Costs," *U.S. News & World Report*, June 7, 2012, http://www.usnews.com/opinion/blogs/joshua-gilder/2012/06/07/obamas-student-loan-proposal-wont-lower-college-costs.

24. Michael Barone, "Obama Losing Rock-Star Status Among Young Voters," *Washington Examiner*, April 30, 2012.

25. Frank Newport, "Young Voters Back Obama, but Many Aren't Poised to Vote," Gallup, April 26, 2012.

26. Esten Perez, "OBAMA BOUNCING BACK, WIDENS LEAD OVER MITT ROMNEY AMONG MILLENNIALS, HARVARD POLL FINDS," Harvard University Institute of Politics, April 24, 2012.

27. Ibid.

28. Lydia Saad, "Majority in U.S. Dissatisfied With Next Generation's Prospects," Gallup, June 4, 2012.

Chapter 8: The Deceit and Division of Obamacare and the "War on Women"

1. Exit Polls: Virginia, CNNPolitics.com, Election Center, February 12, 2008.

2. Exit Polls, *New York Times*, November 5, 2008.

3. "Clinton, Obama try wooing women voters," Associated Press, February 9, 2008.

4. Jeffrey M. Jones, "Obama's Initial Approval Ratings in Historical Context," Gallup, January 26, 2009.

5. Women Members of the House GOP Caucus, "2010: The Year of GOP Women," *Politico*, December 15, 2010.

6. *The EMILY'S List Women's Monitor Poll: Winning Back The Obama Defectors*, available at standwithgabby.org/assets/pdfs/Women_Monitor_Memo.pdf.

7. "Gallup Daily: Obama Job Approval," Gallup Politics, http://www.gallup.com/poll/113980/gallup-daily-obama-job-approval.aspx.

8. National Women's Law Center, September 2011.

9. Michael W. Chapman, "780,000 More Women Unemployed Today Than When Obama Took Office," CNS News, July 6, 2012.

10. Terrence P. Jeffrey, "324,000 Women Dropped Out of Labor Force in Last Two Months—As Number of Women Not in Labor Force Hits Historic High," CNS News, May 9, 2012.

11. Vicki Needham, "Slower jobs growth for women voters could cost Obama in election," *The Hill*, March 25, 2012, 05http://thehill.com/blogs/on-the-money/801-economy/217989-slower-jobs-growth-for-women-voters-could-cost-obama-in-election.

12. Ibid.
13. Ibid.
14. Michael W. Chapman, "780,000 More Women Unemployed Today Than When Obama Took Office." And "U.S. poverty rate for women and children Hit 17-year Record High," InfoWars.com, May 25, 2012, http://www.infowars.com/us-poverty-rate-for-women-and-children-hits-17-year-record-high/.
15. Leslie Bennetts, "Women: The Invisible Poor," *The Daily Beast*, September 14, 2011.
16. 2004 Kaiser Women's Health Survey, Kaiser Family Foundation.
17. Dr. Scott W. Atlas, "Obama policies threaten the most vulnerable," *Washington Times*, May 1, 2012.
18. Ryan Ellis, "Obamacare's Tax War on Women," ATR.org, March 20, 2012.
19. Ibid.
20. Ibid.
21. Ibid.
22. Blake Ellis, "Tanning Salons Burned By Health care Bill," CNN *Money*, March 24, 2010.
23. Ryan Ellis, email to author, May 24, 2012.
24. Helene Cooper and Laura Goodstein, "Rule Shift on Birth Control Is Concession to Obama Allies," *New York Times*, February 10, 2012.
25. "U.S. Bishops Vow to Fight HHS Edict," News Release, February 20, 2012.
26. Ibid.
27. Erik Eckholm, "Both Sides Eager to Take Birth Control Issue to Voters," *New York Times*, February 15, 2012.
28. DCCC: Democrats 2012, "One Million Strong Against the Republican War on Women," http://www.dccc.org/pages/waronwomen.
29. Elise Viebeck, "Anti-abortion groups turn 'war on women' charge against Democrats," *The Hill*, May 3, 2012.
30. Lucy Madison, "Both Sides See Opportunity in Women's Health Fights," CBS News, March 16, 2012.
31. Jeff Poor, "Jackson Lee: Women to be dragged out 'into the streets,' return to 'coat hangers' on abortion act," *Daily Caller*, May 31, 2012.
32. "The Latest Ultimatum by the Federal Government vs. the Catholic Church," *Catholic Voyager*, January 23, 2012.
33. Erik Eckholm, "Poll Finds Wide Support for Birth Control Coverage," *New York Times*, March 1, 2012.

34. Penny Star, "Dems Stage a Single-Witness 'Hearing' to Frame Their 'Reproductive Rights' Argument," CNS News, February 24, 2012.

35. John McCormack, "Georgetown Students Go Broke to Buy Birth Control? Target Sells Pills for $9 Per Month," *Weekly Standard*, February 28, 2012.

36. Catalina Camia, "Limbaugh: Apology to student was 'heartfelt'" *USA Today*, March 5, 2012.

37. Byron Tau and MJ Lee, "Obama, Rush Tangle Over Sandra Fluke," *Politico*, March 6, 2012.

38. Mary Bruce, "Bristol Palin asks Obama: When Should I Expect Your Call," ABC News, March 19, 2012.

39. Rachel Weiner, "Sasha And Malia Dolls 'Inappropriate,' Michelle Obama Says," *Huffington Post*, February 23, 2009.

40. Paul Farhi, "*President Obama's daughters' privacy is difficult to protect in Internet age,*" *Washington Post, March 20, 2012.*

41. David Brody, "Obama says he doesn't want his daughters punished with a baby," *The Brody File*, March 31, 2008.

42. Noreen Malone, "President Obama Invokes Sasha and Malia, Again," *New York Magazine*, May 9, 2012.

43. John McCormack, "Obama Fares Worse Among Women after Month-Long Contraception Mandate Battle," *Weekly Standard*, March, 12, 2012.

44. Lucy Madison, "Poll: Romney Has Slight Edge Over Obama," CBS News, May 14, 2012.

45. Gary Langer, "Romney Rebounds Among Women, While Obama's Favorability Slips," ABC News, May 30, 2012.

46. Timothy P. Carney, "Abortion Lobby Powers the Democratic Money Machine," *Washington Examiner*, May 11, 2011.

47. Cameron Joseph, "Planned Parenthood Endorses Obama With $1.4 million Ad Buy," *The Hill*, May 30, 2012.

48. J. Lester Feder, "HHS Hires Former Planned Parenthood Spokesman," *Politico*, April 20, 2012.

49. "Abortion is Latest Controversy in Health Overhaul," Associated Press, July 21, 2009.

50. Daniel Allott, "Obama's Contraception Plan Won't Cut Pregnancies," *Washington Times*, February 14, 2012.

51. Ibid.

Chapter 9: Obama Condescends to Women

1. Campbell Brown, "Obama: Stop Condescending to Women," *New York Times,* May 19, 2012.
2. Ramsey Cox, "Hill Poll: Romney leads in respect on working women issue," *The Hill,* April 23, 2012. Only 37 percent of likely voters think Obama respects women who stay at home; 49 percent think Romney respects career women, while a mere 27 percent doubt that.
3. Emily Friedman, "Ann Romney Fights Back: Debuts on Twitter to Counter DNC Advisor's Insult," ABC News, April 11, 2012.
4. Amie Parnes, "White House press secretary knows three different Hilary Rosens," *The Hill,* April 12, 2012.
5. Jan Crawford, "Poll reveals gap between married and single women," CBS News, April 18, 2012.
6. "Barely Half of U.S. Adults Are Married—A Record Low," Pew Research Center Publications, December 14, 2011.
7. Ibid.
8. "41 Percent of Babies Born Out of Wedlock," Associated Press, May 7, 2010.
9. Ron Suskind, *Confidence Men* (Harper, 2011), 627.
10. Ibid., 628.
11. Ibid., 277.
12. Ibid.
13. Ibid., 511.
14. Ibid., 629.
15. Ibid., 513.
16. Ibid., 630.
17. Ibid., 654.
18. Ibid., 628.
19. Jodi Kantor, *The Obamas* (Little, Brown and Company, 2012), 146.
20. Ibid., 146.
21. Ibid., 147.
22. Ibid., 148.
23. Ibid.
24. Allison McGevna, "David Letterman Slammed For Sex Jokes About Palin's Teen Daughter," Fox News, June 11, 2009.
25. "David Letterman Jokes About Bachmann's 'Ass,'" Fox News, July 5, 2011.
26. Melissa McEwan, "Unacceptable: Sexist Bill Maher Calls Sarah Palin the C-Word," AlterNet.com, March 29, 2011.
27. Matt Philbin, "Hate and Bile: Left-Wing Attacks on Women Get Little Press," Media Research Center, March 5, 2012.

28. Ibid.

29. Carrie Kahn, "Bill Maher's Obama SuperPAC Donation Causing Stir," National Public Radio, March 28, 2012.

Chapter 10: Obama Ignores Real Women's Rights Issues Abroad

1. Macon Phillips, "Statement released after the President rescinds 'Mexico City Policy,'" whitehouse.gov, January 24, 2009.

2. "Secretary Clinton confirms U.S. thinks abortion access is 'reproductive health'" Catholic News Agency, April 22, 2009.

3. Ibid.

4. Bruce Campion-Smith, "Hillary Clinton stirs the pot on Afghanistan, abortion and the Arctic," TheStar.com, March 30, 2010.

5. Daniel Allott, "Obama's Abortion Imperialism," *American Spectator*, August 2, 2010.

6. Ibid.

7. "White House Spent $23M of Taxpayer Money to Back Kenyan Constitution That Legalizes Abortion, GOP Reps Say," Fox News, May 15, 2010.

8. Daniel Allott, "Obama's Abortion Imperialism."

9. The White House, Office of the Press Secretary, Public Affairs Section, United States Embassy Nairobi, April 2, 2010.

10. Kathleen Gilbert, "Biden Promises Kenya 'Money to Flow' if Pro-Abort Constitution Passes," LifeSiteNews.com, June 18, 2010.

11. "Letter from U.S. Lawmakers Requesting Probe of Obama Admin Support for Kenya Constitution," LifeSiteNews.com, May 11, 2010.

12. Jeff Sagnip, "Probe Sought into Alleged Misuse of U.S. Funds by Obama Administration's Push for New Pro-Abortion Constitution in Kenya," ChrisSmith.house.gov, May 10, 2010.

13. Steven Ertelt, "Obama Admin May Face Probe on Funding of Pro-Abortion Kenya Groups," LifeNews.com, November 8, 2010.

14. "White House Spent $23M of Taxpayer Money to Back Kenyan Constitution That Legalizes Abortion, GOP Reps Say," Fox News, May 15, 2010.

15. Jeff Sagnip, "Probe: Obama Admin Broke Law to Push Abortion in Kenya," LifeNews.com, November 16, 2011.

16. USAID.com, "Supporting the Kenya Constitutional Implementation Process," http://kenya.usaid.gov/programs/democracy-and-governance/1102/.

17. Steven Ertelt, "China: 400 Million Fewer People Because of One-Child Policy," LifeNews.com, September 20, 2011.

18. Steven Ertelt, "100 Members of Congress Tell Obama: De-Fund Pro-Abortion UNFPA," LifeNews.com, October 12, 2011.

19. "Clinton: Chinese human rights can't interfere with other crises," CNN.com, February 22, 2009.

20. "Hillary Clinton's Silence on Chinese Human Rights," *Washington Post*, February 24, 2009.

21. Edward Wong, "China and U.S. Choose Safe Site for Biden Visit," *New York Times*, August 21, 2011.

22. Devin Dwyer, "Biden Under Fire for 'Not Second-Guessing' China's One-Child Policy," ABC News, August 23, 2011.

23. Joseph Abrams, "Obama's Science Czar Considered Forced Abortions, Sterilization as Population Growth Solutions," FoxNews.com, July 21, 2009.

24. Daniel Allott, "It Also Happens Here," *Catholic World Report*, May 10, 2011.

25. Ibid.

26. Pete Kasperowicz, "House rejects bill penalizing doctors for sex-selective abortions," *The Hill*, May 31, 2012.

27. Jonathan V. Last, "The War Against Girls," *Wall Street Journal*, June 24, 2011.

28. Ibid.

29. Laura Bush, "Don't Abandon Afghan Women," *Washington Post*, May 18, 2012.

30. Hillary Clinton, "New Hope for Afghanistan's Women," *Time*, November 24, 2001.

31. Laura Bush, "Don't Abandon Afghan Women."

32. David Brunnstrom and Missy Ryan, "NATO to endorse Afghan exit plan, seeks routes out," Reuters, May 21, 2012.

33. Dino Grandoni, "The Taliban Finds Some Much-Needed Office Space," *Atlantic Wire*, January 3, 2012.

34. Rahim Faiez and Heidi Vogt, "Taliban Poisoned School Girls, Say Afghanistan Officials," *Huffington Post*, June 6, 2012.

35. Dexter Filkins, "Afghan Girls, Scarred by Acid, Defy Terror, Embracing School," *New York Times*, January 13, 2009.

36. "Taliban claims responsibility for killing female politician in Kandahar," Thaindian News, April 13, 2009; "Gunmen kill female Afghan candidate's campaign workers," UK *Telegraph*, August 30, 2010.

37. Emma Graham-Harrison, "Afghan clerics' guidelines 'a green light for Talibanisation,'" *London Guardian*, March 5, 2010.

38. John T. Bennett, "President Obama Goes All In on The Taliban," *U.S. News & World Report*, May 2, 2012.

39. Rajiv Chandrasekaran, "In Afghanistan, U.S. Shifts Strategy on Women's Rights as it Eyes Wider Priorities," *Washington Post*, March 6, 2011.

40. Ibid.

41. Paul Richter, "Status of Afghan women threatens Hillary Clinton's legacy," *Los Angeles Times*, April 8, 2012.

42. Gayle Tzemach Lemmon, "Afghan women are not 'pet rocks,'" *Foreign Policy*, November 21, 2011.

Chapter 11: Obama Divides Catholics

1. Kathryn Jean Lopez, "Dolan: 'We Can't Back Down,'" National Review Online, March 29, 2012.

2. Michael Cooper and Jeff Zeleny, "McCain and Obama Palling Around? Must Be the Al Smith Dinner," *New York Times* The Caucus, October 16, 2008.

3. Jonathan P. Hicks, "At Archdiocesan Gala, No Room for Clinton or Dole," *New York Times*, August 23, 1996.

4. Karina Saltman, "Bush, Kerry not invited to charity dinner," CNN.com, September 14, 2005.

5. Michael Cooper and Jeff Zeleny, "McCain and Obama Palling Around? Must Be the Al Smith Dinner."

6. Julia Duin, "Catholic voters heavily favored Obama, analysis shows," *Washington Times*, November 7, 2008.

7. "How the Faithful Voted," The Pew Forum on Religion and Public Life, November 5, 2008.

8. Laurie McGinley, "Religious institutions' health plans must offer birth control," *Los Angeles Times*, January 20, 2012.

9. David Gibson, "Top Catholic Bishop Feels Betrayed by Obama," *USA Today*, January 25, 2012.

10. James Taranto, "When the Archbishop Met the President," *Wall Street Journal*, March 31, 2012.

11. E. J. Dionne, Jr. "Obama's breach of faith over contraceptive ruling," *Washington Post*, January 29, 2012.

12. Nancy Frazier O'Brien, "St. Joseph Health Services withdraws from CHA membership," Catholic News Service, April 1, 2010.

13. Michelle Boorstein, "Dissent among Catholics seen as nuns' groups back health bill," *Washington Post*, March 18, 2010.

14. Ben Johnson, "Catholic Health Association collaboration with Obama admin on mandate a 'scandal': Catholic leader," LifeSiteNews.com, February 14, 2012.

15. Kathleen Gilbert, "Catholic Health Association: we might have to sue over Obama mandate," LifeSiteNews.com, February 9, 2012.

16. Luiza Oleszczuk, "US Bishops Reject Proposed 'Compromise' on HHS Contraception Mandate," *Christian Post*, May 16, 2012.

17. Helene Cooper and Laurie Goodstein, "Rule Shift on Birth Control Is Concession to Obama Allies," *New York Times*, February 10, 2012.

18. Laurie Goodstein, "Obama Shift on Providing Contraception Splits Critics," *New York Times*, February 14, 2012.

19. Steven Ertelt, "New Poll: HHS Mandate Hurts Obama With Women, Catholics," LifeNews.com, June 9, 2012.

20. Joan Frawley Desmond, "What Did CHA's Carol Keehan Know and When Did She Know It?" *National Catholic Register*, February 14, 2012.

21. Joan Frawley Desmond, "Course Correction: Sister Carol Keehan Now Opposes Obama 'Accommodation' for HHS Mandate," *National Catholic Register*, June 18, 2012.

22. G. Tracy Mehan III, "The Irish Sue the Feds," *American Spectator*, May 22, 2012.

23. Transcript, "Obama's Commencement Address at Notre Dame," *New York Times*, May 17, 2009.

24. Ibid.

25. "Obama, Catholics and the Notre Dame Commencement," The Pew Forum on Religion and Public Life, April 30, 2012.

26. "Campaign targets Obama speech at Notre Dame," *USA Today*, May 11, 2009.

27. Michael Paulson, "Glendon declines Notre Dame medal," *Boston Globe*, April 27, 2009.

28. Dan Gilgoff, "Notre Dame Critics Tally $8.2 Million in Denied University Donations Over Obama," *U.S. News & World Report*, April 27, 2009.

29. Benjamin Mann, "Jews and Evangelicals stand with Church against contraception mandate," Catholic News Agency, January 5, 2012.

30. William Armstrong, Ken Smith and Joe Aguillard, "Why We Have Gone to Court against the Obama Mandate," *Wall Street Journal*, April 23, 2012.

31. Ibid.

32. "Protecting Consciences: Why Conscience is Important," USCCB National Bulletin Insert, June 2012.

33. Donald Wuerl, "Protecting our Catholic conscience in the public square," *Washington Post*, May 23, 2012.

Chapter 12: Obama Attacks Religious Freedom

1. ACOG Committee Opinion, "The Limits of Conscientious Refusal in Reproductive Medicine," No. 385, November 2007.

2. "Ob-Gyn physicians face loss of certification over abortion stance," Christian Medical and Dental Associations.

3. Nancy Berlinger, "The Dog in the Manger: HHS's Continuing Conscience Crisis," The Hastings Center Bioethics Forum, August 26, 2008.

4. "Regulation Proposed to Help Protect Health Care Providers from Discrimination," U.S. Department of Health and Human Services, News Release, Thursday, August 21, 2008.

5. Michael J. New, "Obama Administration Rescinds Bush Conscience Regulations," National Review Online, February 21, 2011.

6. David G. Savage, "This time, election truly could affect 'Roe vs. Wade,'" *Los Angeles Times*, October 7, 2008.

7. Carol Zimmerman, "US bishops' agency denied federal grant to help trafficking victims," Catholic News Agency, October 13, 2011.

8. "The Obama Administration's Attacks on Religion and Religious Freedom," The Alliance Defending Freedom.

9. "Georgetown Says It Covered Over Name Of Jesus To Comply With White House Request," CNS News, May 7, 2012.

10. Adam Liptak, "Religious Groups Given 'Exception' to Work Bias Law," *New York Times*, January 11, 2012.

11. Jonathan V. Last, "Weekly Standard: Obamacare Vs. The Catholics," NPR, February 7, 2012.

12. Robert Barnes, "Supreme Court: Discrimination laws do not protect certain employees of religious groups," *Washington Post*, January 11, 2012.

13. Matt Bowman, phone interview, June 1, 2012.

14. Jill Stanek, "Breaking news: Sebelius vetoes late-term abortion regs," JillStanek.com, April 23, 2009.

15. "Kansas Governor Vetoes a Very Reasonable Abortion Bill with Very Unreasonable Excuses," Kansans for Life press release, April 21, 2008.

16. "Summary of Gov. Sebelius, Dr. George Tiller, ProKanDo PAC information," *Kansas Meadowlark*.

17. Robert Novak, "A vice-president for abortion," *Washington Post*, May 26, 2008.

18. Ibid.

19. "Top Vatican Official Slams Choice of Kathleen Sebelius for Secretary of Health and Human Services," LifeSiteNews.com, March 13, 2009.

20. Remarks by William J. Clinton, Center for American Progress, October 18, 2006.

21. "Georgetown Says It Covered Over Name Of Jesus To Comply With White House Request," CNS News, May 7, 2012.

22. George Neumayr, "Georgetown's In-Kind Obama Donations," RealClearReligion, May 7, 2012.

23. Elise Viebeck, "Fury over birth-control mandate trails HHS Sec. Sebelius to Georgetown," *The Hill*, May 17, 2012.

24. Dr. Susan Berry, "Georgetown Professor Launches Campaign to Nix Sebelius' Graduation Speech," Breitbart.com, May 10, 2012.

25. Vanya Mehta, "President DeGioia defends decision to host Sebelius at Georgetown," *Georgetown Voice* Vox Populi, May 17, 2012.

26. Steven Ertelt, "Biden Stops Backing Komen Over Planned Parenthood De-Funding," LifeNews.com, February 2, 2012.

27. "Bishops Criticize Biden's Abortion Statements," Associated Press, September 9, 2008.

28. "Obama, Catholics and the Notre Dame Commencement," The Pew Forum on Religion and Public Life, April 30, 2009.

29. Carol E. Lee and Jonathan Martin, "Notre Dame speech key for Barack Obama with Catholics," *Politico*, May 17, 2009.

30. "Now the Faithful Voted," The Pew Forum on Religion and Public Life, November 5, 2008.

31. Steven Ertelt, "Pew Poll Finds President Barack Obama Turning Off Catholic Voters Over Abortion," LifeNews.com, April 7, 2009.

32. Human Kahn, "Catholic Church vs. Obama in Election Year Showdown," ABC News, January 30, 2012.

33. John McCormack, "Kathy Dahlkemper: I Wouldn't Have Voted for Obamacare If I'd Known About HHS Rule," *Weekly Standard*, February 7, 2012.

34. Bart Stupak, "Former Democratic congressman key to 'ObamaCare's' passage betrayed by contraception mandate?" *On the Record* with Greta Van Susteren, February 8, 2012.

35. Doug Kmiec, "Endorsing Obama," *Slate*, March 23, 2012.

36. Ibid.

37. Deal. W. Hudson, "Doug Kmiec and the Lure of Obama," *Crisis*, February 20, 2008.

38. Bob Cusack, "Ex-Obama official might not back Obama this year, citing birth-control decision," *The Hill*, February 6, 2012.

39. Caroline May, "Penn. Democratic leader defects to GOP, cites Catholic faith as reason," *The Daily Caller*, May 29, 2012.

40. Jo Ann Nardelli, email interview, June 2, 2012.

41. Ibid.

42. "More See 'Too Much' Religious Talk by Politicians," The Pew Forum on Religion and Public Life, March 21, 2012.

43. Frank Newport, "Catholics' Presidential Pick Differs by Ethnicity, Religiosity," Gallup, May 2, 2012.

44. Maureen Malloy Ferguson, "Obama's grand miscalculation with Catholics," Fox News.com, May 22, 2012.

45. Ibid.
46. Ibid.

Chapter 13: Obama's Politicized Faith

1. Saul Alinsky, *Rules for Radicals* (Vintage Books, 1989), 43.
2. Barack Obama, *The Audacity of Hope* (Vintage, reprint edition, 2008), 214.
3. Ibid.
4. Ibid.
5. David Remnick, *The Bridge* (Knopf, 2010), 175.
6. Edward Klein, *The Amateur* (Regnery, 2012), 37.
7. Ibid., 38.
8. Ibid., 43.
9. "Barack Obama's former pastor says President 'threw him under bus,'" *London Telegraph* May 18, 2010.
10. Eamon Javers, "Barack Obama invokes Jesus more than George W. Bush," Politico, June 9, 2009.
11. "Obama overturns Bush policy on stem cells," CNN, March 9, 2009.
12. Obama Notre Dame Speech, *Huffington Post*, May 17, 2009.
13. Adam Kredo, "'God's partners in matters of life and death,'" *Washington Jewish Week*, August 19, 2009.
14. Daniel Burke, "Obama Uses Sermon on the Mount to Elevate Speeches," *Christianity Today*, April 24, 2009.
15. David Gibson, "Obama and Gay Marriage: The Golden Rule Rules," *USA Today*, May 10, 2012.
16. Peter Baker and Dalia Sussman, "Obama's Switch on Same-Sex Marriage Stirs Skepticism," *New York Times*, May 14, 2012.
17. Christopher Goins, "Pelosi: Her Catholic Faith 'Compels' Her to Support Same-Sex Marriage," CNS News, May 10, 2012.
18. David Nakamura and Michelle Boorstein, "At prayer breakfast and with birth-control decision, Obama riles religious conservatives," *Washington Post*, February 2, 2012.
19. Michael Sean Winters and Brian Roewe, "Protesters, critics greet Rep. Ryan at Georgetown," *National Catholic Reporter*, April 26, 2012.
20. Jeff Jacoby, "Separation of Jesus and Congress," *Boston Globe*, March 6, 2011.
21. Meet the Press transcript for September 7, 2008, http://www.msnbc.msn.com/id/26590488/ns/meet_the_press/t/meet-press-transcript-sept/#.T-4a5Oxn2uI.
22. Ibid.

23. Ibid.
24. Ibid.
25. Amy Sullivan, "Does Biden Have a Catholic Problem?" *Time*, September 13, 2008.
26. Obama, *Audacity of Hope*, 215.

Chapter 14: Abandoning the Faithful

1. "Global Restrictions on Religion," Pew Forum on Religion and Public Life, December 17, 2009.
2. Ethan Bronner, "Mideast's Christians Losing Numbers and Sway," *New York Times*, May 12, 2009.
3. Henry Samuel, "Nicolas Sarkozy says Christians in Middle East are victim of 'religious cleansing,'" *London Telegraph*, January 7, 2011.
4. Cindy Wooden, "Pope says Iraqi Christians experience 'authentic martyrdom,'" Catholic News Agency, June 21, 2007.
5. "Iraqi Christian Targeted in Shooting," Zenit, June 8, 2010.
6. Ethan Bronner, "Mideast's Christians Losing Numbers and Sway."
7. Ibid.
8. "Iraq's Permanent Constitution," United States Commission on International Freedom, March 2006.
9. Edward Pentin, "US might turn blind eye to religious freedom," Zenit, December 8, 2011.
10. "2012 Annual Report," United States Commission on International Religious Freedom.
11. Ibid.
12. Nina Shea, "The world's worst religious persecutors," National Review Online *The Corner*, March 20, 2012.
13. "Global Restrictions on Religion," Pew Forum on Religion and Public Life.
14. Jack Healy, "Exodus From North Signals Iraqi Christians' Slow Decline," *New York Times*, March 10, 2012.
15. "The Catholic Church in the Middle East: Communion and Witness," Synod of Bishops, Special Assembly for the Middle East, 2010, http://www.vatican.va/roman_curia/synod/documents/rc_synod_doc_20100606_instrumentum-mo_en.pdf.
16. Michelle Bauman, "US bishops urge Obama to defend religious minorities in Egypt," Catholic News Agency, October 18, 2011.
17. "Obama Moves away from 'Freedom of Religion' toward 'Freedom of Worship'?" Catholic Online, March 21, 2012.

18. Thomas F. Farr, "Obama administration sidelines religious freedom policy," *Washington Post*, June 25, 2010.

19. Bobby Ross, Jr., "As USCIRF Faces Possible Closure, Funding Divides Religious Freedom Experts," *Christianity Today*, December 9, 2011.

20. "Presidential Memorandum—International Initiatives to Advance the Human Rights of Lesbian, Gay, Bisexual, and Transgender Persons," The White House Office of the Press Secretary, December 6, 2011.

21. Ibid.

22. Ibid.

23. Ibid.

24. Ibid.

25. Geneva Sands, "Clinton: Gay rights and human rights are 'one and the same,'" *The Hill*, December 7, 2011.

26. Ibid.

27. George Neumayr, "Hillary's Surreal State Department," *American Spectator*, December 8, 2011.

Chapter 15: The Post-American President

1. Jonah Goldberg, "The bashing of American exceptionalism," *Los Angeles Times*, November 9, 2010.

2. Amie Parnes, "Obama: My career is 'testimony to American exceptionalism,'" *The Hill*, April 2, 2012.

3. Alicia Colon, "Plenty to be Proud of," *New York Sun*, February 22, 2008.

4. Ben Wallace-Wells, "Destiny's Child," *Rolling Stone*, February 9, 2007.

5. Michael Gledhill, "Who is Barack Obama?" *National Review*, September 1, 2008.

6. Jodi Kantor, *The Obamas* (Little, Brown and Company, 2012), 160.

7. Ibid., 161.

Chapter 16: Obama's Islamophilia

1. Text: "Obama's Speech in Cairo," *New York Times*, June 4, 2009.

2. Ibid.

3. "NASA Chief: Next Frontier Better Relations with Muslim World," Fox News, July 10, 2010.

4. Mark Matthews, "Obama: Science no longer to take a 'back seat' to ideology," *Orlando Sentinel*, April 27, 2009.

5. Elise Viebeck, "Obama to host Ramadan meal," *The Hill*, August 13, 2010.

6. Kristi Keck, "Obama tones down National Day of Prayer observance," CNN, May 6, 2009.
7. Patrick Goodenough, "Religious Tolerance Resolution Backed by Obama Administration Aligns with Islamic Bloc's Interests," CNS News, December 16, 2012.
8. Nina Shea, "SHEA: Wrong way to address 'Islamophobia,'" *Baptist Press*, December 19, 2011.
9. Nina Shea, "A Perverse 'Process,'" *New York Post*, December 16, 2011.
10. Stephen Schwartz, "Obama's Islamic Envoy: Obama Is America's 'Educator-in-Chief on Islam,'" *Weekly Standard*, June 24, 2010.
11. U.S. Department of Homeland Security, *Rightwing Extremism: Current Economic and Political Climate Fueling Resurgence in Radicalization and Recruitment*, http://www.fas.org/irp/eprint/rightwing.pdf.
12. "RADICAL ISLAM'S ALLIANCE WITH THE SOCIALIST LEFT," Discoverthe Networks.org.
13. "Moran: U.S. Has 'Ethnically Cleansed Most of Baghdad,'" YouTube, December 19, 2007.
14. Melanie Phillips, *The World Turned Upside Down* (Encounter Books, 2011).
15. "Global Opinion of Obama Slips, International Policies Faulted," The Pew Center, Pew Global Attitudes Project, June 13, 2012.
16. Laurie Goodstein, "American Muslims Ask, Will We Ever Belong?" *New York Times*, September 5, 2010.
17. Joshua Miller, "Imam Won't 'Barter' Over So-Called 'Ground Zero Mosque' with Florida Pastor," ABC News, September 9, 2010.
18. Andrea Elliott, "More Muslims Arrive in U.S., After 9/11 Dip," *New York Times*, September 10, 2006.
19. Barry A. Kosmin and Ariela Keyser, "American Religious Identification Survey [ARIS 2008]," Trinity College, March 2009, http://commons.trincoll.edu/aris/files/2011/08/ARIS_Report_2008.pdf
20. Ibid.
21. Cathy Lynn Grossman, "Number of U.S. mosques up 74% since 2000," *USA Today*, February 29, 2012.
22. Michael B. Farrell, "Fort Hood Shootings: US Muslims feel new heat," *Christian Science Monitor*, November 17, 2009.
23. Eric Gorski, "Another attack leaves U.S. Muslims fearing backlash," Associated Press, November 7, 2009.
24. Mark Thompson, "Army Gains with Muslim Soldiers May Be Lost," *Time*, November 9, 2009.
25. Gary L. Bauer, "The Myth of the Anti-Muslim Backlash," *Weekly Standard*, December 21, 2009.
26. Ibid.

Chapter 17: Obama Divides Americans over Israel

1. "Report: Sarkozy calls Netanyahu 'liar,'" Ynetnews.com, November 7, 2011.
2. "Obama and Israel," New York Sun, January 7, 2008.
3. Ibid.
4. Mary Bruce, "Obama Says His Commitment To Israel 'Is Unshakable,'" ABC News, December 16, 2011.
5. Herb Keinon, "'US has no better friend than Israel,'" Jerusalem Post, March 11, 2010.
6. Justin Elliott, "Obama's Israel Shuffle," Mother Jones, February 1, 2008.
7. Jim Geraghty, "'Obama used to be very comfortable speaking up for and being associated with Palestinian rights and opposing the Israeli occupation,'" National Review Online Campaign Spot, June 3, 2008.
8. "Obama: Had Wright not retired, I'd have left church," CNN, March 28, 2008.
9. Richard Cohen, "Obama's Farrakhan Test," Washington Post, January 15, 2008.
10. Aaron Klein, "Obama's mystery links to Qaddafi uncovered," Fox News, February 23, 2011.
11. "Obama Church Controversy," PBS, March 9, 2007.
12. Gil Hoffman, "'Jerusalem Post'/Smith Poll: Only 6% of Israelis see US gov't as pro-Israel," Jerusalem Post, June 9, 2009.
13. Barak Ravid, "Visiting Biden slams E. J'lem housing plan," Haaretz, March 10, 2010.
14. Nir Hasson, Avi Issacharoff, and Natash Mozgovaya, "Biden: East Jerusalem plan undermines peace talks," Haaretz, March 9, 2010.
15. "Ax: Israel announcement 'an insult,'" Politico, March 14, 2010.
16. Jeffrey Heller, "Israeli envoy sees 'historic crisis' with U.S.: report," Reuters, March 15, 2010.
17. "Remarks by the President on the Middle East and North Africa," The White House Office of the Press Secretary, May 19, 2011.
18. "Netanyahu: 1967 lines 'indefensible,'" Ynetnews.com, May 20, 2011.
19. "Hamas: we will never recognise Israel," London Guardian, December 8, 2006.
20. Khaled Abu Toameh, "Hamas denounces killing of a 'Muslim warrior,'" Jerusalem Post, May 2, 2011.
21. Gary L. Bauer, "'Two-state solution' not a synonym for peace," Politico, September 3, 2010.
22. Jeffrey Heller and Matt Spetalnick, "Obama, Netanyahu give no sign of narrowing gap on Iran," Reuters, March 5, 2012.
23. "Obama's Iran Abdication," Wall Street Journal, June 18, 2009.
24. John Bolton, "Israel is not the threat, Mr. Obama. Iran is," Christian Science Monitor, April 3, 2012.

Chapter 18: Playing the Hispanic Card

1. "Data Brief: Black Employment and Unemployment in May 2012," UC Berkeley Labor Center, June 2012.
2. Jon Feere, "Obama and McCain at La Raza," Center for Immigration Studies, July 15, 2008.
3. Kristina Wong, "President Obama Says Arizona's 'Poorly-Conceived' Immigration Law Could Mean Hispanic-Americans Are Harassed," ABC News, April 27, 2010.
4. Ibid.
5. Josh Gerstein, "Justice Department sues over Arizona immigration law," *Politico*, July 6, 2010.
6. Stephan Dinan, "Supreme Court casts doubt on Obama's immigration law claim," *Washington Times*, April 25, 2012,
7. Jonathan S. Tobin, "Arizona Immigration Law: Verrilli Strikes Out Again with SCOTUS," *Commentary*, April 25, 2012.
8. "Nationally, 60% Favor Letting Local Police Stop and Verify Immigration Status," Rasmussen Reports, April 26, 2010.
9. Jeffrey M. Jones, "More Americans Favor Than Oppose Arizona Immigration Law," Gallup, April 29, 2010.
10. "Democrats call for elimination of Arizona's new immigration law," CNN, April 28, 2010.
11. Jerry Markon and Michael D. Shear, "Justice Department sues Arizona over immigration law," *Washington Post*, July 7, 2010.
12. Randal C. Archibold, "Arizona Enacts Stringent Law on Immigration," *New York Times*, April 23, 2010.
13. "Obama mocks GOP, jokes they want border moat," CBS News, May 10, 2011.
14. Mary Bruce, "Obama Calls Romney's Stance on Immigration 'Very Troublesome,'" ABC News, April 14, 2012.
15. Ibid.
16. Dylan Smith, "Brewer: 'Heart of SB 1070 can now be implemented,'" *Tucson Sentinel*, June 25, 2012, http://www.tucsonsentinel.com/opinion/report/062512_brewer_sb1070/brewer-heart-sb-1070-can-now-implemented/.
17. Lydia Saad, "Hispanic Voters Put Other Issues Before Immigration," Gallup, June 25, 2012.
18. Jonathan Easley, "Republican senator: Obama's immigration move 'possibly illegal,'" *The Hill*, June 15, 2012.

19.   Lisa Mascaro and Matea Gold, "Marco Rubio calls Obama immigration order a 'short-term answer,'" *Los Angeles Times,* June 15, 2012.

20.   Mike Allen, "Barack Obama's group therapy," *Politico.*

21.   Helene Cooper and Trip Gabriel, "Obama's Announcement Seizes Initiative and Puts Pressure on Romney," *New York Times,* June 15, 2012.

22.   Ibid.

23.   Sarahi Uribe, "After record deportations, Obama's welcome change of immigration policy," *London Guardian,* June 15, 2012.

24.   Steve Freiss, "Obama's policy strategy: Ignore laws," *Politico,* June 16, 2012.

25.   Alfonso Aguilar, "President's hypocritical stance on immigration," *Politico,* June 11, 2012.

Chapter 19: Obama's Divisive Justice Department

1.   "Attorney General Eric Holder at the Department of Justice African American History Month Program," U.S. Department of Justice, February 18, 2009.

2.   Ibid.

3.   "FNC Exclusive: Former DOJ Attorney Discusses New Black Panther Party Voter Intimidation Case," Fox News, June 30, 2010.

4.   William Douglas, "Holder says '60s voting-rights gains at risk,'" *Philadelphia Inquirer,* June 1, 2012.

5.   Ibid.

6.   Ibid.

7.   Krissah Thompson, "Voter registration down among Hispanics, blacks," *Washington Post,* May 4, 2012.

8.   "Holder's Racial Incitement," *Wall Street Journal,* May 31, 2012.

9.   Ibid.

10.   Jerry Markon, "Justice Dept. rejects South Carolina voter ID law, calling it discriminatory," *Washington Post,* December 23, 2011.

11.   Jeremy Pelofsky, "Obama administration blocks Texas voter ID law," Reuters, March 12, 2012.

12.   Ibid.

13.   Ibid.

14.   Robin Bravender, "2012 Elections: Left girds for voting rights battle," *Politico,* June 21, 2012.

15.   "56% Oppose Justice Department's Blocking of Texas Voter ID Law," *Rasmussen Reports,* March 15, 2012.

Chapter 20: Obama's Destructive Race-Baiting

1. Ron Suskind, *Confidence Men* (Harper, 2011), 231.
2. Michael Gledhill, "Who Is Barack Obama?" *National Review*, September 1, 2008.
3. David Remnick, *The Bridge* (Knopf, 2010), 77.
4. Ibid., 238.
5. David Mendell, *From Promise to Power* (Amistad, 2007).
6. Ibid.
7. Illinois Senator Barack Obama, "Keynote address at the Democratic National Convention," July 27, 2004.
8. Helene Cooper, "Obama Criticizes Arrest of Harvard Professor," *New York Times*, July 22, 2009.
9. Roddie A. Burris, "Jackson slams Obama for 'acting white,'" *Politico*, September 9, 2007.
10. Stephanie Condon, "Obama: 'If I had a son, he'd look like Trayvon,'" CBS News, March 23, 2012.
11. Ibid.
12. "'Our Challenges Are Complex,' First Lady Says," NPR, April 17, 2012.
13. Jefferson Morley, "Trayvon's parents go to Washington," *Salon*, March 28, 2012.
14. Renee Lynch, "Trayvon Martin case: 'Blacks are under attack,' says Jesse Jackson," *Los Angeles Times*, March 23, 2012.
15. Erika Harrell, "Black Victims of Violent Crime," U.S. Department of Justice, Bureau of Justice Statistics Special Report, August 2007.
16. Ken LaRive, "Federal Statistics of black on white violence, with links and mathematical extrapolation formulas," Examiner.com, August 1, 2009.
17. Erik Wemple, "NBC issues apology on Zimmerman tape screw-up," *Washington Post*, April 3, 2012.
18. "Spike Lee pays up for wrong-address tweet in Trayvon Martin case," *Los Angeles Times* The Envelope, March 30, 2012.
19. "Mike Tyson on George Zimmerman: 'It's a disgrace he hasn't been shot yet,'" *Grio*, April 12, 2012.
20. Arelis R. Hernandez, "Trayvon Martin: New Black Panthers offer $10,000 bounty for capture of shooter George Zimmerman," *Orlando Sentinel*, March 24, 2012.
21. Rheana Murray, "Man beaten in 'justice for Trayvon' rage," *New York Daily News*, April 24, 2012.
22. Jayson K. Jones and Ana C. Rosado, "McCain Campaign Says Obama Is Playing the 'Race Card,'" *New York Times* The Caucus, July 31, 2008.

23. "NAACP Delegates Vote To Repudiate Racist Elements Within Tea Party," NAACP.org.

24. Jimmy Orr, "Janeane Garofalo says tea parties were for rednecks," *Christian Science Monitor*, April 17, 2009.

25. "Herman Cain: Tea Party racism claims are 'ridiculous,'" CBS News, June 9, 2011.

26. Ibid.

27. Ibid.

28. Donovan Slack and Patrick Reis, "Romney repudiates Jeremiah Wright plan," *Politico*, May 17, 2012.

29. Peter Wallsten and Richard Simon, "Sotomayor nomination splits GOP," *Los Angeles Times*, May 27, 2009.

30. Ward Connerly, "Inestimable Harm," National Review Online, April 5, 2010.

31. Caitlin McDevitt, "Spike Lee: Obama win not a sure thing," *Politico*, June 12, 2012.

32. Barack Obama, *The Audacity of Hope* (Random House, 2006), 245.

33. Ibid.

34. Suzanne Goldenberg, "US election 2008: 'I want to cut his nuts out'—Jackson gaffe turns focus on Obama's move to the right," *London Guardian*, July 10, 2008.

35. Barbara Reynolds, "President Barack Obama's support of gay marriage splits African Americans," *Washington Post*, May 24, 2012.

36. "Data Brief: Black Employment and Unemployment in May 2012," UC Berkeley Labor Center, June 2012.

37. Ibid.

38. Ibid.

39. Corey Boles, "Black Caucus Warns Obama on Jobs," *Wall Street Journal*, August 31, 2011.

40. Steven Gray, "Obama's Message to Black Leaders: "Stop Complaining," *Time*, September 26, 2011.

41. Dana Milbank, "Obama and his foot soldiers go toe to toe," *Washington Post*, October 3, 2011.

42. Tim Mak, "On unemployment rate, black leaders press Obama," *Politico*, September 2, 2011.

43. Michael Muskal, "Rep. Maxine Waters says it's time for Obama to fight," *Los Angeles Times*, August 18, 2011.

44. Daniel Bates, "'I'm exhausted defending you': Middle-class mother confronts Obama at meet-the-voters event," *Daily Mail*, September 22, 2010.

45. Edward Klein, *The Amateur* (Regnery, 2012), 188–89.

Chapter 21: Obama Bullies the Media

1. Brent Baker, "By Nearly 8-to-1, Voters Say Journalists Want Obama to Win," Media Research Center, October 24, 2008.

2. "Canvassing Campaign Media: An Analysis of Time, Tone and Topics," Pew Research Center Publications, October 22, 2008.

3. John Heilemann, "Newt's Base," *New York* magazine, January 27, 2012.

4. Danny Shea, "Chris Matthews: 'I want to do everything I can to make this new presidency work,'" *Huffington Post*, November 6, 2008.

5. Noel Sheppard, "Shocker: 'Barack Obama and the Press Break Up,'" *News Busters*, July 25, 2008.

6. Jodi Kantor, *The Obamas* (Little, Brown and Company, 2012), 157.

7. Michael Scherer, "Team Obama's Petty Limbaugh Strategy," *Time*, March 4, 2009.

8. Ibid.

9. Ben Smith, "Obama Ditches CBC/Fox Debate," *Politico*, April 9, 2007.

10. Jim Vandehei and Mike Allen, "Obama strategy: Marginalize most powerful critics," *Politico*, October 21, 2009.

11. Michael Scherer, "Calling 'Em Out: The White House Takes on the Press," *Time*, October 8, 2009.

12. Ibid.

13. Mike Allen, "Fox 'not really news,' says Axelrod," *Politico*, October 18, 2009.

14. Lynn Sweet, "Rahm Emanuel on CNN's 'State of the Union' Transcript," *Chicago Sun-Times*, October 18, 2009.

15. Brian Stelter, "Fox's Volley With Obama Intensifying," *New York Times*, October 11, 2009.

16. Jonathan Alter, *The Promise* (Simon and Schuster, 2010), 276–77.

17. Chris Rovzar, "Did the White House Lie About Trying to Exclude Fox News?" *New York* magazine, July14, 2011.

18. Jeff Greenfield, "President Obama's Feud with FOX News," CBS News, October 24, 2009.

19. "Top White House Official Says Obama Team 'Controlled' Media Coverage During Campaign," Fox News, October 19, 2009.

20. Andrew C. McCarthy, "Re: Anita Dunn and Mao Zedong," National Review Online *The Corner*, October 6, 2009.

21. Amanda Carpenter, "'Diversity czar' takes heat over remarks," *Washington Times*, September 23, 2009.

Chapter 22: The Imperial Presidency

1. Hayley Peterson, "Obama flexing same powers he once criticized," *Washington Examiner*, January 11, 2012.
2. David Grant, "Why is Obama now supporting super PACS?" *Christian Science Monitor*, February 7, 2012.
3. Michael A. Memoli, "Obama: Overturning healthcare law would be 'extraordinary step,'" *Los Angeles Times*, April 2, 2012.
4. Ibid.
5. Ibid.
6. Ibid.
7. Sahil Kapur, "Dems Warn Of 'Grave Damage' To SCOTUS If 'Obamacare' Is Struck Down," *Talking Points Memo*, March 28, 2012.
8. David Nakamura, "Obama 'confident' Supreme Court will uphold health care law," *Washington Post*, April 2, 2012.
9. "Remarks by the President on the Payroll Tax Cut," The White House Office of the Press Secretary, February 21, 2012.
10. "Obama's Lawless Presidency Close To Totalitarianism," *Investor's Business Daily*, June 18, 2012.
11. Mike Brownfield, "Mike Brownfield: Obama's tyrannical abuse of power," *Orange County Register*, January 5, 2012.
12. Peter Baker, "Obama Making Plans to Use Executive Power," *New York Times*, February 12, 2010.
13. Charlie Savage, "Shift on Executive Power Lets Obama Bypass Rivals," *New York Times*, April 22, 2012.
14. Ibid.
15. Ibid.
16. Z. Byron Wolf, "President Obama Instructs Justice Department to Stop Defending Defense of Marriage Act calls Clinton-Signed Law 'Unconstitutional,'" ABC News, February 23, 2011.
17. "No Child Left Behind: Obama administration grants 10 waivers," *Los Angeles Times*, February 9, 2012.
18. James Risen, "Obama Takes On Congress Over Policy Czar Positions," *New York Times*, April 16, 2011.
19. Charles Krauthammer, "The immigration bombshell: Naked lawlessness," *Washington Post*, June 25, 2012.
20. Juana Summers, "Marco Rubio: Immigration 'all about politics' for some," *Politico*, June 22, 2012.

21. Hayley Peterson, "Obama flexing same powers he once criticized," *Washington Examiner*, January 11, 2012.
22. Ibid.
23. Philip Klein, "The Empress of Obamacare," *American Spectator*, June 4, 2010.
24. Ibid.
25. C. Boyden Gray, "Dodd-Frank, the real threat to the Constitution," *Washington Post*, December 31, 2010.
26. David Limbaugh, *The Great Destroyer* (Regnery, 2012).
27. Bill Haymin, "Americans dangerously close to living in dictatorship," *San Francisco Telegram*, April 25, 2012.
28. Edwin Meese III and Todd Gaziano, "Obama's recess appointments are unconstitutional," *Washington Post*, January 5, 2012.
29. Ibid.
30. Charlie Savage, "Shift on Executive Power Lets Obama Bypass Rivals," *New York Times*, April 22, 2012.
31. Steve Freiss, "Obama's policy strategy: Ignore laws," *Politico*, June 16, 2012.
32. Ibid.
33. Ryan Lizza, "The Second Term," *New Yorker*, June 18, 2012.
34. Ibid.
35. Ibid.
36. Ibid.

Index